S0-ACM-411

THE 12 ESSENTIAL SKILLS FOR GREAT PREACHING

THE 12 ESSENTIAL SKILLS FOR GREAT PREACHING

WAYNE McDILL

BROADMAN
&HOLMAN
PUBLISHERS

Nashville, Tennessee

© Copyright 1994
by Wayne McDill
All rights reserved.
Printed in the United States of America

4220-12
0-8054-2012-6

Dewey Decimal Classification: 251
Subject Heading: PREACHING
Library of Congress Card Catalog Number: 93-38953

Unless otherwise noted, all Scripture quotations are from the *New American Standard Bible,* © Lockman Foundation 1977, used by permission. Scripture quotations marked (NIV) are from the Holy Bible, *New International Version,* copyright © 1973, 1978, 1984 by International Bible Society; and (NKJV) from the *New King James Version,* copyright © 1979, 1980, 1982, Thomas Nelson, Inc., Publishers.

Library of Congress Cataloging-in-Publication Data
McDill, Wayne.
       The 12 essential skills for great preaching / Wayne McDill.
        p. cm.
      ISBN 0-8054-2012-6
       1. Preaching   I. Title.   II. Title: Twelve essential skills for great preaching.

BV4211.2.M334   1994
251—dc20

93-38953
CIP

To the students,

past and present,

who faithfully preach

the Word of God.

CONTENTS

PREFACE

How can preaching be taught? That question has provoked and inspired me for many years. My first preaching class was made up of six men in the Central Baptist Church of Hillsboro, Texas, in 1971. They wanted to learn how to preach, so I attempted to teach them. At the time I was a doctoral student at Southwestern Baptist Theological Seminary in Fort Worth. I never thought I would ever teach homiletics full time.

There is some doubt that preaching can be taught at all, or should be. Some feel sincerely that those who are to preach are born with the talents and supernaturally gifted by God at their call. It is, in that view, a near blasphemy to try to teach someone to do what God has already prepared him for.

I do believe that the gifts for preaching are from God. But I also believe that skills must be developed. We are all stewards of what God has invested in us. As in every aspect of this Christian life, God chooses to use us and holds us accountable for our stewardship. We are ever learning, growing, sharpening our tools for this calling.

So I have persisted in trying to learn it—how to teach preaching. And I am still learning. During recent years I have come to a growing conviction that a *skills development* approach holds much promise in training for homiletics. In one sense all preaching classes must deal with the development of skills, but I am searching for better ways to identify and strengthen the specific skills needed for more effective sermon preparation.

It is obvious that writers and teachers of homiletics of many generations have left their creative marks on these ideas. Very seldom does anyone come along with a really new perspective. Some of those who have, however, are cited in these chapters. Perhaps there is nothing essentially new to today's preaching. But there are new combinations of ideas and new emphases for this day being presented by contemporary teachers. It is a good and rich day to study preaching.

Many have had a hand in this study. Hundreds of preaching students have evaluated class after class, made suggestions, and offered good ideas for improvement. Student assistants and tutors have analyzed with me what we were doing and offered their insights. It is not an exaggeration to say that every semester meant going back to the drawing board in some major area. Out of all this input these methods have evolved, step by step. They are still evolving.

I am also grateful, as ever, for the patient reading and advice of my wife and partner in ministry, Sharon. My son, Michael McDill, has given special help with this study, and will continue to do so as we both teach from these chapters. My thanks go as well to the valuable counsel of my colleague and friend, Austin Tucker.

My prayer is that this study will help some who are called to the greatest mission on earth, proclaiming the gospel of Jesus Christ to a needy world. I praise God for the privilege of making a small contribution to their ministries.

Wayne McDill
Wake Forest, North Carolina

Skill. This does not refer merely to style and delivery, but also to the collection, choice, and arrangement of materials. All who preach eminently well, and the same thing is true of secular speakers, will be found, with scarcely an exception, to have labored much to acquire skill.[1]

John A. Broadus, 1870

INTRODUCTION

STRENGTHENING PREPARATION SKILLS

He made it look so easy. Michael Jordan could run headlong down the court, bouncing the ball on the floor while several other men tried to get in his way, then leap into the air with others clamoring about him and cause a pumpkin-sized ball to slip through a steel hoop as easily as dropping a lump of sugar into your coffee. We celebrated his skill by cheering, and through him we felt some fleeting sense of personal accomplishment. I wish I could do that.

I listened to Itzhak Perlman play a Mozart violin concerto and marveled. He closed his eyes and, in his characteristic way, seemed to delight in every note, his facial expressions animated as though he were singing through the violin. I was caught up in his performance and found myself moving with the flow of the music. I wish I could do that.

But I cannot play basketball like Michael Jordan or the violin like Itzhak Perlman. Neither can you. What do they have that you and I do not? Why can they perform their crafts the way they do while we are only skilled enough to watch? In the first place, they have the gifts for it. Built into the genetic formula for these two very different men is the treasure of a giftedness few people have.

1

Another difference between these two men and the rest of us is the time and effort they have put into developing those gifts. While you and I were watching television as children, Michael Jordan at the same age was dribbling and shooting baskets. Itzhak Perlman was practicing his scales and double stops. They invested their freedom in disciplined practice of their skills while most of us were using up our freedom with something else. Now they have the freedom to perform as one in a million can, while the rest of us are not free to do that.

Factors in Skills Development

No matter what our gifts, everyone needs help. My guess is that somebody, somewhere along the way, helped these two stars with their training. Jordan and Perlman were taught the basic dynamic principles of their crafts, the technique for every skill they would need. Then they practiced. They practiced hours. They practiced devotedly. They were probably driven to practice insatiably while other young people were making softer decisions about their time.

Not only am I not good at basketball or the violin, neither am I good at a host of other activities. Why? It takes time. I heard Robert Schuller say in a pastors' conference, "I determined early in my ministry that I could not afford to be good at golf. You have to choose what you will be good at, because you can be good at only a very few things." What have you decided to be good at? If you have the gifts for performing well at it, then you must develop the skills associated with those gifts.

The premise of this book is simple: *Preachers can significantly improve their preaching by strengthening twelve specific skills used in the preparation of sermons.* Skills development means the gradual growth in your skills in a particular craft, in this case preaching. Here we concentrate on twelve tasks which are necessary to the most effective sermon preparation. Any training program in skills development will involve certain elements that are necessary to practical training. Each of these should also be a part of your own plans to strengthen your preaching.

Def • i • ni´ tion: Skills Development

Skill: proficiency or expertness in a particular craft, gained by training and experience.

Development: the gradual growth which causes skills to become fuller, larger, better.

Skills development, then, is the gradual growth in one's proficiency in a particular craft. *Skills development* focuses on the practical application of the knowledge in a given field. Skills are developed through a step-by-step training program, with sufficient practice in the appropriate tasks. Such a training program requires basic knowledge of the work, explanation of tasks, demonstration of specific steps, supervised practice, and clear standards for the results.

Skills development in preaching is usually limited to delivery, but the method is needed for preparation tasks as well.

It is important to understand the basic concepts behind the skills you are learning. If you understand why something is done, you are more likely to remember how it is done. The skills necessary for effective preaching are based on the principles of biblical interpretation, sermon structure and development, language use, and communication. The better a preacher understands those principles, the more sense the particular skills he needs will make and the more likely he will be to understand the role particular skills play in the work of sermon preparation.

Skills development training requires hands-on experience working with the material of a given craft. You will never develop skills in a particular work just by hearing about it. You have to be a doer and not a hearer only. This will involve an understanding of the properties of the raw material with which you work. If it is basketball, you have to get a feel for the ball and the basket. In the case of sermon preparation, the raw materials are ideas and language, particularly in the words of the text and of your sermon. You are a wordcrafter, handling the words of Scripture and the words of communication. So you have to get the feel of words—judging what they can do and cannot do, exchanging them, matching them, and assembling them for the best results.

Skills are learned best when they are first explained in practical, step-by-step terms. The skills for any performance involve concrete actions that must be accomplished in a certain order. This requires clear instructions. Learning how to do anything is much easier if the task is broken down into achievable steps which can be taken one at a time. If you don't have a personal coach, written instructions should be clear enough for reference and reinforcement as you continue to practice.

Skills development must take into account that each person comes to the task with different experience, background, and expertise in the particular skill. So it is with the development of preaching skills. It is important that you work at your own pace and level. If you are already skilled in a particular task, you will want to move on to other skills you need to strengthen. Different preachers also have different levels of giftedness, creativity, and potential. It is best to deal with the basics while allowing plenty of room for creative freedom as you go along.

Skills development calls for modeling of the particular tasks so that the student can see how it is done by an experienced craftsman. No matter how clear instructions may be, a few good examples are necessary. It is best to have a coach present to demonstrate the particular task you are learning. Less effective is a written example. As you work at strengthening sermon preparation skills, you will need not only instructions, but examples showing what the task looks like on paper.

In skills development there is no substitute for practice. Just because you think you understand something doesn't mean you can do it. Practice is the only way to master a skill, even in sermon preparation. This means writing, writing, writing. Completing a task one time is not practice. At first the work may seem tedious, and you are uncertain. But as you keep working with different texts, you will find yourself more and more at home with each task. Do not work at one preparation task for more than three or four hours at a time. After that you may become mentally fatigued and perhaps frustrated with the task. Regular and consistent practice over the weeks is better than too much at once.

The Missing Ingredient

The same dream comes around from time to time, each time in a little different form. Basically it's about preaching. I am the guest preacher at a grand church—with thousands of seats, balconies, and ornate alcoves. I see myself in the anteroom to the platform waiting for time for the service to start. Then I discover I am missing my coat or my tie. Or my trousers! Something is always missing as I am led to the platform.

Most preachers have had that same nightmare. Something is missing. The preaching experience should be a dynamic time of unfolding the truths of God's Word. It is almost a sacrament, a communion of pastor and people in a wonderful meal from the Bread of Life. But something is missing.

That "something" that is missing could be any number of necessary ingredients for good preaching. There is not one secret answer, not one solution to the call for improvement in your preaching. The answers are many. The formula for effective preaching is complex, but there are clearly identifiable factors which are necessary to the mix. Whatever your style, biblical preaching is best when all the elements in the preaching formula are present.

I have heard it said many a time, "Preachers are born, not made." The assumption behind this statement is that God gifts a person at birth with certain abilities, and there is little or nothing he can do about it. A few are "born preachers," and the others must settle for some level of mediocrity in their preaching. As we look around at the preachers of our day, there seems to be evidence for such a view. How many Billy Grahams are there compared to the thousands of preachers who do only a marginal job in their preaching week by week?

I have been asked by colleagues concerning my preaching classes, "Do you have any good preachers this semester?" Here is the same assumption. Some are good preachers; some are not. I always wince a bit at this idea. It seems to suggest that the study of preaching is in some sense a futile effort. Some who come into the class already have the "right stuff" while others just muddle through as average, run-of-the-mill preachers.

Some courses in homiletics may unintentionally reflect this view. If the giftedness necessary to effective preaching is inborn, what will we teach in preaching courses? We cannot expect too much in terms of real growth. All we are doing is helping the students discover the gifts they have and polish them a bit. So we concentrate on a survey of preaching: history, heroes of the pulpit, various kinds of structure, some basics in interpretation and outlining, some advice about preaching in the pastoral ministry, and so on. The course concentrates on knowledge and values because skills are predestined.

What about the pastor who has completed his seminary work and has received all the training he is likely to get in preaching? What is his view of the issue of giftedness? He can name the stars of the pulpit for this generation. He knows what good preaching sounds like. Even though he thinks he would do well on a conference program, in his heart he suspects he is not in the same league with the speakers he most admires. There is again that sense of destiny. Somehow he does not have what it takes to excel.

Most pastors are committed to good preaching. Few, however, are really satisfied with their own sermon preparation or its results. On one hand, preaching is an academic discipline. It calls for serious study, for expert training. On the other hand, preaching is a spiritual exercise. Its basis is the Word of the living God. It comes with much prayer and hopefully with the Spirit's enabling. Poor preaching, then, reflects badly on the preacher's scholarship as well as his spirituality.

But what to do about it? Most of us are very uncomfortable with any situation in which our preaching is criticized. I always advise pastors' wives to wait until Tuesday or Wednesday to offer any criticisms about Sunday's sermon. A tired, frustrated pastor will not take well to "helpful" criticisms on Sunday, or even Monday morning.

Preaching is a very personal expression of our sincere commitment to God. Criticism of our sermons goes too much to the heart of our calling and ministry. We much prefer to learn on our own how to strengthen our preaching. I know that sounds like an indictment of our pride and self-centeredness, and maybe it is. But we are human. We are not eager to have our most heart-felt expressions evaluated and critiqued. But we also need the opportunity to study this vital area without others standing in judgment on our best efforts.

This book is designed with a self-improvement format, a do-it-yourself approach which will let you concentrate on your own skills, at your own pace, and in the areas you see need to be strengthened. You and I know we are not self-sufficient. We need help. Working for improvement in our preaching is a continual adventure of growth and development. I have been preaching for thirty-five years, but I am still working on it. It is too important to neglect and too complex to take for granted.

Kinds of Learning

In any learning process there are three basic kinds of learning which take place: (1) knowledge, (2) values, and (3) skills. Strengthening competency in preaching calls for growth through each of these kinds of learning. If you are to improve your sermons, you will have to have the necessary knowledge of several fields. You will have to understand and embrace the values appropriate to effective preaching. You will have to understand and develop the skills necessary to function in the sermon preparation process.

The first kind of learning, knowledge, deals with the **what** *of the subject being studied.* There is really no end to the extensive knowledge you might acquire on the subject of preaching. You could study the history of preaching, the various approaches to preaching, preaching in the great religions of the world, the lives of great preachers, the theology of preaching, and so on.

The preparation of sermons calls for knowledge of at least three disciplines. Every preacher should study *homiletics*, which deals with the preparation of sermons and with preaching in general. Preaching courses also involve the study of *hermeneutics*, the science of literary interpretation. Knowledge for preaching also must include some understanding of *speech communication,* including general communication theory as well as a particular emphasis on oral presentation.

A second kind of learning concerns values, which deals with the why of the area of study. The learner wants to know whether this knowledge is important, whether it will make a difference for him personally. Values, therefore, deal with the convictions and desire of the learner as he seeks the new knowledge and puts it to work in his own experience. Without an understanding of the value of new learning, most learners will consider it irrelevant and forget it as soon as the study is over.

The third kind of learning is the development of skills, which is essentially the application of the knowledge the learner has acquired. In some courses of study, the development of skills is not a part of the teaching aim. A history course might have little to offer for skills development because it is difficult to do history. A course in chemistry, on the other hand, not only aims to impart knowledge, but also attempts to teach the students how to handle chemicals properly in the lab.

The diligent student of homiletics—whether in a seminary lab or in the parish ministry—should aim for greater and greater mastery of all three areas of learning: knowledge, values, and skills. We are concentrating here on skills. But skills must be based on sure knowledge and motivated by Christian values.

Gifts

We are not all equal in intelligence, quickness of wit, that sparkle of dynamism in personality. Emotionally we are different. Some are more passionate, more caring, more fiery by nature. Some have clearer articulation by nature, while others seem to mumble or stutter. Some are naturally dramatic and extroverted, relishing the spotlight, while others churn with dread at standing before a crowd.

We use the word *gift* to mean a natural quality or endowment that we see as conferred by God Himself. We use the term to mean spiritual gifts in addition to natural abilities. The New Testament discussion of spiritual gifts includes preaching as a distinct endowment from God given by the Holy Spirit (1 Cor. 12:10, 28, 29). Talent means a gift committed to one's trust to use and improve. This use of the word comes from the parable of the talents. So talent has come to mean any natural faculty, ability, or power.

We inherit these natural characteristics from our forebears through complex and unique genetic patterns. I have experienced the strange and delightful sense of recognition as I made some gesture, stood in a certain way, or laughed, and felt the presence of my dad in it. I am like him in so many ways, and that's as it should be. That package of inherited traits is what I have to work with as I try to become the best preacher possible for me to be.

Moses complained as one of his many excuses, "Lord, I have never been eloquent . . . for I am slow of speech and slow of tongue." But God's answer was pointed, "Who has made man's mouth? . . . Now then go, and I . . . will be with your mouth, and teach you what you are to say" (Ex. 4:10–12). Moses was not a "born preacher," but God planned to use him anyway.

Jesus, in the parable of the talents, acknowledges that we are not all endowed with the same gifts (Matt. 25:14–30). God, in His sovereignty, has done as He pleased to give each of us what He chooses. The issue in the parable is not how much each receives, but what he does with it. Whatever the level of giftedness, each is to account to his Lord for the use of what he receives.

Skills

The idea of skills, however, is different from gifts and talents. Skill has to do with unusual ability or proficiency, the expertise at some art or craft. A skilled person is one who has acquired an ability, usually gained through special experience or a regular program of training. Though we may not be able to change our gifts or talents, we can work on the skills that express them. We can develop natural talents and spiritual gifts alike through training and experience.

A call to preach comes with the gifts necessary to that calling.

John Broadus wrote 120 years ago that the preacher needs "the capacity for clear thinking, with strong feelings, and a vigorous imagination; also capacity for expression, and the power of forcible utterance."[2] Though they are not all developed to their fullest, you have the gifts necessary for these qualities if you are called. Though each of us is unique, and our gifts come in different combinations, we are responsible for what we do with that one talent, two talents, or five talents. The sharpening and maximizing of those gifts is what we mean by skills development.

It may be easier to focus on your limitations, using your lack of talent as an excuse for poor preaching. You can rationalize that weakness by pointing to other areas of ministry you feel are strengths. Then you don't have to put out the effort to develop preaching skills. You are exempt from the discipline and hard work required to develop your skills to your best. You can just shrug your shoulders and say, "Some have it and some don't."

But we know well that this rationalization is not easy to swallow. Every minister I know wants to be an effective preacher of the Word of God. No matter what else you do well, if you are weak at preaching there is no way to make it up. It hangs over your head like a cloud of accusation. You become defensive about your preaching. You may try to laugh it off when your people make jokes about it. You may become angry. But neither you nor they will ever be satisfied with poor preaching.

Sermon Preparation Skills

In this study we will focus on the skills necessary to sermon preparation. Though delivery skills are important, most experienced preachers are fairly comfortable in the pulpit. They have developed a style in the preaching of their sermons that is personal, communicative, and forceful. The delivery style is not the critical factor in what we recognize as great preaching. Great delivery without effective content is often only "sound and fury, signifying nothing." On the other hand, striking content is of real interest to the hearer, even if the delivery is weak.

You may wonder how we can approach the study of sermon preparation in the same way someone would teach a welding class, since we usually associate skills development with a training program for some technical occupation. Studying sermon preparation as a general subject may not help the preacher much; the job must be broken down into doable tasks. Then the preacher must master each of those tasks by the same techniques used in any skills development: understanding the task, seeing a step-by-step demonstration, and practicing the steps until each is mastered.

The preparation of sermons involves a series of tasks that the preacher must accomplish one at a time. Most preachers work out their own system of sermon preparation by trial and error. The more organized sorts plan their work in detail, while the rest just muddle through. Most preachers fall into a pattern of sermon preparation not designed so much for good preaching as it is to suit their temperaments and life-styles.

What I have detailed in this study is a series of exercises you can use to strengthen sermon preparation skills at your own pace. Each task addresses a specific aspect of good preparation and can become a part of your own sermon preparation system. Each skill is based on sound principles of interpretation or communication, and results in specific benefits to your final product. Go through the book in the order of the chapters to get a feel for each of the exercises, then concentrate your efforts on the skill you feel is your neediest point. After mastering that one, move on to the next area of need.

The particular skills I have chosen to emphasize are critical to the overall result of good sermons. The first three skills prepare you for a thorough inductive study of the text. Chapters 4, 5, and 6 focus on skills important for getting the textual idea to the contemporary world of your audience. Chapters 7 and 8 help with skills needed for planning the way you will organize the sermon. Chapters 9 through 11 deal with skills needed for finishing the development of sermon ideas. Finally, chapter 12 concentrates on your purpose in preaching.

Twelve Skills for Sermon Preparation

1. *Getting the Text in View:* Recognizing and noting the relationship of various ideas in the text.

2. *Seeing What Is There:* Recognizing and noting the significance of details in the text.

3. *Asking the Right Questions:* Asking questions leading to the best research to interpret the writer's meaning.

4. *Naming the Textual Idea:* Naming from themes in the text the one idea that unlocks the text's meaning.

5. *Touching Human Needs:* Tracing from textual truths to the hearer's particular need for those truths.

6. *Bridging from Text to Sermon:* Constructing an interpretive bridge for bringing the truth of the text to its expression in the sermon.

7. *Writing Sermon Divisions:* Wording divisions clearly to state the teachings of the text on its subject.

8. *Planning Sermon Design:* Determining the arrangement of sermon materials for the most effective communication.

9. *Developing Sermon Ideas:* Planning development for the understanding, acceptance, and response of the hearer.

10. *Exploring Natural Analogies:* Finding natural analogies that precisely and vividly picture sermon ideas.

11. *Drawing Pictures,* Telling Stories: Using vivid language to create word pictures of biblical and contemporary scenes and stories.

12. *Preaching for Faith:* Planning every aspect of sermon design toward the aim of a faith response in the hearer.

Assumptions for this Study

My views about preaching should be clear to you already, not only in what you have read so far, but in what you can read between the lines. To conclude this introductory chapter, I want to go over a few simple beliefs I have about learning how to preach. Some of these views you will already have noticed; others will help complete the picture of assumptions about preaching which are foundational to the ideas in this book. Here are some of my convictions about the strengthening of preaching skills.

Sermon preparation is a supernatural endeavor. I am amazed that God has chosen to make Himself known through preaching. If you were God, would you trust the kingdom into the hands of the preachers you know? Paul asked the right question, "Who is adequate for these things?" (2 Cor. 2:16). Every aspect of preaching calls for earnest prayer. We preach by faith, and it is God who makes it work for His purposes.

Effective preaching is not a mystery talent for only the most gifted. Of the hundreds of students in my classes through the years, there have been a few ten-talent ones, many five-talent ones, and a few one-talent ones. I am uneasy with the idea that only the good preachers can learn homiletics. The keys to growing in this, as in any other skill, are desire, consistency, and hard work. Training in homiletics should be designed to equip the one-talent person along with the more gifted.

Anyone can learn the methods used in the preparation of good sermons. Any reasonably intelligent person can learn to discern the truths in Scripture and declare them to the profit of the hearer. Though we think of the heroes of old and the stars of today as our models for preaching, most Christians hear from rather humble and nondescript pastors week by week in the thousands of small churches across the country. While we thank God for those who preach to thousands, we also thank Him that those who preach to dozens can do so effectively.

Preaching is a science before it is an art, calling for discipline before freedom. At times these methods seem mechanical and wooden, a "fill-in-the-blank" approach to sermon preparation. These exercises represent a deliberate effort to break down into simple steps the normal process for effective sermon preparation. Since we deal with the canon of Scripture, we must be careful students before we can be inspiring faith-builders. It takes hard work before the freedom comes.

Old habits resist new methods and require objectivity and discipline. If you have read this far, you are probably already preaching or plan to do so. Maybe you have been preaching for several years. If so, you already have methods of preparation and delivery that work for you. It is difficult to set those methods aside to look objectively at a new approach, but that objectivity is necessary if this study is to do much good. You won't learn much if you set out to defend and justify your own methods against those presented here. Just suspend judgment a while and take advantage of anything here you can use.

The great weakness of preaching is fuzzy, ill-defined ideas. Unless the preacher is clear about his ideas, those who listen will surely not be. But we must recognize this failure if we are to work at a correction.

The preacher is a wordcrafter who clarifies his ideas carefully and precisely with the right words. There is little chance of really knowing what you want to say until you put it into words. The verbalizing itself gives shape to the thought and distinguishes it from other ideas. Wordcrafting, the craft of the preacher, is as much a science and an art as any other craft.

Biblical preaching allows the text to shape the sermon. There are many and various definitions of biblical preaching. Perhaps the simplest way I can describe it is to say that a biblical sermon is one in which the text shapes the sermon. The purpose, the theme, the structure, and the development of the sermon are to reflect the text.

The Bible is a rich and unlimited source for fresh, timely preaching. I am not smart enough to think of something theological and helpful to say for half an hour, three times a week, for years and years. Neither are you. We must not follow that common pattern of preaching in which the sermon is about 90 percent the preacher's ideas and about 10 percent biblical exposition. The Bible is the written record of the revelation of God. It is our source for the best, freshest, most meaningful preaching.

This study can deal with but one approach to preaching. Most introductory courses are surveys. They cover the history and the contemporary views on the subject. This study will not attempt that much. It is designed to deal with a basic method of sermon preparation in terms of twelve skills which can be strengthened for more effective preaching.

Summary

Skills for any performance are a reflection of gifts and the hard work of learning and experience. Preachers can strengthen preaching skills by learning and practicing twelve selected tasks for sermon preparation. Skills development means the gradual growth in the skills of a particular craft. As part of learning and experience, skills development requires clear instructions, hands-on familiarity with the material, working at one's own pace, examples to follow, and consistent practice.

Preaching is an expression of the deepest devotion and convictions of the preacher. Most preachers prefer to work on their own at improving their skills. Three kinds of learning—knowledge, values, and skills—are all needed for improving preaching. The gifts necessary to the preaching ministry come with the call to that ministry, but the preacher is responsible for what he does with his gifts. Most preachers develop a sermon preparation method by trial and error, but can strengthen it by an intentional skills development plan. I believe that preaching is a supernatural endeavor, but that anyone can learn the necessary skills with discipline, hard work, and a commitment to clear thinking and Bible-based sermons.

Now that these introductory ideas are before us, we will move along to the skills related to inductive Bible study.

Study Questions

1. What does a skills development approach to preaching improvement mean?

2. What are some of the features of a skills development program?

3. What are the differences in talents, gifts, and skills?

4. What are three basic kinds of learning?

5. According to the author, what is the greatest fault of poor preaching?

6. What are the author's assumptions about your potential for preaching?

---

1. John A. Broadus, *A Treatise on the Preparation and Delivery of Sermons,* revised 1898 by Edwin Charles Dargan (New York: George H. Doran, 1926), 9.
2. Ibid., 9–10.

A sermon should be like a tree. . . .
It should have deep roots:
As much unseen as above the surface
Roots spreading as widely as its branches spread
Roots deep underground
In the soil of life's struggle
In the subsoil of the eternal Word.[1]
                    H. Grady Davis, 1958

CHAPTER 1

GETTING THE TEXT IN VIEW

They stood at the laboratory table, Harvard freshman Nathaniel Shaler and his professor, who was about to give him his first assignment. It was 1858. The professor was Louis Agassiz, renowned naturalist and opponent of Darwinian views. He opened a specimen jar, and a foul odor escaped to worsen the already unpleasant smell of the lab. He removed an odd-looking fish and placed it in the pan.

"You are to examine this fish and record everything you see," Professor Agassiz said, his Swiss accent adding to the aura of academia. Then he warned that the student was, on no account, to talk to anyone about it or read anything about fishes. "When I return, I will see what you have observed."

As the professor left, the student looked around the otherwise empty lab, placed his paper and pen on the table, and took a tentative look at the smelly fish. He recorded a few observations, then a dozen, finally twenty. Though always within call, Professor Agassiz concerned himself with Nathaniel no further that day, nor the next, nor for a week.

Finally, on the seventh day, he returned for a report, sitting down on the end of the table, puffing his cigar. "Well?" he asked. After an hour's report on the fish from the eager student, he turned to leave again, saying, "That's not right." Mr. Shaler threw himself into the task anew, discarding his old notes. After another week of ten-hour days, he was able to give a report which satisfied his professor. Next Agassiz placed a half-peck of bones before him and said, "See what you can do with these."

What was the point of it all? Observation. Louis Agassiz later said, when asked about his distinguished career as a naturalist, that his greatest contribution was to teach students to observe, to look and really see what was there.[2]

Inductive and Deductive Thinking

This emphasis on observation is critical to the scientific method. Whatever the area of study, it is vital to let the data speak for itself. This approach is inductive, examining the particulars in order to come to some conclusion about what you see there and what it means. Deductive thinking, on the other hand, begins with assertions of truth and moves to the particulars which might come from such truths.

One of the mental tendencies of preachers is a fondness for deductive thinking. They tend to think more in terms of general truths than particular situations. The preacher sees the particulars in his world as evidence of convictions he already holds. As a result he may approach his biblical study with a head full of preaching ideas looking for a place to touch down. Contrast that with a research scientist who must work inductively. The scientific method requires him to examine every detail before coming to a conclusion about what it means.

Def • i • ni´ tion: Deduction and Induction

Deduction: act or process of reasoning from the general to the particular, or from the universal to the individual, or, specifically, from given premises to their necessary conclusions.

PREMISE: all squirrels climb trees

premise: this animal is a squirrel

conclusion: this animal climbs trees

Induction: act or process of reasoning from a part to a whole, from particulars to generals, or from the individual to the universal.

observed: seventy-five squirrels climbing trees

conclusion: all squirrels climb trees

As a result of this deductive mindset, preachers may not be as observant as they need to be of the particular factors which affect their preaching. One factor affecting our preaching is the complex world of the biblical text. Here it is too easy to glance casually at the surface appearance of the passage and make a quick evaluation from our own ideas. Another set of factors has to do with the life needs of the people we serve. Here is human nature on parade. But rather than carefully examining what we see, we may tend to respond deductively and make judgments too quickly, bringing the *generals* of our beliefs to bear on the *particulars* of human life.

A debate has been joined in recent years over inductive versus deductive approaches to sermon structure.[3] The traditional sermon outline tends to be deductive, beginning with general truths and moving from there to particular applications. Those calling for inductive preaching say that modern audiences will respond better to preaching which begins with the particular knowledge and experiences of the hearer and moves from there to the universal truths of the faith. This makes sense, of course, because people are always interested in their own personal concerns.

Isn't it obvious that the preacher needs to think deductively at times and at other times inductively? The challenge for us is to determine when inductive thinking is appropriate and when we should proceed deductively. We can declare the timeless truths and move from them to the particulars which show them to be true. But we can also learn to study the particulars of contemporary life and of the Scripture in such a way as to arrive at the general meaning of those details.

Inductive Bible Study

In this chapter and the two following we will outline elements of an inductive study of the text. In this approach the preacher will come to the text to discover for himself what is there. Only after completing his own analysis will he search out what someone else says about the text and state some conclusions.

In this chapter we will concentrate on an inductive look at the biblical text, with a special emphasis on the writer's organization of his thoughts. The skill we are seeking to strengthen is this: *recognizing and noting the relationship of various ideas in the text.* To help develop this skill you can practice with an exercise called the *structural diagram.* The purpose of this exercise is to get on paper the basic structure of the text in the writer's own words.

Before we introduce this skill and the structural diagram exercise, however, it will be helpful to take a closer look at inductive Bible study. We will define this approach to your textual study and discuss its advantages and results.

Approaching the Text

The cartoon shows a pastor in a discouraged mood, his face in his hands, elbows on a large desk. Behind him are hundreds of books on bookshelves which reach to the ceiling. The caption reads, "I can't think of anything to preach." I like to show this cartoon to my classes because of the assumptions behind it. In the first place, it is on target with the stress of pastors about what to preach. Another assumption, however, is that the pastor should be looking in all those books to find something to preach.

Our image of the pastor preparing his sermon may picture him at a large desk covered with open books, his paper before him, writing with inspiration and the furrowed brow of earnestness. He moves from commentary to commentary to find the meaning of his biblical text. He finds a snappy quote in one book and a fresh insight on the text in another. He puts it all together and sits back with a sigh of satisfaction. He has his sermon for Sunday.

Sermon preparation in the real world is a different story. Pastors are often frustrated with their sermon preparation, particularly the handling of the biblical text. Many do not have a clearly defined method for approaching a text. Their technique may involve praying, thumbing pages, reading, staring, and searching commentaries. They all seem the things to do, but don't work very satisfactorily. Effective text study isn't achieved by earnestness alone; neither can it be assured by the amount of time you put in. The key may well be the approach you take to the task, your study methods.

Some preachers may have a lack of confidence in their own scholarship. They are not sure they can bring out the deeper meaning of their texts. They just don't recognize all those insights the commentators find in Scripture. Since they don't want to lead their congregations astray, they make sure what they say is backed by a real scholar.

On the other hand, some find it easier to prepare topical sermons. That way they don't have to dig into the text for all the hidden insights that are probably there. They can just do an overview of the topic and come up with some aspects of that subject they know are generally consistent with Scripture. The sermon is biblical only in the sense that it doesn't contradict the Bible.

A growing number of preachers are finding that the best approach to their text study is inductive. This means you come to your text to examine it as thoroughly as possible in order to understand its meaning. You try to avoid coming with your mind already made up about what it means. You are reasoning from the particulars (specific information in and about the text) to the generals (teachings the text reveals). Those who use an inductive study method are continually amazed at the riches their study produces.[4]

Text-based preaching particularly requires an inductive approach to Bible study for sermon preparation. It is important that the preacher's intention be to let the text speak. He will be tempted repeatedly with the "sermonizer's trap," the tendency to look for a sermon instead of examining the details for the meaning of the text. This fallacy usually results in only a surface understanding of the riches of the text. Not only should the preacher's intention favor inductive study, his methods for his Bible study must also follow an inductive approach. For one thing, that means waiting until your own analysis is complete before consulting commentaries and other helps.

Def • i • ni´ tion:
Deductive & Inductive Bible Study

Deductive Bible Study: bringing your own or others' ideas to the text in order to find support and verification for them in the text.

  subject: brought by the preacher

  aspects: determined by the preacher

  purpose: confirm the preacher's ideas

Inductive Bible Study: carefully examining the text for whatever information it contains on the subject it addresses and seeking to discern the universal principles thus revealed.

  subject: revealed by the text itself

  aspects: observed in the text's ideas

  purpose: receive the writer's teaching

The nature of the Bible itself invites inductive study. It is a book of particulars, with the universal truths of the revelation of God presented in specific historical settings. The prophets and preachers and writers of Scripture communicate in particulars. The natural step from study to sermon is much easier with inductive methods. The reasons for choosing an inductive approach to your study are numerous. Let's consider some of the values of inductive Bible study more closely.

Values of Inductive Bible Study

Not only is the inductive approach to textual study valuable because of the nature of the biblical materials, but there are a number of advantages to the preacher and the congregation. Let's consider some of the advantages of inductive Bible study.

With inductive Bible study, you can get to work whether you are particularly inspired or not. Let's face it. Most of us preachers are looking for something to light our fire. We want an insight, a spark of inspiration, an angle on the truth which will get us moving with some enthusiasm. The problem with this is that the emotional measure of truth is not that dependable. We may spend a lot of time looking for something to stimulate us rather than actually studying. The inductive method described here is somewhat mechanical. You can work at your Bible study, inspired or not. I promise you, however, that somewhere along the way the ideas you discover will ignite your enthusiasm.

In an inductive approach to Bible study, the preacher is a first-hand user of the primary documents, the Scriptures. A basic principle for effective research is the use of primary documents. Though a preacher might think his best source of information on his text will be commentaries, he is ignoring this basic principle if he begins there. What someone else says about the text is not nearly so important as what the text itself says.

Inductive Bible study begins with what the text actually says and involves a careful and systematic examination of it. What someone else thinks it says is given consideration in a later stage, after the preacher has observed for himself what is in the text and systematically raised the questions which come to his mind about it. When he seeks the expertise of others, he does so for answers to his own questions.

As a result of beginning with the text itself, the preacher is less dependent on the interpretations of others. As we have said, many a preacher is uncertain about his own qualifications to interpret the Bible. He is sure that the mysteries of its meaning are known only by that exclusive circle of scholars able to discern its secrets. He does not realize that an inductive method of Bible study will allow him to open its meaning for himself. The Bible was given to reveal God, not to hide Him. As the preacher learns to examine the text carefully, he will be amazed to find that his favorite commentators often note the same insights he has already discovered.

Inductive Bible study also allows the preacher to be more receptive to the Holy Spirit. Jesus promised, "When He, the Spirit of truth, comes, He will guide you into all the truth" (John 16:13). Not only did the Holy Spirit inspire the writing of Scripture, He also illumines the reader to understand its meaning. If the preacher's sermon preparation method has him using Scripture merely to support his own ideas, he will frustrate this ministry of illumination. If he examines the text inductively, however, he suspends his own conclusions to let it speak, opening the way for the Spirit to disclose its meaning.

The inductive approach to Bible study means the preacher has more enthusiasm for truths he has discovered himself. Oletta Wald named her book on inductive Bible study *The Joy of Discovery*.[5] It is a most appropriate title. Inductive Bible study is a process of discovery. The preacher comes to the Bible with a commitment to let the text speak. His careful examination of every aspect of the passage leads to the discovery of insights he never noticed before. He is eager to share those "new" insights in his sermon. His enthusiasm is far beyond what he experiences relating some expert's interpretation. And his audience can tell the difference.

The preacher is more creative in his interpretation of the text's meaning when his method is inductive. His joy in personally discovering insights from the text gets his creative instincts moving. His mind begins racing to analogies, metaphors, descriptions, other passages, and contemporary meanings for textual insights. He finds himself writing as fast as he can to record the explanations, the images, the evidence, and the applications which come to mind. By the time he completes his inductive study he has more than enough material for his sermon, and it is the fruit of his own study.

Inductive Bible study assures that the preacher is better prepared for every kind of preaching. In this book are directions for preparing a theological outline of the text as the sermon structure. This traditional structure is probably the most familiar way to organize an expository sermon. There are other varieties of sermons which can also be effective. The oldest form is the verse-by-verse interpretation and application, called a homily. You may want to try an inductive or life situation structure or take a narrative approach. Whatever the organization of the sermon, however, an inductive study of your text will better prepare you with content.

Planning Inductive Bible Study

If you are to take an inductive approach to your textual study, you will have to plan it out in step-by-step fashion. There are three phases in an inductive study of your text. Phase 1 is *observation*, in which the preacher seeks to examine the text in every detail. Phase 2 is *interpretation*, as the preacher comes to an understanding of the meaning of the text. Phase 3 is *proclamation*, as the text's meaning is expressed in a form designed for communication. At this point we will focus on phase 1.

Inductive Bible study begins with observation. The aim of your study in this phase is to examine every aspect of the text in order to come to an understanding of the writer's meaning. You are like Sherlock Holmes attempting to unravel a mystery. With his double-billed cap, his pipe, and his large magnifying glass, he explores every possible avenue of information. So it is with the expositor. Every bit of information can be helpful. You do not know at first which particular details will turn out to be critical for an understanding of your text. There are two general kinds of observation you want to pursue.

(1) The first kind of observation is the *panoramic view*, a look at the larger picture. This is like standing on a mountain to look down on a farm in the valley below. You can take in the entire farm at once. You can see the layout of the land and how the various buildings, fields, and equipment are related. You can see the surrounding area, the terrain, adjoining farms, woods, and water. In a similar way you want to begin with an overview of your text in its context.

(2) The second kind of observation is the *microscopic view*, a look at the details within the text itself. You will examine every shred of evidence you can in the words and phrases of the text in order to discern the writer's meaning. We will discuss the microscopic observation in the next two chapters. At present we will begin with the panoramic view.

Before you begin to examine the text itself, read a background sketch of the book in a Bible dictionary. You will learn something about the writer and the readers, the places where they lived, the occasion of the writing, the kind of literature it is, and the important themes of the book. In any inductive study you will want to have some background information before you examine the text itself. This will help you to see the text in its setting. But you will avoid research concerning the interpretation of the text until after your own examination is complete.

Carefully read the chapters on either side of your text, preferably several times. This will usually require reading the entire book. When you are preaching a series of sermons through a book, you will read it over and over, noting how the ideas in the text fit into the writer's overall message. In your text study you may want to use a different translation than you do in the pulpit.

A literal translation such as the *King James Version,* the *New King James Version,* or the *New American Standard Bible,* is best for study because of its closeness to the Greek or Hebrew text of the passage. Some prefer a dynamic equivalent translation such as the *New International Version,* in the pulpit because it emphasizes the use of contemporary language. [6]

Seeing Structural Relationships

A key element in the panoramic view of the text is the writing of a structural diagram. As we have said, the purpose of this exercise is to diagram the text in terms of the structural relationship of various ideas in it. At this point you are not working with sermon structure. You are only analyzing the text writer's structure for this passage.

This exercise will open your understanding of the text as a whole and help you see the way the writer deals with his subject. Though it might be best to diagram the text in the original language, we will work here in English. It is possible that your study of significant words in the text will later uncover some needed adjustment to your structural diagram. If you use a literal translation, however, you will be able to do the diagram in English with good results.

As you gain experience using it, the structural diagram will give you more and more insight into the relationship of ideas in the text. Here are some of the relationships to watch for.

Def • i • ni´ tion: Structural Diagram

A *structural diagram* is a phrase-by-phrase chart of the text in the exact word order of the translation you use. Its purpose is to show in graphic form the relationship of various ideas in the text.

The structural diagram is one exercise in an inductive study of the text. It is part of the observation phase in which the particulars of the text are examined in detail. The structural diagram helps give an overview of the writer's thought. A similar form of this exercise has been called a "syntactical display," "block diagram," or "mechanical layout."[7]

The structural diagram is constructed by copying the text wording in order, one phrase at a time. Beginning with the first independent clause, main ideas are set to the left and subordinate ideas to the right. Equal ideas are thus lined up vertically. Connectives are set apart in brackets.

The main ideas in the text will usually have the most support from secondary ideas. This is the principle of proportion, which concerns the amount of space the writer gives to various ideas in a given discussion. For example, 1 Peter 1:3–5 (NKJV) has a number of significant theological words in it, but the structural diagram shows us that the writer comments the most on three ideas: (1) "has begotten us again," (2) "to an inheritance," and (3) "for you who are kept." As these ideas flow one to the other in the text, the diagram shows them to be key centers of support in the writer's thoughts. Each idea has a series of subordinate concepts which enlarge the reader's understanding of it. The three main ideas, with their clusters of support, cover everything the writer says in these verses.

Secondary ideas in the diagram will provide vital information about the concepts they support. "Support" means that these secondary ideas are helping to explain and describe main ideas. In the example from 1 Peter, we noticed the clusters of support material for certain ideas in the text. The phrase "has begotten us again" is supported first by (1) "according to His abundant mercy." Note that this phrase doesn't follow "begotten," but is before it. It nonetheless tells us something about the reason for God's action in giving us new birth. Other supportive ideas to "begotten us again" follow in a series: (2) "to a living hope," (3) "through the resurrection," and (4) "to an inheritance." So we see a cause, a means, and two results of the new birth.

Some ideas will be related in terms of cause and effect. This will be a key aspect of the diagram to see. Notice, for example, in Matthew 5:13, that the loss of its flavor by the salt results in four effects: (1) "how shall it be seasoned," (2) "it is then good for nothing," (3) "it is to be thrown out," and (4) "it is to be trampled underfoot." The last two effects may be one, but they are distinct enough to list separately. Noting these four effects of the loss of flavor helps to see how the salt metaphor might apply to the disciple's life in Jesus' thinking.

Notice the placement of the four outcomes vertically as a series. We had to ask whether to place those results under "salt," since that is the main subject, or under flavor, since that is what is lost? I chose to place them under "loses" because they are the results of losing. They tell us nothing about salt or flavor, but support the idea of losing the flavor. So as you deal with conditional statements, be careful to discern the pivotal word for the results which follow the condition.

**Structural Diagram
1 Peter 1:3-5 (NKJV)**

Blessed be the God
    [and] Father
        of our Lord Jesus Christ
who
    according to His abundant mercy
  has begotten us again
  to a living hope
  through the resurrection
      of Jesus Christ
      from the dead
  to an inheritance
    incorruptible
[and] undefiled
[and that] does not fade away
    reserved in heaven
      for you
        who are kept
           by the power of God
           through faith
           for salvation
              ready to be revealed
                in the last time.

Questions and answers create a dialogue structure as the writer assumes both sides of the conversation. Questions usually indicate an argument in which the writer is focusing attention on a particular point. In Galatians 3 Paul uses eight questions in his argument for justification by faith alone. In verse 2 a question serves to make the central point clear, "Did you receive the Spirit by the works of the law, or by the hearing of faith?" Isaiah uses questions most effectively, as in Isaiah 40:21, "Did you not know? Have you not heard? Has it not been declared to you from the beginning? Have you not understood from the foundations of the earth?"

The progression of thought will show the writer's ideas moving toward some end or conclusion. As you examine the movement of the writer's message, ask the simple question, "Where is this discussion going?" In the structural diagram of 1 Peter 1:3–5, the writer links one idea with another to move steadily toward the final words about "the salvation ready to be revealed in the last times."

Watch the Connectives

One of the simplest keys to the structure of your text is to look carefully at the connectives. You have set them apart in brackets for emphasis in your structural diagram. Each connective reveals the nature of the relationship between the ideas it links together. In doing so, these terms open the structure of the text to you so that you can properly interpret the relationship of ideas in the writer's thinking. Watch for the following kinds of structure as they are signaled by connectives.[8] The most common connective is "and," used to indicate logical sequence, as in any series of ideas.

Comparison shows ideas to be alike, similar, or of equal weight in the writer's thinking. Watch for "like," "as," "also," and "too" as connectives. Of course "and" can be a comparison connective as well, though its common use may cause you to overlook it. In Psalm 1:3 the godly man is described as "like a tree firmly planted by streams of water."

Contrast means two elements are unlike, possibly opposites. Some connectives of contrast are "but," "nevertheless," "even though," "much more," "yet," and "although." In Exodus 32:34 God says, "My angel shall go before you; nevertheless in the day when I punish, I will punish them for their sin."

Conditional statements reveal a relationship in which a particular condition is said to lead to a predictable result. They are often indicated by the "if ... then" pattern, though not all conditional statements use the terms "if" and "then." In Matthew 5:13 there is the conditional statement, "if the salt loses its flavor." We have already noted the "then" or result of the condition.

Structural Diagram
Matthew 5:13 (NKJV)

You are the salt
          of the earth;
[but]
[if] the salt loses its flavor,
          how shall it be seasoned?
It is [then] good
          for nothing
        [but] to be thrown out
        [and] trampled underfoot
          by men.

Correlative structure shows two elements to be related to each other reciprocally. It is seen in the use of pairs of connectives: "both ... and," "as ... so also," "so ... as," "for ... as." In Ephesians 5:24 we see this correlative relationship, "But as the church is subject to Christ, so also the wives ought to be to their husbands in everything."

Connectives of reason point to arguments which show that one element is the reason behind another: "because," "therefore," "for this reason," "for," "since." In Genesis 22:18 God promises Abraham, "And in your seed all the nations of the earth shall be blessed, because you have obeyed My voice."

Purpose statements are often apparent by connectives like "that," "so that," and "in order that." These connectives may also indicate result, but you will be able by the wording to tell which is meant. In Luke 5:7 the result relationship is clear, "And they came, and filled both of the boats, so that they began to sink." In Ephesians 1:18 the ideas are related by purpose: "I pray that the eyes of your heart may be enlightened, so that you may know what is the hope of His calling."

Sequence or time connectors help you to note the order of events: "now," "until," "when," "after," "before," "since," "while." Also note the geographical connector "where."

Guidelines for the Exercise

You will find that the structural diagram will help with the overview of the text for any kind of material. You will notice relationships among the ideas in the text which you might never see without the diagram. For long narratives, the diagram may not be of such value because the progression of thought is already obvious. You will find, however, that for critical sections of a narrative passage, a structural diagram will help get the text in view.

At first you may not be sure of the placement of phrases. Just ask the question, "What does this phrase tell about in the line above?" If it is a new idea, it will go to the left margin. If it is part of a series, it may relate to a word several lines above. Always try to line up with the specific word in the previous material which it most clearly supports. Though you might debate that with yourself, try to follow the writer's intention as best you can discern it.

Structural Diagram
Hebrews 4:12–13 (NKJV)

[For] the word of God is living
      [and] powerful
      [and] sharper
         [than] any two-edged sword,
           piercing
              even to the division
                  of soul [and] spirit,
                [and] of joints [and] marrow,
        [and] is a discerner of the thoughts
           [and] intents
              of the heart.

To get started choose a short, familiar passage and practice the structural diagram. Jot down the observations you make as you look at the structure of the text. Go back to a sermon you have recently preached and write out the text in a diagram. See if any new insights come which you had not noticed in your previous study of the text. Remember, there may be differences of interpretation as you come to difficult placement decisions. Make your best choice, but make sure your reasons are clear.

Once you have constructed a few dozen structural diagrams, it will become much quicker and easier for you to do. Then you will find that, as you read, the structure of a text will be more apparent to you. You will begin to develop an eye for relationships between the various ideas and the difference that makes in your interpretation. This, of course, is the aim of this exercise, to develop the skill of observation in this panoramic view of the text.

Remember as you practice this exercise that your aim is to get the text in view. You are attempting to understand the structure of the biblical writer's message just as he wrote it. Your ultimate aim for the preparation of biblical sermons is to let the text shape the sermon. The text will give you its subject, its structure, its development, and its purpose. The structural diagram helps get you started in seeing them.

Completing the Structural Diagram

Here are the steps you will take in preparing a structural diagram of your text. As you get into your diagram, the order of these steps will no longer apply. They are not rules to follow so much as procedural instructions. You want to be flexible as you construct the diagram. Keep in mind the aim of graphically portraying the structure of the passage. An important benefit of this exercise is that you must write out the text yourself, word for word. That familiarizes you with the exact wording of the text. You notice details and relationships just because you are copying it word for word.

STEP 1: Write the first independent clause as your starting point. An independent clause expresses a complete thought without the aid of other phrases and contains at least a subject and verb. All texts, however, do not begin with independent clauses. Sometimes your text will begin with a supporting phrase rather than a main idea. In this case, find the first independent clause to establish your anchor line at the left margin. After writing it, place the preceding phrase(s) above it, but still in position to indicate their relationship to the independent clause. This is necessary to maintain the exact word order of the text. Look, for example, at Genesis 1:1, "In the beginning God created the heavens and the earth." The first independent clause begins with "God created. . . ." The "in the beginning" part must wait to be placed in relation to that first clause.

STEP 2: Place supporting phrases, clauses, and words starting directly under the words they relate to. "What does this phrase relate to?" will be your main question throughout the exercise. Sometimes placement under the most appropriate word of the phrase above calls for an interpretation decision. For instance, is "piercing" in Hebrews 4:12 the equivalent of "living," "powerful," and "sharper" in a series? Or does "piercing" modify "sword" and thus explain how the Word of God is sharp? Though it may not make a difference in the meaning of the text, you must decide where you think the "piercing" phrase goes. It will make some difference in the structure as you picture it.

STEP 3: Line up any series of equal words, phrases, or parallel thoughts vertically. This will happen automatically when you properly construct your diagram. A series may include supporting ideas of various kinds that reveal different information about the subject. Notice the clear series of terms describing the Word of God in the diagram of Hebrews 4:12. The Word is said to be "living," "powerful," "sharper than any two-edged sword," "piercing," and "a discerner."

STEP 4: Place connectives in brackets and set apart from the main ideas. Connectives are very important for indicating the nature of the relationship between elements of the text. Setting them apart lets the phrase or clause stand alone and emphasizes how the connectives relate one idea to another.

STEP 5: Place parentheses around words italicized in the text and around forms of address. In a literal text (KJV, NKJV, NASB) words not in the original language are placed in italics to indicate that they are editorial additions for the sake of smoothness of wording. "Brothers" and other forms of address are not usually a part of the structural relationships.

Summary

This chapter presents the structural diagram exercise designed to help strengthen skill in noting the relationship of ideas in the text. The frustration of many preachers with their text study methods can be remedied with an inductive study approach, of which the structural diagram is a part. Inductive study has a number of advantages: working without "inspiration," dealing firsthand with the Scriptures, less dependence on others' interpretations, better receptivity to the Spirit, more enthusiasm for discovered ideas, more creativity in interpretation, and better preparation for any structure.

The observation phase of inductive Bible study includes the panoramic view (the broad look) and the microscopic view (the details). The panoramic view considers the context of the passage, the background, and the structure. The structural diagram will display the structure of the text in several ways. Main ideas can be recognized by the support the writer gives them. Cause and effect relationships can be seen. The use of questions and the progression of thoughts reveal structure. The most revealing feature of the text's structure may be the connectives, which indicate comparison, contrast, condition, correlation, reason, and purpose in the relationship of textual ideas.

Now that we have worked on the structural diagram exercise, we are ready to move on to immediate observations, the next part of the observation phase in our inductive Bible study.

Study Questions

1. What is the difference between inductive and deductive thinking?
2. Why is inductive Bible study important for the preacher's intention?
3. What are the seven advantages of inductive Bible study?
4. What are the three phases of an inductive Bible study?
5. What are two general kinds of observation?
6. What is the main purpose of the structural diagram exercise?
7. What are the eight kinds of structure signaled by connectives?

---

1. H. Grady Davis, *Design for Preaching* (Philadelphia: Fortress, 1958), 15.

2. Nathaniel Southgate Shaler, "Chapters from an Autobiography," *Atlantic Monthly,* 103 (February 1990): 221–22.

3. The current debate began with Fred B. Craddock, *As One Without Authority: Essays on Inductive Preaching* (Nashville: Abingdon, 1971). Years earlier, however, H. Grady Davis discussed inductive preaching in *Design for Preaching,* 174–77. See also Ralph L. Lewis and Greg Lewis, *Inductive Preaching: Helping People Listen* (Westchester, Ill.: Crossway, 1983), plus other books by these authors.

4. The ideas here on inductive Bible study are adapted from Farrar Patterson, *Inductive Bible Study for Sermon Preparation* (Fort Worth: By the author, 1977), and from Oletta Wald, *The Joy of Discovery,* revised edition (Minneapolis: Augsburg, 1975). Also see a similar approach taken by Josh McDowell, *Guide to Understanding Your Bible* (San Bernardino, Calif.: Here's Life, 1982).

5. Though this little book is not designed for pastors and sermon preparation, it is a good introduction to some methods for inductive Bible study.

6. See Robert L. Thomas, "Bible Translations and Expository Preaching" in *Rediscovering Expository Preaching*, ed. John MacArthur, Jr. (Dallas: Word, 1992), who prefers a literal translation; and Gordon D. Fee and Douglas Stuart, *How to Read the Bible for All Its Worth* (Grand Rapids: Zondervan, 1982), chap. 2., who argue for the dynamic equivalents.

7. Patterson, *Inductive Bible Study,* 9–10. See Walter C. Kaiser, Jr., *Toward an Exegetical Theology* (Grand Rapids: Baker, 1981), 99, 165–81; and Donald L. Hamilton, *Homiletical Handbook* (Nashville: Broadman, 1992),36–37.

8. McDowell, *Guide to Understanding Your Bible,* 53.

Structural Diagram

Text ___Psalm 1:1–2 (NKJV)___ Name ___W. McDill___ Date_____

Identify the first independent clause and copy it word for word from your text. Then copy succeeding material phrase by phrase, locating each phrase carefully under the word it supports. This will place main ideas to the left margin, with supporting ideas falling to the right below them. Copy any words before the first independent clause above, with placement indicating the word it supports. Any series of equal ideas should be lined up vertically. Set connectives apart in [brackets]. Put *italicized* words in (parentheses). Underline verbs and circle words carrying the main themes of the text.

Blessed is the man

    who walks not

       in the counsel

         of the ungodly

     [nor] stands

       in the path

         of sinners

    [nor] sits

      in the seat

        of the scornful

[But] his delight is in the law

       of the Lord

[and] in His law

   he meditates

    day [and] night

Structural Diagram

Text ___Ephesians 1:3–5 (NKJV)___   Name __W. McDill__   Date_____

Identify the first independent clause and copy it word for word from your text. Then copy succeeding material phrase by phrase, locating each phrase carefully under the word it supports. This will place main ideas to the left margin, with supporting ideas falling to the right below them. Copy any words before the first independent clause above, with placement indicating the word it supports. Any series of equal ideas should be lined up vertically. Set connectives apart in [brackets]. Put *italicized* words in (parentheses). Underline verbs and circle words carrying the main themes of the text.

Blessed be the God
　　　　　　[and] Father
　　　　　　　　　　of our Lord Jesus Christ
Who has (blessed) us
　　　　　　　　with every spiritual blessing
　　　　　　　　in the heavenly (places)
　　　　　　　　　(in Christ)
[just] as He (chose) us
　　　　　　　in Him
　　　　　　　　　before the foundation
　　　　　　　　　　　of the world
　　　　　　[that] we should be holy
　　　　　　　　　[and] without blame
　　　　　　　　　　　(before Him)
in love having (predestined) us
　　　　　　　　to adoption
　　　　　　　　as sons
　　　　　　　　　(by Jesus Christ)
　　　　　　　　to Himself
　　　　　　　　　according to the good pleasure
　　　　　　　　　　　　of His will
　　　　　　　to the praise
　　　　　　　　　of the glory
　　　　　　　　　　　of His grace . . .

38

Structural Diagram

Text _____ Name _____ Date _____

    Identify the first independent clause and copy it word for word from your text. Then copy succeeding material phrase by phrase, locating each phrase carefully under the word it supports. This will place main ideas to the left margin, with supporting ideas falling to the right below them. Copy any words before the first independent clause above, with placement indicating the word it supports. Any series of equal ideas should be lined up vertically. Set connectives apart in [brackets]. Put *italicized* words in (parentheses). Underline verbs and circle words carrying the main themes of the text.

Perhaps there is no property in which men are more
distinguished from each other, than in the various
degrees in which they possess the faculty of observation. The great herd of mankind pass their lives in
listless inattention and indifference to what is going
on around them, . . . while those who are destined to
distinction have a lynx-eyed vigilance that nothing
can escape.

William Wirt, 1828

CHAPTER 2

SEEING WHAT IS THERE

Just before Christmas 1988 Pan Am Flight 103 exploded over
Lockerbie, Scotland. All 259 people aboard were killed, plus 11
more on the ground. The question: Who planted the bomb? The
first step in the investigation was to reconstruct the plane and its
parts from hundreds of thousands of fragments scattered across
845 square miles of Scottish countryside. In late 1989 a Scottish
investigator going through a bag of burned clothing found a
fingernail-sized shred of green plastic embedded in a piece of
shirt. The tiny piece of plastic was traced to a timing device, the
shirt to a small store in Malta. From these apparently insignifi-
cant details the case was broken and indictments issued.[1]

The success of the investigation lay in the details. Tirelessly
the investigators combed through the wreckage, leaving not even
the smallest clue unexamined. What the untrained layman
would overlook as meaningless, they analyzed in every way
possible. They worked from information gathered in previous
experiences of this kind. They reconstructed not only the entire

plane, but the sequence of events leading to the crash. As important as gathering the information was the interpretation of it.

The Power of Observation

The key to the big issues is often a trivial detail. Police investigators find and identify a piece of carpet fiber. An auditor notices an unusual ledger entry. An astronomer logs a star where none is supposed to be. A geneticist traces a gene structure he doesn't expect. What gift do these specialists have that leads to such breakthroughs? We call it the power of observation. Very simply it is the alertness to detail of one who is trained to really see when he looks.

We might think that a person either has this special gift of visual perception or he doesn't, and there is something to the idea that it is a gift. But the power of observation is also a skill to be developed. This has been proved in the training for such highly demanding jobs as FBI and Treasury agents. Though a person may not be accustomed to the alertness to detail these jobs require, he can learn it.

Most people tend to be observant in some area of interest while not paying attention in other areas. For instance, a husband may not notice what his wife is wearing as they get in the car to go out for the evening. But his eye is immediately drawn to a tiny scratch in the paint of their new car. His attention is selective. His wife, on the other hand, can tell him that the old friend they met unexpectedly at the restaurant had dyed her hair. But she cannot describe how they got to the restaurant and couldn't find her way there again. We are observant in the things of interest to us.

Spiritual Blindness

Not only do we tend to be selective in our natural power of observation, the Bible teaches that we suffer from spiritual blindness. Throughout Scripture the theme of blindness is used for the perception of the things of God. When the covenant was renewed with Israel after the wilderness wandering, Moses told them, "Yet to this day the Lord has not given you a heart to know, nor eyes to see, nor ears to hear" (Deut. 29:4).

The sin of God's people results in a blindness to God's truth. In his call, Isaiah was told to go and tell the people, "Keep on listening, but do not perceive; Keep on looking, but do not understand" (Isa. 6:9). Even though Isaiah preached God's message to them, they would not grasp it because of their sin. God spoke to Jeremiah of His judgment for their sin, "Here this, O foolish and senseless people, Who have eyes, but see not; Who have ears, but hear not" (Jer. 5:21). Ezekiel was told by the Lord, "Son of man, you live in the midst of the rebellious house, who have eyes to see but do not see, ears to hear but do not hear; for they are a rebellious house" (Eze. 12:2).

This spiritual blindness of man is a theme in the New Testament as well. Both Jesus (Matt. 13:14–15) and Paul (Acts 28:27) applied Isaiah's words to their own generation, particularly to the Jews. Paul wrote that "their minds were hardened; for until this very day at the reading of the old covenant the same veil remains unlifted, because it is removed in Christ" (2 Cor. 3:14). He said the gospel was veiled as well to those "in whose case the god of this world has blinded the minds of the unbelieving, that they might not see the light of the gospel" (2 Cor. 4:4). Jesus challenged the church at Laodicea to recognize their spiritual blindness, to use "eye salve to anoint your eyes, that you may see" (Rev. 3:18).

This spiritual blindness of the fallen man affects his intellectual perception as well where the revelation of God is concerned. Isaiah expressed the problem as he wrote, "'For My thoughts are not your thoughts, Neither are your ways My ways,' declares the Lord. 'For as the heavens are higher than the earth, so are My ways higher than your ways, and my thoughts than your thoughts'" (Isa. 55:8–9). The thinking of God is foreign to the mind of man.

Paul follows the same theme, but distinguishes between the natural man and the spiritual man. "But a natural man does not accept the things of the Spirit of God; for they are foolishness to him, and he cannot understand them, because they are spiritually appraised" (1 Cor. 2:14). This hopeless situation is remedied by the new powers of the regenerate man. "But he who is spiritual appraises all things" (1 Cor. 2:15). This new discernment comes because "we have the mind of Christ" (1 Cor. 2:16). He reproves the Corinthians for their immaturity because they are unable to receive the meat of God's truth. Even as believers, their carnality had dulled their spiritual discernment so that they could not grasp the deep things of God.

Jesus promised, however, that the Holy Spirit would come as the "Spirit of truth." In that role "He will guide you into all truth; for He will not speak on His own . . . for He will take of what is Mine and declare it to you" (John 16:13–14). Paul recognized the need for the grace of God in receiving His truth. He prayed for the Ephesians that God "may give you the spirit of wisdom and revelation in the knowledge of Him, . . . the eyes of your understanding being enlightened" (Eph. 1:17–18). Here is the power of observation from the biblical view, an endowment of the grace of God.

Preachers are no different from anyone else in their need for this special sight for the Word of God. Not only do we need the supernatural ability to see in the spiritual dimension, we need to cultivate our natural alertness to the written text. Spiritual enlightenment enhances mental perception. Even for the most experienced of us, there is always room to grow in our insight into the subtleties of the biblical text. Even though we have the gifts and the grace of God necessary for this aspect of our sermon preparation, we also know that as stewards of this grace we must develop these skills.

In this chapter we will introduce the exercise we call *Immediate Observations*. The skill we hope to develop with this exercise is this: *recognizing and noting details in the wording of the text and their significance for its meaning.* It is one thing to identify the relationship of various ideas in the text, and quite another to dig into the details of the text's wording. We have referred to one as the panoramic view and the other as the microscopic view. Each exercise, however, calls for careful observation and analysis. This is why we are addressing the matter of your power of observation.

Developing Observation Skills

For expository preaching the text is a constant. Every time you read it the words are the same. It does not vary its message from one reader to another. How is it, then, that one person will find insights in a text that another never sees? The text is the same for each. The difference is in what they see. One looks but does not see, while another looks and sees what is only apparent to an alert and attentive eye.

What does it take to have this power of observation? For one thing it will take a certain amount of basic talent and intelligence. We believe, though, that anyone called of God to the preaching ministry will have the gifts necessary to the preparation and delivery of sermons. But giftedness is not the same as skill. Remember, the premise of this book is that a preacher can strengthen certain skills and thus improve his preaching. Consider some of the factors involved in strengthening your power of observation.

Skill in observation depends heavily on one's motivation. Most people are not very observant because they don't have to be. They get along pretty well not having to pay close attention to what is going on around them. Some vocations do call for special power of observation—an auditor checking over the corporate books, a Secret Service agent carefully watching the crowd while the president speaks, or an auto plant inspector running his hand over the finish of a new car. They are all motivated to be observant because it is their job. When a preacher realizes it is his special calling to find the truth his people need to hear, he will be motivated as well. There is no substitute for desire.

Skill in observation demands an eye for the details. Inductive thinking begins with the details, the particulars. The goal is to arrive at a conclusion based on these specifics. The attention must not be focused on that aim but on the particulars. In one sense an able observer learns to think small. He knows that it is the close attention to the little things that is the secret to success in business, in art, in science, in every pursuit of life. So it is with preaching as well, particularly in the study of the biblical text.

Def • i • ni ´ tion: Observation

Observation means the act or practice of noting and recording facts and events, as for some scientific study. For Bible study observation means noting and recording what the student sees in a careful examination of the details of the Scripture passage. The aim of recording these observations is to understand the intended meaning of the writer.

Observations are of two kinds: (1) The *panoramic* approach, seeing the whole. This involves looking at the overall message of the writer in its context and noting the relationship of ideas in the text. (2) The *microscopic* approach, seeing the parts. This involves carefully examining the writer's message in its smallest parts and noting every detail of what he wrote.

Recording *immediate observations* is one step in the microscopic approach of the student's observation of the text. This exercise is a key feature of an inductive method for Bible study.

Skill in observation calls for a healthy learner's curiosity. There are several kinds of curiosity. One is motivated by the pride of knowing more than others. A second kind of curiosity is driven by the carnal desire to know the private affairs of your neighbors. A third kind of curiosity comes from a thirst for knowledge, and it is that which enables us to develop the power of observation. This tendency to probe and investigate strengthens our attention to detail. We continually find ourselves asking how many, what kind, what color, which way, why, who, in what order, and so on. A learner's curiosity on the part of the preacher will have him probing into the corners and between the lines of his text.

Skill in observation needs discernment as to what is worthy of close attention. I do not like to play Trivial Pursuit. Not only do I find myself not knowing the details of knowledge in many categories, I am not interested in knowing. This is not to say that world affairs, even remote events, are not important to us. We must choose, however, what we are to give full attention. Since you cannot pay attention to everything, the skill of observation is focused on those matters of consequence. As a preacher gains experience in his inductive study of the text, he will learn where to dig in for the most fruitful results.

Skill in observation requires a willingness to postpone judgment. Most of us are prone to jump to conclusions. With even one "fact" in hand, we tend immediately to assume we know where it leads. The skilled observer, however, will intentionally wait to make a judgment, even though he may see the beginnings of a trend. Unless he waits until sufficient particulars are clear, he may find himself trying to prove a hasty conclusion and thus ignoring other particulars which do not support it. Another discipline needed at this point is the setting aside of opinions. Otherwise our own biases crowd in to force themselves on each new situation. The discipline of suspending judgment is at the heart of inductive Bible study. The preacher records all the observations he can before coming to a conclusion about what they mean.

Skill in observation demands a ruthless realism about the facts. A "fact" is something which has actually happened or actually exists. There is a marked difference between a fact and a supposition, between reality and guesswork. We are tempted to want the facts to favor our views and to "see" them in that light. We also tend to be selective about which facts to note and which to ignore. Or we may tend to call a "fact" what is only conjecture or guesswork. In all these possible pitfalls, the skilled observer will be strict in dealing with the facts realistically. A preacher must take care to avoid these same pitfalls in his study of the Bible: adjusting the text to his views, avoiding what does not support his views, and claiming biblical support by inference.

Skill in observation requires knowing what to look for. An observant person has to have some knowledge of the area of inquiry. An astronomer can search the skies with skill because he knows what to look for. An auto mechanic can often tell you what is wrong with your car merely by listening to it because he knows what to expect. A physician can diagnose your trouble by examining you and asking questions because he knows what to look for. So it is with the preacher in his Bible study: he has to know what to look for in the text or his search will be frustrating.

Your power of observation as a preacher is valuable not only in textual study, but also in the study of your congregation and their needs. They are a part of the larger tribe we call mankind, so whatever we note about human nature will apply to them. But they are also Christians, an identity that calls for a different set of expectations. Beyond that, your flock is part of a regional identity and a local community. Watch and learn. Learn who they are, and you will make the communication contact much more readily.

The Immediate Observations Exercise

The immediate observations exercise is designed to help develop the skill of noting and observing the details of the text. As you complete this exercise with text after text, you will notice that you have an eye for the details you did not have before. Let me remind you, however, that there is no substitute for working on paper. You just cannot do this exercise in your head. After you have considerable experience with it, you will not need the written exercise as much but will still find it valuable.

Remember that this is not the time for research. You are to record what you see without the aid of lexicons, commentaries, or other helps. This emphasis on observation is the great value of inductive Bible study. The preacher is involved in a "hands-on" relationship with the text. As a result, he becomes more and more capable as a serious student of the Bible. Research is important in your study of the text, but it comes at a later phase, after you complete your inductive analysis.

Complete each exercise in order for the entire text. The first exercise for observation was the structural diagram. This exercise, immediate observations, is followed by the third, interpretive questions. At each step be careful not to jump ahead. This keeps you from becoming distracted from your observations until you have examined the whole passage one step at a time. For now, avoid asking questions. That will come after your immediate observations are complete.

Approach the immediate observations exercise as a brainstorming session. Even though you are the only one involved, operate with the rules we usually set when a group "brainstorms" a problem. Write down every idea that comes up. Do not try to evaluate or sort out which are good ideas at this point. The purpose is to come up with as many ideas as the subject will evoke. If you start second-guessing yourself and trying to evaluate your observations, you will stifle your creativity and squelch your attention to detail. There will be time later to sort out your ideas.

Let me mention again that your aim in the observation phase of your study is to look carefully at the text itself. You are asking, "What do I see in the text?" and "What is the author saying?" You are not searching for a sermon in there somewhere. If you will complete a thorough inductive study of the text, you will be able to state the theological ideas found there. These ideas then become the ideas in your sermon. So don't jump ahead to sermonizing before you have allowed the text to speak in its own terms.

Those with little Bible study and preaching experience may be quite unsure of their ability to make valid observations from details in the text. Most of the material in the text will not be familiar. The temptation will be to look for the "answers" in commentaries and other reference books. With more and more experience, however, the preacher will grow in his knowledge of the Bible. He will begin to recognize recurring themes, common metaphors, historical references, etc.

This recognition factor will become an increasingly valuable strength as you study the Bible for your preaching ministry. You will find that the Scripture is consistent throughout. The central themes will come up again and again in the Old Testament and the New. The more significant Bible terms will become familiar to you. The figurative language will make increasing sense. Like flowers springing up here and there in a field, the great theological themes of Scripture will appear and you will recognize them in each new context.

Experienced preachers may have a different kind of reluctance as they approach the immediate observations exercise. Those of us who have been preaching for some time know that we know something about the Bible. The temptation for us is to examine the text in terms of our own knowledge, rather than in terms of the writer's intention. Seeing a particular theme mentioned, we may jump to the conclusion that we understand the text and that there is no need to dig deeper. But discipline yourself to the inductive method and withhold your conclusions until your observations are complete.

What to Look For

The power of observation requires some knowledge of what you are looking for. So it is with the immediate observations exercise. Consider, then, what you expect to see in the text.

Begin by reviewing the observations you have noted from your structural diagram. The purpose of that exercise was to strengthen your skill in recognizing and noting the relationship of various ideas in the text. So watch for the following patterns: (1) main themes which get more space in the writer's discussion; (2) supporting ideas which clarify the meaning of primary concepts; (3) cause and effect structure; (4) questions and answers which focus special attention on an idea; (5) the writer's progression of thought.

The structural diagram also reveals relational observations by examining the connectives. Note the following as you see them: (1) comparisons, (2) contrasts, (3) conditional statements, (4) correlative structure, (5) reasons, (6) purpose, and (7) results. Simply write, for example, "the godly man compared with a tree." Or note, "the godly contrasted with the wicked." You may write "purpose of the writer in this section."

After writing your observations from the structural diagram, look for other features in the text.

Identify significant words you see in the passage. By significant we mean those words which carry the weight of meaning in the text. They may be nouns, verbs, or modifiers. They will carry key theological themes from which you will later select a dominant theme you believe is the writer's subject. Notice, for example, the significant words in the first verse of Psalm 1: blessed, walks, counsel, ungodly, stands, path, sinners, sits, seat, scornful. Each of these words is full of meaning and deserves close examination.

Note the verb tenses you can see in the English text. These can be very important as you identify past events already accomplished, present action which continues, and future action yet to come. Later on, as you research the original language you may find more subtle distinctions in tense which the English text does not convey. Notice in Mark 11:24 the very interesting verb tenses, "all things for which you pray and ask, believe that you have received them, and they shall be granted you." In this case the verb tenses dramatically affect the interpretation.

Watch for descriptions the writer uses. The way he describes events and ideas will provide details and shades of meaning not otherwise apparent. Consider whether any descriptive wording differs from the usual scriptural portrayal of the subject. The description of the Philistine champion, Goliath, is vivid in 1 Samuel 17. Note his height, his armor and its weight, his weapons and their size and weight. These descriptive details will be an aid in understanding the size of the man and in picturing him in your sermon.

Note any repetition of words, phrases, or ideas. This will usually indicate that the theme in question is a primary one in the passage. See if the repeated idea is given different shades of meaning or remains constant with the repetition. In the account of Jesus' response to Nicodemus in John 3:3–8 the word "born" appears eight times in these six verses. Surely this indicates something about the theme for this passage.

Identify figurative language of any kind. There are a number of distinctive figures of speech you will want to identify, though some have only uncommon and technical uses.[2] You may find that you can identify figurative language without being able to use the technical term for it. You want to see how the figurative language portrays the subject and opens the door to better understanding of the writer's intention. Look at the figurative language in Psalm 1:1. Though you might not see all these terms as figurative at first, a closer look will reveal that they are not literal: walks, stands, path, sits, seat. The meaning of these figures will be most important for the interpretation of this text.

Observations to Note

- Main themes emphasized by amount of discussion
- Supporting material which clarifies main ideas
- Cause and effect relationship of ideas
- Questions and answers focusing attention
- Progression of thought toward a climax or conclusion

- Comparisons between ideas or persons
- Contrasts of ideas, character, or behavior
- Conditional statements in the "If . . . then" pattern
- Correlative structure
- Reasons cited by the writer
- Purpose statements
- Results

- Significant words which carry the weight of meaning
- Verb tenses apparent in the English translation
- Descriptions used by the writer
- Repetition of ideas, words, and phrases
- Figurative language of various kinds
- Assertions carrying the writer's firm convictions
- Commands or admonitions applying theological truths
- Promises revealing the intentions of God

Note assertions the writer makes. An assertion is a statement which is affirmed positively and declared with assurance. Assertions stand out from supporting comments which elaborate on them. Assertions often carry special significance because they contain the key elements of the writer's thinking. In John 14:6 Jesus asserts clearly, "I am the way, the truth, and the life; no one comes to the Father, but through me." This statement is intended as a clear affirmation of a conviction of Jesus.

Identify commands or admonitions to the readers. These statements are important because they usually carry the application of the theological ideas the writer is discussing. To clarify this you may want to trace them back to the doctrinal basis for the particular call to action. As you make the connection, you will see how this action reflects the conviction behind it. Paul writes in Ephesians 4:1, "I . . . beseech you to walk worthy of the calling with which you were called." Much of the rest of the book gives the details of how to do so.

Watch for promises expressed in the passage, either plainly or by implication. The Bible contains thousands of promises to the believer. A study of the promises of Scripture reveals much about God and His character, His will, and His intentions in His dealings with man. Many of the promises are universal in application so that they speak just as surely to our generation as to the one addressed in the text. Moses delivered the promise of God to Israel, "He will not leave you nor forsake you" (Deut. 31:6), which is later quoted in Hebrews 13:5. As a direct promise of God with universal application, it has special significance in telling us of God's intentions.

Completing the Exercise

Let me summarize some guidelines for getting started: (1) work with a single translation; (2) pray expectantly for the guidance of the Holy Spirit; (3) come with the attitude and intention of a learner; (4) be alert to the "sermonizer's trap;" (5) expect to do a lot of writing, especially at first; (6) keep in mind that the goal is to discern the thought in the mind of the original writer in his historical situation.

STEP 1: Your first step for the immediate observations exercise is to divide a sheet of paper into two columns. You may want to design a special form for this exercise similar to those used as examples in this chapter. In reality, however, it is nothing more than a sheet of paper divided into two columns. I prefer to write this exercise by hand because I am able to look at the whole passage at once by spreading out my worksheets; others, however, like the flexibility and quickness of the word processor.

STEP 2: In the left column copy one phrase or verse of the text, word for word. You will need to experiment with how much to copy at once. Texts from the New Testament epistles, for example, are so packed with meaning that you will copy only short phrases to note observations. Other material, such as narratives in both Testaments, may be copied in longer portions because you are not likely to have as many observations per verse. As with all of the exercises, it is best just to start writing, and adjust after you begin to get the feel of it.

STEP 3: In the right column record your observations from a look at the details of the one phrase. Review the possibilities of "what to look for" that are listed in this chapter. Do not expect to find all the different kinds of observations in one verse or phrase. You will be able to note a number of different kinds, however, so do not stop until you have exhausted the possibilities. Remember, this is not the time for asking questions; that step comes next. And do not move to that step until you have completed your immediate observations for the entire passage.

Summary

An important skill for many professions is the power of observation, the alertness to detail which comes with training and experience in a particular field. The Bible indicates that man suffers from spiritual blindness, an inability to perceive the spiritual dimension. The regenerated man, however, is able to discern the things of God with the help of the Holy Spirit. Preachers especially need this spiritual sight in addition to natural skills. The sermon preparation skill addressed in this chapter is recognizing and noting the details in the wording of the text and their significance for its meaning. The exercise is immediate observations.

The text of Scripture is the constant in preaching. Differences in giftedness and skills will result in different levels of effectiveness in preaching. Skill in observation depends on one's motivation, demands an eye for details, calls for a healthy learner's curiosity, needs discernment as to what is worthy of close attention, requires a willingness to suspend judgment, demands a ruthless realism about the facts, and requires knowing what to look for. The preacher should be observant of his people as well as his text.

The immediate observations exercise calls for a sheet of paper divided into two columns, one for the words of the text and the other for observations. It is not the time for research into the views of others about the text, but for the preacher's own observations. The exercise is a brainstorming session for noting everything you see in the text. The preacher will need to keep before him a list of the kind of observations he might make.

Now that we have examined the first two exercises in the observation phase of your text study, we are ready to move to the third, interpretive questions. We have diagrammed the structure of the biblical writer's message in its original context. We have looked at the details of his wording for observations. Now we will raise the questions which come to mind about the text and go to study helps for some answers. These questions will open the way to a sound interpretation of the text for today's audience.

Study Questions

1. What is the power of observation?
2. What is the skill the observations exercise aims to strengthen?
3. Identify the factors involved in strengthening your power of observation.
4. What area besides the study of the text calls for a preacher's careful observation?
5. What is the recognition factor?
6. What are some of the things to look for in the text?
7. When making immediate observations, why is it important to suspend judgment?
8. What is the goal of the observations exercise?

---

1. Helen Gibson, Farah Nayerl, and Elaine Shannon, "Solving the Lockerbie Case," *Time,* November 25, 1991, 62.

2. See a list of figures of speech in Howard G. Hendricks and William D. Hendricks, *Living by the Book* (Chicago: Moody, 1991), 266-267. A different list with some similarities can be found in Al Fasol, *Essentials for Biblical Preaching* (Grand Rapids: Baker, 1989), 84-85.

Immediate Observatons

Text _____ Psalm 1 _ Name W. McDill _____ Date_____

Copy the text in the left column, one phrase at a time. Look closely at the words and phrases of the text and write observations you note there in the right column. Look again at your structural diagram for ideas as to what the text is saying. Note not only what is obvious, but also what is suggested and implied by the words of the text in its context.

Watch for observations in several categories: (1) historical details; (2) literary details; and (3) theological details. Your purpose is to examine the text for every bit of information possible about its message.

Phrases of the Test	Your Observations
How blessed is the	Here is a means of fulfillment.
man	There is a great extent ("how")
	A person meeting certain requirements.
Who does not walk in	"Walk" is probably manner of life.
the counsel of the	Counsel is advice on influence.
wicked	The wicked is probably the ungodly.
	This man does not follow the advice of sinners
	in his lifestyle. Walk may mean values as
	well.
nor stand in the path of	"Stand" seems to mean position, where he
sinners,	places himself. "Stand" could indicate
	loyalties, values.
	The "path" of sinners is their normal traffic
	pattern. This man refuses to position himself
	in the way sinners go and is blessed. The
	blessing may be inherent in obedience.
nor sit in the seat of	The third condition of his blessing seems to be
scoffers	a progression here.
	"Sit" and "seat" also figurative May mean
	judgment or conclusion, like a judge "sitting"
	So the three conditions complete the man's
	responsibility.

Immediate Observatons

Text John 3:1–8 (NASB)   Name   W. McDill   Date

Copy the text in the left column, one phrase at a time. Look closely at the words and phrases of the text and write observations you note there in the right column. Look again at your structural diagram for ideas as to what the text is saying. Note not only what is obvious, but also what is suggested and implied by the words of the text in its context.

Watch for observations in several categories: (1) historical details; (2) literary details; and (3) theological details. Your purpose is to examine the text for every bit of information possible about its message.

Phrases of the Test	Your Observations
Now there was a man	Beginning of a story
of the Pharisees,	A particular man, a "historic character"
named Nicodemus.	Belonged to the Pharisees, with certain beliefs, values, etc.
	He may be mentioned in other places.
a ruler of the Jews	Ruler means member of the ruling council.
	Was a leader among the Jews
	Was a Jew himself
	Possibly had a leadership agenda
	May have come representing Jewish leaders.
this man came to Him	The same man
by night	He apparently sought out Jesus.
	May have had an appointment
	May have come at night for secrecy
	May have been no other time to see Jesus; too busy; no privacy.
	John means something significant in mentioning "by night."
	Could be symbolic, following the light and darkness theme in John

Immediate Observatons

Text __Ephesians 1:3 (NKJV)__ Name __W. McDill__ Date_____

Copy the text in the left column, one phrase at a time. Look closely at the words and phrases of the text and write observations you note there in the right column. Look again at your structural diagram for ideas as to what the text is saying. Note not only what is obvious, but also what is suggested and implied by the words of the text in its context.

Watch for observations in several categories: (1) historical details; (2) literary details; and (3) theological details. Your purpose is to examine the text for every bit of information possible about its message.

Phrases of the Test	Your Observations
Blessed be the God	God is to be praised for what follows
and Father of our Lord	God is identified through Jesus Christ.
Jesus Christ,	Could mean He is already blessed, fulfilled
	He is the Father of Jesus Christ.
	Jesus is "our" Lord.
who has blessed us	Past tense—already blessed us
with every spiritual	We (us) are the objects of blessing.
blessing in the heav-	The blessings are "spiritual."
enly (places) in Christ	We have been given "every" spiritual blessing.
	The blessings are located in the heavenly
	(places), the heavenlies.
	"Places" is italicized, not in the Greek.
	All blessings are focused in Christ. (thru Him,
	by Him, because of)
just as He chose us in	We are objects of His choice. Choosing us
Him before the	means grace, election. This choosing is in
foundation of the	Christ.
world.	We were chosen before the foundation of the
	world. "Foundation" means creation. "The
	world" is the created order. "Just as" con-
	nects with "blessed" in the previous clause.

Immediate Observatons

Text _____ Name _____ Date_____

Copy the text in the left column, one phrase at a time. Look closely at the words and phrases of the text and write observations you note there in the right column. Look again at your structural diagram for ideas as to what the text is saying. Note not only what is obvious, but also what is suggested and implied by the words of the text in its context.

Watch for observations in several categories: (1) historical details; (2) literary details; and (3) theological details. Your purpose is to examine the text for every bit of information possible about its message.

Phrases of the Test	Your Observations

Asking the right questions is of crucial importance, for asking the wrong questions will undoubtedly result in receiving wrong answers. One of the weighty issues in hermeneutics is, therefore, how to ask the right questions.[1]

Sidney Greidanus, 1988

CHAPTER 3

ASKING THE RIGHT QUESTIONS

Interpreting the world around us is an everyday part of life. We watch the television meteorologist to hear his interpretation of air currents, temperature, barometric pressure, and other factors which tell him what our weather is likely to be in the next few days. Sometimes he is even right. We read experts' predictions about the economy as they interpret the various indexes of economic activity. We listen carefully as the physician goes over the results of our annual exam and what they mean. All of these are interpretations of the available information that explain what it all means to us.

You and I are interpreters as well. You receive a letter from Uncle Jack and try to decipher what it says and then what it means. You examine the spots on the leaves of a rose bush, try to figure what is causing it to look so bad, and what to do about it. You hear a noise in the night and go downstairs to stalk around in the dark in search of the source. In every case you are asking three basic questions: (1) What do we have here? (2) What does it mean? and (3) What is its significance for us? These are the larger questions of interpretation.

The word *interpret* means simply "to explain the meaning of something." In order to explain the meaning of anything, you must first examine the phenomenon carefully to see what is actually there. This analysis requires some knowledge of the field, a skilled eye for indicators of one sort or another, and an understanding of what the indicators mean. A dentist who examines your teeth has to know something about teeth, what to look for in teeth, and the meaning of what he finds.

We also use the idea of interpretation to go beyond meaning to significance. The meteorologist can tell you what the weather patterns mean, but you want more. You want to know their significance for your local weather tomorrow. Significance means the bearing the meaning has on you. You are glad for your dentist's expertise in describing the condition of your teeth, but you want more. You want to know what it will take to fix them and how much it will cost.

Hermeneutics

Interpretation of the Bible is called *hermeneutics*. The word comes from the name of the Greek god, Hermes, who served as a messenger for the other gods. He was also the god of eloquence. So hermeneutics is the science of interpretation, particularly as it is applied to the Bible.

Interpreting written material such as the Bible is like interpreting anything else, but also has its special features. We still aim to discover what is there, in this case what the text says. We seek to discern what it means, particularly its theological message. And we want to understand the significance of that meaning for ourselves and our hearers. The Bible, however, has three features which make its interpretation different from the weather or a letter from your Uncle Jack.

In the first place the Bible is old. Its message comes from a time long ago, from several ancient periods of history with their own unique characteristics. Second, the Bible is fixed and stable as a written document. Unlike talking with a person face to face, you cannot read body language or emotion. The words are set for all time. It will hold still for you while you study it week after week. A third special feature of the Bible for the interpreter is this: it is about God and His dealings with mankind. That purpose in its writing requires the interpreter to deal with the Bible on its own terms, as what it was intended to be.

In the two previous chapters we focused on the skills of observation: (1) seeing the relationship of ideas in the text and (2) recognizing and noting details in the text and their meaning. Now we move to the second phase of inductive Bible study, interpretation. The exercise we introduce in this chapter is *Interpretive Questions*. The skill we hope to develop with this exercise is this: *asking questions for the best research to interpret the writer's meaning*.

Effective interpretation depends on the asking and answering of the right questions. A detective investigating a crime, an attorney defending a case, a physician dealing with a mysterious ailment—each will make careful observations and ask penetrating questions if they are to find the right answers. So it is with Bible interpretation. If you ask the right questions, your research will follow the right paths and lead you to the information you need for interpreting the text. Some of the information will be found in the Bible itself. Much of it will be found in other resources.

A Different World

I had never been to Russia. In April 1993, however, I was asked to teach a one-week intensive course in biblical ethics at the International Academy of Modern Knowledge in Obninsk. I enjoyed the trip, especially the people. It is true that people everywhere are much the same, but I couldn't help noticing the barriers I had to cross to relate to them in even the most surface way. I never once forgot that I was a foreigner and out of my element.

The first and most obvious barrier was the eight-thousand-mile distance from my home in North Carolina. We spent nineteen hours by air, in airport layovers, and in ground transportation getting there. Other barriers to cross had to do with language; Russian is an East Slavic language written in the Cyrillic alphabet, which is based on Greek letters. The culture is quite different from my own, especially since they are only recently breaking free of the seventy-five year dominance of Soviet Communism. The climate, architecture, dress, currency, diet, technology, and many other factors are different from what I am used to at home.

The world of the Bible is also a very different world from ours. The people, the politics, the times of the Bible are just as much foreign lands to us as Russia was to me. We need help to operate there. I do not mean to say that a person cannot read the Bible today and understand it. There is much there that is as understandable as if it were written here yesterday. But preaching calls for a study of the texts of Scripture at a deeper level. For that task we need interpreters for ourselves, and we must become interpreters for our hearers.

Though the world of the Bible is different from our own, some things are the same. We open our Bibles with two issues already settled in our minds. First, we believe that God is the same now as He was in the days of the Bible accounts. We believe He is immutable, that He never changes. Therefore His power and goodness and wisdom do not change. Second, we also believe that human beings are the same as they were then. Technology has changed so that now persons use a computer to keep records, drive or fly to get where they want to go, and pick up a phone for instant communication to the world. But the nature of mankind hasn't changed. It is still a mixed nature—made in the image of God on the one hand, but fallen into sin on the other and seriously injured in that fall.

So as we read of the strange and foreign world of the Bible, we can recognize the personal dimension. The people described there are much like us. We see ourselves in them, in their hopes, their doubts, their struggles, their failures, their faith. Their story is our story as we see God dealing with them in love and know that He is the same yesterday, today, and forever. We read of the mighty acts of God in that history, and we are encouraged to trust Him with our own history. So their story is faith's mirror image of our own.

While these unchanging factors make the Bible familiar to us, the differences from our world make it a mystery. The distance from where we live now to the lands of the Bible is many thousands of miles. But that distance is not our greatest barrier in getting inside the Bible world. There are other distances we must deal with which cause us to raise questions as we study the Bible.

The *historical distance* to the world of the Bible raises questions. A number of major civilizations march across the pages of the Bible, along with countless minor people groups and tribes. Some of these cultures were the setting for major portions of the Bible as God's people recorded His revelation—ancient Mesopotamia, Canaan, Egypt, Assyria, Babylon, Greece, and Rome. Their lives were very different from ours. How can we understand the Bible without knowing about their world—the geography, the customs of the people, their world view, politics, science, art, and daily lifestyle? Now, after two thousand years, the sands of those passing years have buried entire civilizations and the personal stories of countless lives. In many cases the Bible is the only record of what happened then, so studying its pages naturally raises the questions of history.

The *literary distance* to the world of the Bible raises questions. We must deal with it as a literary document containing various forms of literature, some strange to us. Though we have excellent English Bibles, we know it was written originally in Hebrew and Koine Greek, with some brief references in Aramaic. These languages are not like English. The alphabets, different grammatical structures, and ways of communicating a thought are different. Though it is best for a preacher to study these languages and literary forms, very few of us will ever be experts in the languages of the Bible. We will need a number of reference books to help us as we raise literary questions in our study of the Bible.

Your Reference Library

Bible Atlases will answer your geographical questions by showing the location and relationship of various places mentioned in the text.

Bible Dictionaries deal primarily with words used in the Bible, but also present much other material similar to that found in an encyclopedia. Almost any subject related to the Bible can be found there.

Bible Handbooks offer information similar to that in dictionaries, with perhaps more emphasis on the text of various books of the Bible.

Commentaries offer an explanation of the text and its meaning, with features varying from one commentary to another.

Concordances list the words which appear in the Bible and show the references where they appear, their meaning, and Greek or Hebrew roots.

Interlinear Bibles offer the Greek or Hebrew text between the lines of the English translation.

Lexicons deal with the Greek or Hebrew words as to their meaning in various forms and contexts.

Topical Bibles list many texts of the Bible under various topics, printing the complete wording of major ones and the reference of others.

Word Studies provide language, background, and usage information on words from the English Bible.

The *theological distance* to the world of the Bible raises questions. One theological mystery has to do with the religions of the ancient peoples who were neighbors, enemies, and captors of God's people. You will want to know about the gods of ancient Mesopotamia at the time of Abraham. For another text you will study the religion of Egypt that Moses confronted. You will ask about Baal and Molloch and Ashtoreth. You will confront the beliefs of the Hebrews at various stages in their history, along with the religion of the Greeks and Romans. Beyond these mysteries we must plumb the depths of Jesus' theology and Paul's, the theological error they addressed, and the consistency of biblical views. We have many theological questions to raise as we examine our preaching texts.

The Interpreter's Challenge

Biblical interpretation is a challenge for three important reasons: (1) the nature of the believer; (2) the nature of the Bible; and (3) the difference between the Bible world and our own. We have just discussed the distances we face in this third challenge.

The nature of the modern believer is a challenge as he works to interpret his Bible. The problem lies in his subjectivity, which means he naturally interprets everything (including the Bible) in terms of his own views and interests. Realizing it or not, he brings all that he is to his interpretation. In one sense his mind is already made up, with opinions and ideas on most issues. But the meaning we seek in a passage is not the meaning we give to it out of our own thinking, but the objective meaning to be found in the words of the original writer.

The pressure to find something to preach is always on a pastor. His approach to the text is naturally going to reflect his goal of preparing a sermon. Most of us, then, come to Scripture looking for sermons like children looking for Easter eggs in the grass. The text of Scripture can seem merely a place where some really colorful sermons are cleverly hidden. The temptation is to ignore the larger fabric of the text, snatch up a sermon, and keep moving.

The nature of the Bible itself presents a second challenge for interpretation. It is a divine/human book, written by men but containing the very Word of God. The interpreter must deal with the tension this dual source creates as he tries to sort out the very human qualities of the writers from the divine source of their

65

message. He finds that the stamp of individual personality is on each text he studies. Paul is not like Peter, and Luke is not like John. Their choice of content, their writing styles, vocabularies, and favorite themes all demonstrate their distinctiveness. Even so it is the Spirit of God who inspired each one with the divinely intended message.

The Bible also contains another tension for the interpreter, the particular/universal nature of its message. It comes out of particular situations in history and yet contains universal truths valid for all time. The interpreter must deal with the specific circumstances of those who wrote it and the timeless nature of their message. In fact, he can only discern the timeless truths by understanding what the original audience heard for their situation.

As we have already discussed, the third challenge for the interpreter is *the difference between the Bible world and our own.* John R. W. Stott describes the preaching task as bridge building. He says the preacher must build a bridge between the biblical world and the modern world to span the "broad and deep divide of 2000 years of changing culture."[2] He says two mistakes are common to modern preachers in dealing with what he calls a communication chasm. Some tend to stay on the Bible side and never quite build a bridge to the contemporary audience. Others tend to stay on the contemporary side and build no bridges to the biblical record of the faith.

If the preacher is to be a faithful interpreter, he must deal carefully with these three challenges: (1) the nature of the believer, (2) the nature of the Bible, and (3) the distance to the biblical world. He can do so only if he determines to let the text speak, standing with one foot firmly planted on the biblical side and one on the side of his contemporary audience.

Letting the Writer Speak

One of the greatest challenges for a preacher comes because he is trying to prepare a sermon. He may find himself trying to cross the hermeneutical bridge between the biblical world and the contemporary world before he has completed his task on the biblical side. He is tempted to snatch up some little homiletical tidbit and run across the bridge with it, leaving unexamined the depth of the writer's message. To change the metaphor, we preachers are too often like the wide receiver so intent on reaching the goal line that he turns to run before he has a good grip on the football. The preacher who wants to preach the Bible must make sure his aim is to discern the message of the original writer.

Gordon Fee has written aptly that "the text cannot mean what it never meant."[3] The only way to be sure of the timeless meaning which can speak today is to discover the original meaning on the occasion of its writing. Scripture was not written in a vacuum. The writer had a purpose and chose his words accordingly. There were needs, problems, and conflicts which called forth the ideas he expressed. His vocabulary, his audience, his concerns, his argument, and the progression of his thought were all related to his moment in time. His message was bound in history and is opened today like a time capsule from another age. That capsule contains, however, a revelation from God that speaks in the present moment of both generations.

Principles of Interpretation[4]
William D. Thompson

1. *Simplicity*. What is the natural and obvious meaning? The starting point for biblical interpretation is the clear, plain meaning of the passage.

2. *Intentionality*. Why is this text there? God intends the Bible to communicate His creative and redemptive purposes in Jesus Christ.

3. *Correspondence*. What connection is there between what God said then and is saying now? The basic interpretative process involves correspondence between the biblical and the contemporary worlds.

4. *Polarity*. What opposing ideas do I see? In every biblical passage, opposing forces are moving against each other.

5. *Contextuality*. What else is going on? Knowledge of a biblical passage's context or contexts may enhance its meaning significantly.

6. *Genre*. What kind of material is this? The literary form of the text profoundly influences its interpretation.

7. *Language*. What does the wording indicate? Knowledge of the role and use of language facilitates the discernment of meaning.

8. *Identification*. Where do I see myself and my hearers in this passage? Meaning is shaped by the placement of oneself and ones hearers in the dynamics of the text.

9. *Multiplicity*. What various meanings does this text yield? A text may yield a variety of meanings.

10. *Perspective*. How does this passage point to the death and resurrection of Christ? The Bible is a witness to the saving activity of God in Jesus Christ, the meaning of whose life, death, and resurrection controls the meaning of every passage.

So we come to the text to discover first what the writer intended to say. The Bible says his words were "God-breathed" (2 Tim. 3:16). Not only did the writer have a definite intention in what he wrote, the Holy Spirit was working to see that what He intended to communicate was faithfully recorded. We must not come to so carefully prepared a document tramping about looking for a sermon. We must come humbly—to listen, to learn, to discover. We must come with respect and appreciation for that writer as we carefully examine every word and phrase, that they may speak again now as clearly as they did then.

The writer has written what he intended to say in code. It is not a cryptic code, however. The code he used is designed to reveal his thought faithfully rather than to hide it from his readers. That code is language. Except for apocalyptic material and some parables, the biblical writers chose the words that would best convey their thought in the clearest fashion as the language was commonly used in their day.

Where does the modern interpreter fit into this communication process? In one sense he is an outsider attempting to decode a message never intended for him, like reading someone else's mail. The biblical writers never imagined that a space-age believer would one day be laboring over their words, attempting to understand their meaning and proclaim it anew. Old Testament writers lived in a variety of cultures across thousands of years. New Testament writers saw themselves as living in the last days. Many expected the return of Christ in their own lifetime. Even though their writings contained the foundational concepts for Christian theology, they were designed to speak to that generation.

The intention of the Author behind the writers went beyond their limited aim. The Holy Spirit saw to it that those writings, however limited their intended audience, contained the timeless truths of divine revelation for succeeding generations. The Spirit's intention was not in conflict with the human writers, but it was much greater in scope. It is that divine intention for Scripture which includes us as legitimate hearers. In that sense we are not outsiders, because the message is for us as well as for its original audience.

Because the message was originally written to address conditions in a specific time, we must begin with that intended message in our study. God's method of revelation is incarnational. He uses human experiences, thought processes, and language to convey His message to men. Even though we seek to discern theological truths which transcend the original occasion of writing, we can only discover them within the fabric of that original message. This important principle bears repeating. Our first task in discovering God's message to this generation is to understand the inspired writer's message to his own generation.

Three Areas of Inquiry

The questions you ask of the text will fall into the three categories we have already discussed as distances to the biblical world. There is the historical distance, the literary distance, and the theological distance.

You should raise questions about your text as an historical account. You will want to know the situation the text describes or the occasion upon which it was written. You will ask questions about any customs, political activity, economic conditions, glimpses of everyday life, business and trades, worldview— anything to do with the cultural context of the passage. Find out about people mentioned in the text, their races, other important figures, and names used in passing.

You will ask about geographical locations, distances, transportation, agriculture, and the topography of the land. You may want to consult a time line for placing your text historically in relation to other biblical and secular events. The historical questions are almost unlimited. Use your imagination to place yourself back in the world of your text. Ask anything you think of to complete the picture you have of that time.

Some of your historical questions may be answered in a study of other passages in the Bible itself. For instance, the author and readers may be mentioned in the larger context of your text.

Beyond the Bible, you will want to use a good Bible dictionary. It will have most Bible topics listed for the very information you need. Look up persons, cities, groups, movements, aspects of culture, etc. by name.

You should raise questions about your text as a literary work. First you will want to identify the kind of literature this is. This is what we call "genre," which simply means "kind" or "form." The Bible contains many different forms of writing: narrative, poetry, prophecy, and letters. There is quite some variety in the categories of literary forms different writers list. It is better to keep it fairly simple for sermon preparation purposes.

Questions will arise also about the definition of words, about grammar, syntax, structure, the kind of argument, figurative language, verb tenses, noun forms, mood, etc. Some of these answers will be in your structural diagram. You may want to study the writer's style as compared to other biblical writers. You will always want to ask "What is this about?" for each paragraph or section of your text. We will look at this question in detail in the next chapter.

You should raise questions about your text as a theological document. You will want to begin by identifying the theological themes that appear in the text. As we will discuss in the next chapter, each text may contain multiple themes in various relationships. Clarifying these themes and their relationships in the text is necessary to discovering the writer's central idea. The theological themes are best interpreted by other passages in the Bible that explain, illustrate, argue, or apply their meaning. Your aim is to draw from the text the theological message the writer intended and make it the message of your sermon.

Questions to Ask

These historical, literary, and theological distances can be examined in many ways. Here are three sets of questions you can ask. One set is the traditional journalist's questions. The second set deals more with the intentions of the biblical writer. A third set follows the principles of interpretation we have listed from

Thompson. Though you will notice some overlap in them, these three sets of questions will all be helpful as you raise issues for needed research.

The first set of questions you can ask are the standard journalistic questions used to get the facts in a story. They are who, what, when, where, why, and how. You can see immediately how helpful such simple questions could be. Who is the person referred to here? What is the issue Paul is addressing? When did this episode take place with reference to other events in the gospel account? Where is Laodicea? Why does Paul say, "You would have plucked out your own eyes and given them to me" (Gal. 4:15)? How did passenger traffic on ships work in those days (Jonah 1:3)? These questions are seeking basic information, but some of that information will affect the interpretation of the text and the presentation of the sermon.

A second series of questions deals with the writer's intentions as he wrote. The definition question asks, "What does this word mean?" This sends you to language studies for the meaning and background of the word in this context. The reason question asks, "Why did the author use this term?" This focuses on word choices and seeks to discern sometimes subtle differences between similar terms. The implication question asks, "What does this statement imply?" This question seeks to read between the lines and find the meaning of what was not stated directly.

A fourth question is the relationship question, "How are these ideas related?" You will be able to answer this more readily because you have completed the structural diagram to discover the relationship of ideas in the text. The progression question also deals with structure, "Where is this thought going?" Again, the structural diagram will help indicate the progression of thought, along with a careful examination of the context. The assumption question asks, "What is the assumption behind this statement?" This may lead to a search of corollary passages. It also may require reasoning from effect to cause to determine the basis for an assertion.

A third set of questions can be raised following the principles of interpretation quoted from William D. Thompson. Examine that set of questions for additional possibilities. If the questions suggested here do not give all the answers you seek, raise any questions you like.[5]

The Interpretive Questions Exercise

The skill we are aiming to strengthen in this chapter has to do with asking the questions which will lead to an understanding of the text writer's meaning. The exercise is Interpretive Questions.

A careful inductive exegesis of the text is an investigation. As our inductive Bible study method requires, you begin by observation. You sharpen your skills by learning to see what you might not have noticed before. Now, as we move from observation to interpretation, we still need our observation skills as we examine the text in terms of what mysteries are in it. We must look for what we do not understand, what will require research in other texts and in resources beyond the Bible.

Begin the process of asking questions only after completing your immediate observations for all verses in the text. This may be a difficult discipline to maintain. Observations you note about the text will often bring questions to mind. For instance, you will notice a significant word and need to ask what it means. Write for your observations, "significant word." Then wait for this step to raise the question about the definition of the word.

The interpreter needs to have a working knowledge of basic principles of interpretation, like those from Thompson. These hermeneutical principles are like the "tricks of the trade" for an interpreter. They guide him in his examination of the text so that his work is kept within the bounds of legitimate hermeneutics. The assumption behind these principles is that, properly handled, the text will disclose its meaning to the interpreter. Overall, interpretation raises three broad questions: (1) What do we have here? (2) What does it mean? (3) What is its significance for us?

In asking questions of the text, you may ask whatever you wish. Remember, however, that your aim is the proper interpretation of the text's message as the writer intended it. As you raise questions, you may not be sure which ones will lead you to the answers you need for your interpretation. As in recording your observations, do not second-guess yourself at this point. It is better to raise too many questions than to talk yourself out of one which might have proved fruitful. More experience with this exercise will give you a feel for the best questions.

Write everything down. Use a worksheet with space for your text phrases, the questions you will raise, and answers to those questions. Before you begin writing your text down a phrase at a time, there may be some questions which address the passage as a whole. Write these general questions first as you can, but allow yourself the freedom to bring them up at any time later as well. Some of your questions will be suggested by the structural diagram you have already drawn. Others will come from observations you have made. Check back to these earlier exercises as you work your way through the text with your questions. Do not begin to search for answers to your questions until you have asked every question you can.

Completing the Exercise

The Interpretive Questions exercise is designed to help strengthen your skill in asking the questions which will lead to the research necessary for a valid interpretation of the text. As with the last exercise, you will begin with a sheet of paper divided to provide two columns for your work. The following steps may be rather obvious to you, but let's go over them one by one.

STEP 1: Copy the first phrase of your text in the left column, word for word. Choose as large a portion as you can handle effectively at once. Different kinds of material require smaller or larger portions because of the nature of the content.

STEP 2: Look closely at the phrase and write the questions you need answered for a complete understanding of it. Number your questions so you can use the same numbers for recording answers later. Consult the lists of questions in this chapter to prompt you. Do not second-guess yourself. It is better to ask questions that prove unfruitful than to talk yourself out of them before you know where they will lead.

Complete the process of asking questions about your text, phrase by phrase. Then go back and check whether you can think of other questions you need to ask. Begin your research only after you have raised all the questions you can.

STEP 3: Begin your research with your first questions, seeking out whatever resources you need. On a separate paper, number your answers to correspond to your question numbers. Be sure to cite sources with page numbers for what you find. You may want to begin with word studies, then move to historical information, and so on. Use whatever process works best, but avoid looking for sermon outlines and other sermon material specifically. You want the text to shape the sermon, not from someone else's interpretation, but from your own.

Summary

This chapter is about raising questions which will lead to research to help you in your interpretation of the text. Interpretation is a normal part of everyday life as we raise the questions of what something is, what it means, and what significance it has for us. Interpretation of the Bible is called hermeneutics. Bible interpretation takes into account that it is old, its words are fixed, and it is essentially about God.

The world of the Bible is very different from our own. We do assume, however, that God has not changed, nor has the nature of man changed. Three major distances remove the Bible from our immediate understanding: the historical distance, the literary distance, and the theological distance. Interpreting the Bible is a challenge because of the subjectivity of the believer, the nature of the Bible, and the distances to the biblical world. The Bible presents two special tensions: its divine/human origin and the particular/universal nature of its message.

The aim of the interpreter is to discern the message intended by the biblical writer. For this he must deal carefully with the biblical world and build a bridge from there to the contemporary audience. Only in the history bound message of the biblical writer will the timeless message for today be found. The Holy Spirit intended us as part of a broader audience than the writer had in mind.

The interpreter will ask questions about his text—historical, literary, and theological questions. To help in asking every possible question, he can consult at least three sets of questions: the traditional journalist's questions, questions about the writer's intentions, and questions from principles of interpretation. The Interpretive Questions exercise will follow a step-by-step plan in which all questions will be asked before research begins.

Now that we have examined the text by constructing the structural diagram, noting observations, and asking questions, we are ready to move on to further steps in our interpretation of the text. Next we will examine the text to discover and name the writer's central idea.

Study Questions

1. What are three basic questions for interpretation?
2. What is a definition of "hermeneutics"?
3. What are three factors that make interpretation of the Bible unique?
4. What are two issues that are set for the Bible interpreter?
5. What are three major distances between the modern interpreter and the world of the Bible?
6. What are three reasons biblical interpretation is a challenge?
7. What is the preacher's first task in discovering God's message for his generation?
8. What are the journalist's questions?
9. How has finding the writer's intended message by asking questions helped your Bible study in the past?

---

1. Sidney Greidanus, *The Modern Preacher and the Ancient Text* (Grand Rapids: Eerdmans, 1988), 17.
2. John R. W. Stott, *Between Two Worlds: The Art of Preaching in the Twentieth Century* (Grand Rapids: Eerdmans, 1983), 137ff.
3. Gordon D. Fee and Douglas Stuart, *How to Read the Bible for All It's Worth* (Grand Rapids: Zondervan, 1982), 26–27.
4. William D. Thompson, *Preaching Biblically* (Nashville: Abingdon, 1981), 45–77.
5. See Howard G. Hendricks and William D. Hendricks, *Living by the Book* (Chicago: Moody, 1991), 304ff for nine rather specific questions to ask for application, probably better used later in the development of the sermon.

Interpretive Questions

Text <u>Psalm 1 (NASB)</u> Name <u>W. McDill</u> Date_____

Copy the text in the left column, one phrase at a time. Look closely at the words and phrases of the text and write questions you need to have answered in the right column. Work phrase by phrase and do not stop to answer the questions until you have completed questions for the whole text. Ask questions which will search out the writer's meaning in context.

Three categories of questions can be asked: (1) historical questions; (2) literary questions; and (3) theological questions. Your purpose is to let the text suggest questions you need answered to interpret its meaning.

Phrases of the Text	Your Questions
Vs. 1 How blessed is	1. What does "blessed" mean in Hebrew?
the man who does not	2. How was the figurative "walk" understood?
walk in the counsel of	3. What does "counsel" mean and signify in a figurative
the wicked,	sense?
	4. Who are "the wicked"?
	5. How would these figures be understood in the day of
	original writing?
	6. In what sense is he blessed?
	7. Is there an inherent blessing in his refusal of the advice
	of the wicked?
Nor stand in the path	8. What do the figures "stand" and "path" mean in this
of sinners,	context?
	9. How does the term "sinners" differ from "the wicked"
	above?
	10. Does "stand" have a particular theological meaning?
Nor sit in the seat of	11. Does this threefold separation from the world intend
scoffers!	main categories?
	12. What do the metaphors "sit" and "seat" mean here?
	13. Who are "the scoffers"? How do they differ from "the
	wicked" and "sinners"?
	14. Is there a progression in the "walk," "stand," "sit"
	order here?

Interpretive Questions

Text ___Ephesians 1:3 (NASB)___ Name ___W. McDill___ Date_____

   Copy the text in the left column, one phrase at a time. Look closely at the words and phrases of the text and write questions you need to have answered in the right column. Work phrase by phrase and do not stop to answer the questions until you have completed questions for the whole text. Ask questions which will search out the writer's meaning in context.

   Three categories of questions can be asked: (1) historical questions; (2) literary questions; and (3) theological questions. Your purpose is to let the text suggest questions you need answered to interpret its meaning.

Phrases of the Text	Your Questions
Vs. 1 Blessed be the	1. What does "blessed" mean, especially in this context?
God and Father of our	2. What would the original reader understand by
Lord Jesus Christ,	"blessed"?
	3. What significance does this theological formula
	have for Paul in this text?
who has blessed us	4. How does "blessed" here differ from the usage above?
with every spiritual	5. Who is meant by "us"?
blessing in the	6. In what sense are the blessings spiritual: nature,
heavenly (places) in	source, etc.?
Christ.	7. Does "every" mean there are none withheld?
	8. What and where is "the heavenly"?
	9. How are the blessings "in Christ"?
	By His redemption, Christ as source?
	10. How are we blessed? Potentially, actually,
	metaphorically, corporately?
	11. What is the significance of the past tense verb,
	"has blessed"?
	12. Of what use are spiritual blessings in the material
	world?
	13. How are the blessings appropriated?

Interpretive Questions

Text _____ Name _____ Date_____

Copy the text in the left column, one phrase at a time. Look closely at the words and phrases of the text and write questions you need to have answered in the right column. Work phrase by phrase and do not stop to answer the questions until you have completed questions for the whole text. Ask questions which will search out the writer's meaning in context.

Three categories of questions can be asked: (1) historical questions; (2) literary questions; and (3) theological questions. Your purpose is to let the text suggest questions you need answered to interpret its meaning.

Phrases of the Text	Your Questions

The words "subject" and "theme" are used by many interchangeably, but it is a loose use of terms, the result of hazy thought and indefinite aim. The subject is general; the theme is particular. "Faith" is a subject; "The Promptitude of Faith" is a theme. "Faith" is broad and general; it makes no affirmation or denial; it suggests no limit or purpose. "The Promptitude of Faith" is specific, gives definite relations and has an unmistakable purpose.[1]

Arthur S. Hoyt, 1905

CHAPTER 4

NAMING THE TEXTUAL IDEA

A young pastor was having breakfast with the men of his church when one of them made a comment about how "curious" a particular person was. As the conversation continued, the pastor could tell they were using the word in an unusual way. The more he listened, the more clear it became that by "curious" they meant strange or peculiar. He asked about it, and learned that in this particular area the word was used that way. He told the group that the word "curious" ordinarily meant inquisitive. They looked at him blankly in a moment of silence. Then one of them said, "Preacher, around here we don't even know what 'quizzative' means."

After thinking about that episode, the preacher started to make a list of other terms used in ways he thought unusual. He noticed, for instance, that "ill" didn't mean sick; it meant irritable and angry. He also started to think about the words he might be using which did not say to his audience what he meant by the use of them. It is one thing to know what you want to say and another to put it into the best words for communicating it to a particular audience.

Thought and Language

There is a basic assumption by mankind that somehow language can carry the thoughts in our minds accurately and clearly to the minds of others. At best, though, it is a matter of approximation. We hope to get at least close enough to the idea in the words we use that those around us can generally understand. It is not that our language cannot handle precise communication. It is rather that we are too careless with our words and do not choose them with the hearer in mind. As preachers, however, we must take the communication task seriously. We cannot be satisfied with an indistinct, murky expression of our thoughts.

Maybe it's a naive notion that our thoughts can be perfectly or even adequately expressed in verbal symbols. There are so many ways to miscommunicate. The speaker can be unclear about his ideas, or make poor word choices, or mispronounce the words. The hearer, on the other hand, can be inattentive, unfamiliar with some word used, confused by body language or tone, or place an unusual meaning on a word because of his own experience.

Some words may sound similar but carry a very different meaning. A favorite story of mine is about an elderly couple sitting on the porch in the cool of the evening. They sat in silence until the woman came out of her reverie with what she intended to be a romantic comment, "I'm proud of you, old man." Her hard-of-hearing husband turned, cupped his hand to his ear and asked, "What was that?" She leaned toward him and said it again louder, with an admiring smile on her face, "I said I'm proud of you, old man." He looked at her in bewilderment and then huffed in response, "I'm tired of you too, old woman."

In oral communication the one speaking carries the greater burden for making contact with the hearer. We expect the preacher to cover most, if not all, the distance to his hearers to complete the communication connection. The hearer is seen as generally passive, not only expecting clarity from the preacher, but something of interest as well. Each hearer sits before you as a complex bundle of experiences and understandings. One word from you can unknowingly trigger the replay in his mind of something from his own background which has little or nothing to do with your sermon.

You said "lonely" and one woman in the congregation spent several minutes going over her Saturday visit with her widowed mother. The word "father" brought one young man a mental replay of harsh words he had with his father only weeks before he died. You mentioned "camping" and another man spent several minutes going over the repairs needed to his RV. Their attention is not hindered nearly as much by distractions in the auditorium as it is by distractions in their own minds.

In normal use our words and thoughts are so inseparable that it is very difficult to distinguish them. The thought uses the word to give it expression, but the uncertain thought is also clarified by the word. If our thinking is clear and precise, it may well come from a careful use of language. Muddled attitudes and ideas are always connected with muddled language, and we preachers are not immune to this confusion. The greatest weakness of preaching is fuzzy thinking. The sharp focus of precise thought is lost in the flow of slogans, platitudes, and other "preacher talk" that seems designed to sound good rather than to communicate clearly.

Language is not only the vehicle of thought; it is a great help in the thinking process. Thoughts are often vague and nebulous until they are forced to take on the clothing of words. Simply put, you may not really know what you think until you try to put it into carefully chosen words. Counselors have learned this in many a session with some perplexed or distraught person. Just talking out his trouble will allow him to get it into focus and set it before him in clear terms. Then, seeing the nature of his problem, he is able to deal with it. He goes away grateful for the help of his counselor, who did little more than listen.

Listening is as vital a part of communication as speaking. The effective preacher will learn to listen to his people. He will learn who they really are as he listens carefully in the ordinary interactions of life. He will learn about their relationship with God as he listens to their prayers and how they talk about their faith. He will learn about them in the silence of their body language as they hear his sermons. The effective preacher must also listen to the biblical writers. He must determine to let the texts of Scripture speak, in their own terms, in their own context, and in their timeless message.

In this chapter we will introduce the exercise we call *Naming the Textual Idea.* The skill we hope to develop with this exercise is this: *discovering the writer's idea in the text and designating it with precise terminology.* After completing the previous exercises with a text, you will be able to identify the writer's idea. The task then is to express that concept with such careful wording that you can communicate exactly what you mean. We will do this by using a formula for wording a concept as subject and complement.

The Skill of a Craftsman

Verne Griffith of Beaverton, Oregon, was a woodcrafter. He loved wood—the look of it, the feel of it, the smell of it. He collected scraps and pieces of wood of various kinds and sorted them in storage racks in his shop. He would take a piece and show it to me with loving admiration. "This is myrtle wood," he said. "It grows in only two places, in the Holy Land and here in the Northwest. Look at this marbled grain. Isn't it beautiful!" Verne made clocks, bowls, platters, and other such items out of various woods. He knew in his mind what the thing would look like before he began, but only in the making of it was it defined. He would glue pieces together in intricate designs, then turn and shape the laminate into a bowl or plate. When he was finished the natural beauty of the wood would show in the combination of grains and colors.

As professional communicators we are called to be *wordcrafters.* Just as some are skilled with wood, clay, paints, or the tones of music, so the preacher is to be skilled in the use of words. Several different skills are necessary to any craft. You need to understand the raw material you handle, its possibilities and limits. You need to be skilled in the use of the tools necessary to that craft as you prepare and shape your material. You also want to be skilled at combining the stuff of your craft, and in the finishing of your product with smooth edges, vibrant color, the right touch.

Are you a wordcrafter? Do you love words? Do you like the look of them, the feel, the smell? Are you impressed with their texture, their color, their uniqueness? Are you skilled in the use of wordcrafting tools—dictionaries, thesauruses, lexicons, concordances, style manuals? Can you identify one kind of word from another and tell how each might be used best? Do you rummage around for the exact word, the precise word, the right word? Or do you just pick up any old sound and send it forth to confuse the ears of those who hear you?

Some today see preaching as more experience than communication. It's something that "happens" which may or may not carry any definable ideas. It is an "event" in which participation is more important than understanding. Of course preaching is an event. It can be a significant experience on the part of preacher and hearers. But if it does not contain clear and transferable ideas, its essential purpose is lost. Preaching is communication. Its value is measured by the message it carries and how effectively it is expressed.

Def • i • ni´ tion: The Wordcrafter

Like a craftsman in wood or clay, the preacher is to be a skilled *craftsman in words*. He is to be skilled in the handling of the Word of God in Scripture. He is to be skilled in the work of proclamation. He is to be skilled in bridging the distance between the biblical world and the world of his contemporary audience.

The wordcrafter learns the possibilities and the limitations of his material, words. He studies the combinations of words for dynamic and creative *communication*. He seeks out the best words for clarity, force, and beauty in his preaching.

Like any dedicated craftsman, the wordcrafter works to develop his skills. He acquires the best tools for his craft and uses them with skill. He respects the Word of God as a divine masterpiece of communication. He trusts the Spirit and the Word of God that the Word he proclaims may be a word from God to those who hear.

Let me emphasize again that the great fault of preaching is fuzzy thinking. A high percentage of sermons we hear are uncertain and imprecise as to the sermon theme. Good things may be said. Some thoughts may be helpful. The text may be used. But even with those good qualities, it may seem that the preacher is wandering in the wilderness (and we with him) and unable to find the crossing into the promised land of clear thinking. Even if his delivery is effective, the main issue is still content. Did he say anything worth hearing? Did I really grasp what was said?

Becoming a skilled wordcrafter demands the capacity for critical thinking. By critical thinking we mean analyzing thoughts, sorting out ideas, distinguishing one concept from another, evaluating arguments, and making judgments about the best way to express ideas. It requires levels of precision and craftsmanship not necessary to casual thinking. Critical thinking means you cannot be satisfied with terminology which merely comes close to an accurate wording of the idea. You want to find the words which exactly express the idea. You want to distinguish it from ideas that are similar but not quite the same. It is this kind of thinking that is so needed among preachers today.

At no other point is this capacity for critical thinking more needed than in discerning the writer's thoughts as they are revealed in the words of the text. It is always difficult to be completely objective, but we must try. We must avoid reading into the text some idea we bring with us. Our goal is to let the text speak. As we hear what the text is saying we are identifying the textual idea. That is what you seek because it will become your sermon idea as well. This brings your wordcrafting skills to their real test, as we will see.

A Concept Needs a Name

Once the textual idea begins to emerge out of your careful inductive study of the text, you face your next challenge, naming the textual idea. I know that may sound strange to you. Why do we need to name the textual idea? Why not just call it what it already is? Are we trying to come up with an impressive name? Won't it be clear what the idea is, without naming it something?

By naming the textual idea, I am saying you have to call it something. You have to choose words which will name it best, which will identify that idea in as clear and precise terms as are possible in language. Finding the right words for the textual idea can be a difficult task, but there are several important reasons why it is vital to your sermon preparation.

In the first place the preacher needs to name the idea carefully so as to *define it precisely in his own mind.* Unless it is clearly defined by a careful choice of words, the idea remains vague in his own thinking and may be confused with similar concepts. He may know the idea is there. He "sees" it in his mind, but he does not see it clearly until he names it. When he keeps working at his craft until he finds just the right words to name the idea, he knows, "That's it!" It is like looking through a file of photographs until you see someone you know.

A second reason for accurately naming the textual idea is *to make sure it reflects what the biblical writer is saying.* How can you take an idea through the text, verse by verse, to see if it is on target, unless you give it a precise name? You want to see if what you are calling the subject is actually what the writer is talking about.

Third, you must give the textual idea an accurate name *so that the same words can be used in the sermon idea.* Our aim is for the textual idea to become the sermon idea. We want to maintain a straight line of thought from the text to the sermon. Unless we find the right words to identify the textual idea, how will we ever preach that idea?

The words used to name the idea are not the idea. Those words are the label, the designation, the name we give the idea so that we can identify it clearly and distinctly. Neither are the words we name it, nor the idea in our minds, the same as the reality we are thinking and talking about. The idea of God's mercy and the words we use to talk about it are both distinct from the reality of this attribute in God. God's mercy is a reality whether we think about it or talk about it at all.

My wife and I enjoy birdwatching and try to learn more about the birds native to our area. We have bought books and studied the photographs and descriptions of the birds. So when my wife asks me what I saw this morning as I had my coffee on the porch, I can answer "a male spotted thrasher" or "a female American robin." I wouldn't say "an animal," "a bird," or "a big bird and two smaller birds." Those descriptions are too vague. Those birds have names which precisely identify them, so I use those names. But the bird is not the same as my mental representation of it or the name I call it. The bird is a reality distinct from the idea and the name that designates that idea.

By separating the concept from the name of the concept and the reality behind it, we express several convictions about our study of the text. For one thing, we acknowledge that there is an idea in the text which was in the mind of the writer as he wrote it. Whether or not we are able to name that idea with suitable words does not affect the idea. It was there in the mind of the writer and is there in the words of the text. But the preacher will never be sure he also has it in his mind until he can name it.

Separating the idea from its name also acknowledges that the idea is a mental representation of an actual reality. That idea represents not just a word, but envisions a condition, a resource, a relationship, a quality of character, a response to God, etc. We call it by a name, but it is more than its name. Unless we name it accurately, the corresponding reality in human experience will not be recognizable to the hearer.

Wording the Textual Idea

An idea can be more easily worded by breaking it down into its component parts. This helps as you identify the core of the textual idea, which later becomes the basis for the sermon idea. Though it is best to state the textual idea and the sermon idea as complete sentences, the concept that is the basis for those sentences can be stated in two words. Haddon Robinson says that in its basic structure an idea is made up of a subject and a complement.[2]

Def • i • ni´ tion: Textual Idea

The textual idea is a concept derived from the words of the biblical writer that the preacher takes to be the writer's intended message to his original readers. This idea is discovered in a careful study of the biblical text in its historical, literary, and theological context. The textual idea is designated by two words carefully selected as subject and complement.

The one-word *subject* answers the question, "What is the writer talking about?" It is the dominant theme of the text. The one-word complement is a second theme from the text which focuses and defines the subject. It answers the question, "How does the writer limit the scope of what he is talking about?"

The two themes in combination identify as precisely as possible to the preacher the idea presented in the text. The full statement of the textual idea requires a complete past tense sentence, including the subject/complement with the historical context from the text. The subject/complement of the textual idea becomes the subject/complement of the sermon idea as the text shapes the sermon.

An idea is not really an idea unless it has both a subject, the central theme of the idea, and a complement, the defining focus of the idea. When we talk about the subject of a text, we mean the theme which, in one word, best answers the question, "What is the writer talking about?" The subject could be a broad theme like "love" as in 1 Corinthians 13. But that subject is too broad, covering much more than the text itself covers. So we must limit and define the subject, "love," in the same way the text limits it.

That limiting element in formulating an idea is called the complement. This word completes the expression of the idea by answering the question, "How does the writer limit the scope of what he's talking about?" Since he doesn't intend to say all that can possibly be said on his subject, what is the limiting factor in his discussion of the subject? In the example from 1 Corinthians 13, we have said our subject is "love." That's what the writer is talking about. Now we must ask how he seems to limit his comments about "love." A careful inductive study of the text has called to our attention Paul's introduction of the passage by these words, "And yet I show you a more excellent way" (1 Cor. 12:31). From that statement and the tone of the text, we might conclude that the writer seems to limit his comments by the theme of "excellence."

If we think the subject is "love" and that the limiting factor in the discussion of love is "excellence," we have a subject and a complement. I usually write it as subject/complement in this case, love/excellence. So our textual idea might be entitled The Excellence of Love. It is not love only, but the excellence of love. "Love" is always an interesting subject, but adding the term "excellence" strikes a spark and expresses an idea with some real impact. Where did we get that idea? From the very words of the writer.

So a subject alone is not an idea. Just as cartoon writers depict an idea as a light bulb shining in one's imagination, so an idea is an expression of creativity. It is a eureka experience, for you have found it. Such an idea much better expresses the particular thrust of a text than a broad theme does. No text says all that can be said about its subject. It treats the subject in a particular way. It is that particular treatment of the subject that is dynamic.

Look at the story of Paul and Silas in the Philippian jail (Acts 16:25–34). As you try to determine the theological subject of this passage, you are looking for the most plain and obvious theme. Perhaps you will choose praise because the most remarkable turn in the text is their singing in the night. If you choose praise you know immediately that the text does not completely cover the subject of praise. So you look through the text for a complement to limit and define the idea with the particular angle on praise it presents. Their situation will lead you to pain, trouble, or some other such word. So you have praise/trouble, which appears to be a strange combination of words. But it carries the meaning of the experience in the text, praise in the midst of trouble.

This is a most helpful way to understand the difference between a subject and a complete idea. This exercise calls for you to choose a one-word subject to answer the question, "What is the writer talking about?" Once you are satisfied that this is indeed what the writer intended to talk about, then you add the complement which limits and focuses the subject to complete the idea. The complement asks, "How does the writer seem to limit his discussion of what he is talking about?"

Guidelines for the Exercise

This exercise is Naming the Textual Idea. It is designed to help strengthen your skill in identifying and designating the writer's idea in carefully chosen words. This is the climax of the interpretive process. At this point you have constructed the Structural Diagram, you have written Immediate Observations about the text, and you have asked and answered Interpretive Questions. Now you are ready to name the textual idea in the best words to communicate it precisely. The work you have done in the previous exercises may make the idea obvious. Now here are some guidelines for arriving at the best wording of the idea.

Carefully identify all the theological themes in the text for insight into its central idea. The task of identifying a subject/complement to name the textual idea is complicated by the number of biblical themes in a text. By "themes" I mean theological subjects you will find in different combinations in texts throughout the Bible. As you look at the text before you, you may see themes like faith, obedience, grace, sin, mercy, and so forth. Of these many themes, you must decide which one is the dominant theme and how the other themes support it. Look at the structure for which ideas have the most support in the writer's wording. Look for repeated words. You can usually recognize the theological themes in the text by looking at the significant words you see there. The subjects of justice, law, grace, love, sin, life, time, and other such themes are carried by particular words used by the biblical writers.

Consider the plain and obvious meaning of the text for indications of the textual idea. Is there a "plain and obvious" subject? Matthew 7:7–12 is the well-known passage about asking, seeking, and knocking. If you look at this text for the simplest and most obvious meaning, you will probably think of "prayer." Though the word "prayer" is not in the text, the theme is still clear. It is wise, then, to make "prayer" your subject. As you look further for a complement, you may be impressed with the repeated promises in this passage. You could choose "confident" as your complement, the idea being prayer/confident.

Carefully examine the apparent intention of the writer for an insight into his central idea. The questions are, "Why is this text here? What is its intended message?" In Luke 18:1 the writer made his intention and that of Jesus clear, "Now He was telling them a parable to show that at all times they ought to pray and not to lose heart." What Jesus and Luke intended for this parable is clear, so your subject is not difficult to name as "prayer." Again, the challenge will come in naming the complement. But look at the intention of the writer again. He speaks of praying "at all times" and "not losing heart." Does that suggest "persistence" as a complement? If so, our subject/complement would be prayer/persistence, or persistent prayer.

Examining the context of the text may help identify the writer's central idea. Examine the literary context, the chapters and verses before and after your text. James 1:2–4 has a good many themes in it: joy, trials, faith, maturity, endurance, completeness, and so on. Which of these might be the primary theme of the text? Look at the context. The previous verse is James' greeting to the scattered tribes. Why were they scattered, we ask? Because of persecution. The following section begins, "If any of you lacks wisdom, . . ." How does a lack of wisdom connect with verses 2–4? Could it be that their hard times called for seeing matters from God's perspective (wisdom)? The context, then, seems to support "trials" as the primary theme. A good complement might be "response." Thus you have trials/response, or response to trials as a textual idea.

Discern the meaning of figurative language for insight into the writer's subject. In Matthew 5:13–16 Jesus says that His disciples are the "salt of the earth" and the "light of the world." Unlike some other figures he uses, he does not explain what he means by "salt" and "light." We may assume that we all know, but it is better by far to translate the metaphors into a conceptual term. In this case you will have the subject of this text. Some thought and study may lead you to see that Jesus is here talking about the "influence" of His followers on their "world." Since the figurative terms dominate this passage, they may well carry the textual idea. But do not use these terms as your subject or complement because they are not universal theological concepts. They are illustrations which must be translated into conceptual terms such as influence/world.

Look for a pivotal verse in the text which may contain the main theme. Though every text does not have a pivotal verse, many will. It will be that one verse which seems to summarize the meaning of the entire section. As you look for that key verse, it may appear that two or even three verses might qualify. When this is the case, compare the theme which dominates those verses with other indicators in the text, such as we have outlined here. As I studied Revelation 3:14–22, it seemed that verse 19 was pivotal to the meaning of the entire passage as a call to repentance. As I looked through the text, that theme held up as the dominant idea.

Words Not to Use

There are several kinds of words which are best not used as a subject or complement for the textual idea.

Do not use "instructions" or "commands" because that identifies a type of written or spoken material, but says little about the content.

Do not use "God" as your subject or complement; all subjects are theological, but using God as a subject (unless that is the explicit content of the passage) says the obvious and does not frame a dynamic idea.

Avoid using words like "appropriate," "true," "authentic," "genuine," "real," etc. for your complement. These do not really limit and describe the subject; they only say you are positive about it.

Do not use places, persons, or objects as your subject or

complement; they cannot be theological ideas.

Avoid using figurative words in the text as subject words. You will not have a legitimate subject if you simply bring the metaphors of the text over to the sermon.

Do not use "not," "never," or any other negation for the complement. The terms you use for your subject and complement are all to be understood as plus-or-minus values. Whether it is discussed as positive or negative does not change the nature of the concept itself. "Godliness" as a subject can be either positive (plus) godliness or negative (minus) godliness.

Completing the Exercise

Using the worksheet at the end of this chapter, follow the three steps to complete the exercise, Naming the Textual Idea. Base your choice of words on evidence in the text itself. Do not play a guessing game.

STEP 1: Write down all the one-word possibilities the text seems to suggest which might serve as subjects or complements. These are words from the text plus others which designate ideas in the text. There is no essential difference in the words you use for subject or complement. As you write a list of possible terms, keep in mind that you may use one of them as the subject and another as the complement. The dynamic of the idea comes in the combination of the two words.

STEP 2: Take the most likely word from your list and ask of the entire text, verse by verse, "Does this word identify what the writer is talking about?" If the word you choose seems to be suitable with only a part of the text, choose another, and see if it covers the whole passage. Some of the ideas in the text are only aspects of the overall subject and may be the basis for division statements. It is important to see how the ideas in the text are related and which of the words on your list could be the main subject, which the complement, and which the core of the division statements.

STEP 3: Once you have settled on a subject word, now choose another word for your complement. This word is not to modify the subject so much as to identify the limit placed on his treatment of the subject by the writer. The addition of the complement makes a creative combination of two themes which form a complete idea. The word for your complement may not be in the text, but rather suggested by the situation described, the progression of thought, or the overall message of the text.

STEP 4: Turn your subject / complement into a working title for the sermon. It may turn out to be the title you keep. This title, from the text subject and complement, will keep your sermon on track with the text.

Summary

This chapter has been about the relationship of thought and word and how precisely our words can express our thoughts. This issue is vital to the preacher's interpretation of the words of Scripture and his careful choice of words to communicate the message he finds there. Words not only express our thoughts, they can help clarify them. Naming the Textual Idea is the exercise designed to strengthen skills in designating the text writer's idea.

The preacher is to be a wordcrafter who skillfully discerns and uses words in his sermon preparation. The great fault of preaching is fuzzy thinking, which can be overcome through the use of precise language. The textual idea is named by the preacher by the use of a subject and complement. The subject identifies the dominant theme of the text. The complement is a secondary theme which limits the scope of the subject.

Chapter 3, Asking the Right Questions, was the first of three chapters on skills for interpreting the text. This chapter was the second. Now we move to the third, Touching Human Needs, where the text will be interpreted in terms of the human element.

Study Questions

1. What is the greatest weakness of preaching?
2. What is the aim of the skill exercise in this chapter?
3. What is a wordcrafter?
4. What are three reasons that naming the textual idea is vital for sermon preparation?
5. Define the textual idea.
6. What are the two basic components of an idea?
7. What is the difference between the subject and complement of the textual idea?
8. What are some of the guidelines you might follow in wording the textual idea?
9. How does the idea of being a wordcrafter fit into your concept of the teaching and preaching ministry?

---

1. Arthur S. Hoyt, *The Work of Preaching* (New York: George H. Doran, 1905), 98.
2. Haddon W. Robinson, *Biblical Preaching* (Grand Rapids: Baker, 1980), 39–40. Robinson follows H. Grady Davis, *Design for Preaching,* chap. 3 "Anatomy of the Idea." (Philadelphia: Fortress, 1958). He uses the terms subject and complement to designate the sermon subject and its completion in the outline. I am using the two terms as component parts of the textual idea to make a complete concept of it.

Naming the Textual Idea

Text ___Psalm 1___ Name ___W. McDill___ Date_____

Follow the steps below to discover and name the textual idea, jotting your possibilities down as you go. Avoid terms that are either too general or too narrow for the text treatment. The test will be whether the words you choose work throughout the text to name its main idea.

Begin by listing all the theological theme words in the text. These are the Bible themes which are in various texts in different combinations.

blessedness	law (of God)	(the) wicked
walk (figurative)	medication	prospering
sit (fig.)	fruitbearing (fig.)	chaff (fig.)
stand (fig.)	wither (fig.)	knowledge (of God)
delighting	streams (fig.)	righteous
judgment	perish	

1. Look at the passage for the "plain and obvious" meaning of the text. Think of telling a child in one word what the text is about.

   (the) godly (man)

   blessedness

2. Focus on the writer's intended original meaning. The text cannot mean what it never meant. What did the writer seem to have in mind?

   godliness

   wickedness

3. Look at the larger context of the chapter and book. What is the writer's progression of thought? Where does your text fit into that sequence of ideas?

   praise (to God)

4. Discern the meaning of any figurative language in the text. Translate all figurative language into its theological meaning for naming as a subject.

   [largely figurative]

5. See if the text seems to have a pivotal verse, a single key verse which captures the point of the whole text. If so, what is the best word to name it?

   v. 6 Contrast of the godly and wicked

Now write the word that seems best to identify the dominant theme of the text in the most simple and direct way. The subject answers the question, "What is the text writer talking about?"

Subject of the text in one word: ___godly___

Choose another term to focus and define the subject, either one of the words above, or another that works better. The complement answers the question, "How does the writer limit the scope of what he is talking about?"

Complement to the subject in one word: ___contrast___

Subject/complement as a working title: ___The Godly and the Wicked Contrasted___

Naming the Textual Idea

Text _____Ephesians 1:3–6_____ Name __W. McDill__ Date_____

Follow the steps below to discover and name the textual idea, jotting your possibilities down as you go. Avoid terms that are either too general or too narrow for the text treatment. The test will be whether the words you choose work throughout the text to name its main idea.

Begin by listing all the theological theme words in the text. These are the Bible themes which are in various texts in different combinations.

praise (to God)	creation	adoption
blessings	holiness	will (of God)
spiritual (realm)	blamelessness	grace
heavenlies	love (of God)	giving (of God)
chosen	predestination	Christ

1. Look at the passage for the "plain and obvious" meaning of the text. Think of telling a child in one word what the text is about.

    blessings

    in Christ

2. Focus on the writer's intended original meaning. The text cannot mean what it never meant. What did the writer seem to have in mind?

    praise

    identity (believer)

3. Look at the larger context of the chapter and book. What is the writer's progression of thought? Where does your text fit into that sequence of ideas?

    grace

4. Discern the meaning of any figurative language in the text. Translate all figurative language into its theological meaning for naming as a subject.

    adoption = chosen

    by God for Himself

5. See if the text seems to have a pivotal verse, a single key verse which captures the point of the whole text. If so, what is the best word to name it?

    v. 5 "predestined to

    adoption as sons"

Now write the word that seems best to identify the dominant theme of the text in the most simple and direct way. The subject answers the question, "What is the text writer talking about?"

Subject of the text in one word: ___chosen___

Choose another term to focus and define the subject, either one of the words above, or another that works better. The complement answers the question, "How does the writer limit the scope of what he is talking about?"

Complement to the subject in one word: __grace__

Subject/complement as a working title: __Chosen by the Grace of God__

Naming the Textual Idea

Text _____Philippians 2:5–11_____ Name _W. McDill_ Date_____

Follow the steps below to discover and name the textual idea, jotting your possibilities down as you go. Avoid terms that are either too general or too narrow for the text treatment. The test will be whether the words you choose work throughout the text to name its main idea.

Begin by listing all the theological theme words in the text. These are the Bible themes which are in various texts in different combinations.

attitude	servanthood	exaltation
Christ	incarnation	name
pre-existence	humility	worship
divinity (Jesus)	death	confession
self-emptying	cross	glory (to God)

1. Look at the passage for the "plain and obvious" meaning of the text. Think of telling a child in one word what the text is about.

   attitude

   Christlikeness

2. Focus on the writer's intended original meaning. The text cannot mean what it never meant. What did the writer seem to have in mind?

   humility

   conduct

3. Look at the larger context of the chapter and book. What is the writer's progression of thought? Where does your text fit into that sequence of ideas?

   attitude

4. Discern the meaning of any figurative language in the text. Translate all figurative language into its theological meaning for naming as a subject.

   (none)

5. See if the text seems to have a pivotal verse, a single key verse which captures the point of the whole text. If so, what is the best word to name it?

   v. 5 follow the

   attitude of Jesus

Now write the word that seems best to identify the dominant theme of the text in the most simple and direct way. The subject answers the question, "What is the text writer talking about?"

Subject of the text in one word: ___attitude_____

Choose another term to focus and define the subject, either one of the words above, or another that works better. The complement answers the question, "How does the writer limit the scope of what he is talking about?"

Complement to the subject in one word: ___Christlike___

Subject/complement as a working title: _A Christlike Attitude_____

Naming the Textual Idea

Text _____ Name _____ Date_____

Follow the steps below to discover and name the textual idea, jotting your possibilities down as you go. Avoid terms that are either too general or too narrow for the text treatment. The test will be whether the words you choose work throughout the text to name its main idea.

Begin by listing all the theological theme words in the text. These are the Bible themes which are in various texts in different combinations.

_____   _____   _____

_____   _____   _____

_____   _____   _____

_____   _____   _____

_____   _____   _____

1. Look at the passage for the "plain and obvious" meaning of the text. Think of telling a child in one word what the text is about.   _____

2. Focus on the writer's intended original meaning. The text cannot mean what it never meant. What did the writer seem to have in mind?   _____

3. Look at the larger context of the chapter and book. What is the writer's progression of thought? Where does your text fit into that sequence of ideas?   _____

4. Discern the meaning of any figurative language in the text. Translate all figurative language into its theological meaning for naming as a subject.   _____

5. See if the text seems to have a pivotal verse, a single key verse which captures the point of the whole text. If so, what is the best word to name it?   _____

_____

Now write the word that seems best to identify the dominant theme of the text in the most simple and direct way. The subject answers the question, "What is the text writer talking about?"

Subject of the text in one word: _____

Choose another term to focus and define the subject, either one of the words above, or another that works better. The complement answers the question, "How does the writer limit the scope of what he is talking about?"

Complement to the subject in one word: _____

Subject/complement as a working title: _____

> If I were asked what is the first thing in effective preaching, I should say sympathy; and what is the second thing, I should say sympathy; and what is the third thing, I should say sympathy.[1]
>
> John A. Broadus, ca. 1870

CHAPTER 5

TOUCHING HUMAN NEEDS

Mrs. Lentsch was my fourth-grade teacher at Cheek Elementary. She was a rather thin, freckled lady with reddish hair. From my viewpoint as a nine-year-old, she was not a regular person. She was instead a member of that special and unique tribe called "teacher." She could see behind her without turning around, and I was never quite comfortable around her.

She wrote notes on my report cards about "living up to his potential" and things like that. She was completely absorbed with math and grammar and history and chalk and worksheets with smelly purple ink. She was always a mystery to me. I could not imagine her as a wife or mother or laughing out loud or having her hair messed up or going barefoot.

My one-dimensional view of Mrs. Lentsch may have been partly her creation. She never spoke of herself or her family, never gave any indication she had a thought about anything outside the school. She couldn't have had a regular life; she just materialized in her classroom each morning in time for us to file in.

The Preacher's World

Sometimes preachers seem to be a lot like Mrs. Lentsch. They are not regular people. They live in a mysterious world of study and prayer and old books and stained-glass windows. They don't have bad thoughts or lose their tempers or say anything colorful if they mash their fingers. Maybe they don't even mash their fingers.

Of course, people in the congregation know better. They see the pastor's family. They have occasions for social visits and idle conversation. But deep in their inner perceptions is that image of the pastor as an entirely different category of person. He can seem removed from the real life of his people because of his preoccupation with institutional and theological concerns.

It is an occupational hazard of the pastorate that he has the church on his mind. He is responsible for the overall ministry of the church. He receives credit when the church grows and prospers and is often blamed when it flounders and declines. He seems to be the only person consistently concerned about attendance and tithing and witnessing and new members. These institutional concerns show up regularly in his preaching.

The pastor, as the primary preacher/teacher in the church, is also interested in the ancient world of the Bible. He studies about the Israelites, the Canaanites, the Jebusites, and other ancient peoples. He is also on close terms with Abraham and Moses and Daniel, as well as Peter and Paul. He uses Bible terminology and seems to think everyone understands it. So the pastor may well seem like a non-regular person because he is so interested in these theological concerns.

The other members of the church get the idea they should be more interested in these important subjects. The pastor seems to think so. But they have other issues on their minds. They are thinking about their own personal concerns—family finances, work, mortgage payments, health, children, marriage, leisure, etc. They are especially occupied with these personal concerns when problems arise.

So the preacher has one set of interests on his mind, and the people in the pew are thinking about another set. When the time comes for a sermon, the pastor's ministerial interests inevitably push their way into his preaching, no matter the text. And those in the congregation are meditating on their own personal concerns, no matter the sermon subject. They are sitting in the same room with their interests in two different worlds.

Occasionally the preacher will touch on a real life concern of his hearers. When that happens, it is like a cool drink on a hot, dry day. The hearer sits up, attentive to every word, alert and eager for help for his needs from the Word of God. All too often, however, it is a false hope. The apparently real and practical help soon dissolves into vague admonitions and spiritual generalities. The hearer relaxes his attention and sighs like a fisherman who thought he had a bite, but found a slack line.

Sometimes it seems the pastor is preaching to an audience that doesn't really exist. His subject matter, his terminology, his attitude—all seem to indicate he feels the congregation should be just as interested in church matters as he is. It sounds at times as though he thinks they live only to attend church and discuss religion. They do not. They live in the real world, beyond the church building. They want to know how to live the Christian life out there. They want to be addressed in terms of their own life-styles, their own needs, their own language, their own interests. Unless Christianity works for the real person in the real world, it does not work.

There are four ingredients necessary for a preaching situation: the preacher, the sermon, the Scripture, and the audience. Which of these is the primary element? Is it the preacher, for without him there would be no telling of the message? Is it the Scripture, for without that there is no word from God? Is it the sermon, for without it nothing is said? Some thought will lead you to the conclusion that it is the audience. Without the people, none of the other ingredients would be necessary.

We have devoted our first four chapters to interpretation of the biblical text. Now we look at our understanding of the audience as we continue the work of sermon preparation. The exercise we introduce here is *The Need Element.* The skill we hope to strengthen is this: *tracing from theological concepts in the text to the corresponding needs in contemporary hearers.* Preaching is more effective if the practical and personal needs of hearers are a factor in interpretation as well as preparation and delivery.

Real World Preaching

The human element as a factor in our preaching is such a part of our environment that the preacher may take it for granted and thus overlook it. It is like water to the fish, air to the bird, or earth to the mole. We are surrounded by the common human experience. It is all we know. The very language of man is the language of human experience. Whatever his dialect, he cannot communicate except in terms of human experience. But God has entered into the experience of man in a very personal way. That human experience is the arena, and the only arena, of His revelation.

Preaching to people where they live will have to begin in the thinking of the preacher. He will have to shift his thoughts out of churchworld thinking into realworld thinking. By virtue of his calling and his leadership position, the pastor is probably the only one thinking all week about the church and its welfare. If we are to bridge the gap successfully between the biblical revelation and the contemporary audience, we must rethink our attitudes toward the congregation and the world they live in.

A beginning point for examining your thinking might be to look at your own concept of what is meant by "church." Does that word mean only the gathered congregation in the church building? Does it mean the organization with its committees, its officers and teachers, its budget and needs? Or does "church" mean the people, with their diversity, their own personal concerns, their ministries? And what is the pastor's role in the church? Is he there to exploit their energies and resources for the benefit of the institution? Or is he to edify the people for the life and ministry they have in Christ? Is his goal to squeeze something out of them or build something into them?

Another way to enhance your realworld preaching is to keep in touch with that real world. Not only can a pastor profit by keeping in touch with his own flock, he is helped by a study of the nature of humanity. Jesus did not need anyone to interpret man to Him because He already knew what was in the heart of man. The preacher also must become an interpreter of human nature, an expert on the real person in this contemporary age. He can do this by reading best-sellers, keeping up with the news, understanding trends, and just paying attention.

Preaching to real people also calls for an attitude of compassion and understanding in the preacher. People will listen to your preaching when they know you respect them and really care about their needs. If all the preacher has to say is critical and negative, if he demonstrates a spirit of impatience and disapproval, if he seems only to want to use them for keeping the church running, he will not preach much to real people because they will tune him out.

Compassion in preaching is not an end in itself. Some preachers seem to feel that a caring analysis of the suffering of their people is somehow a remedy. They can point out all the causes and ramifications of the trouble with compassion and understanding, and that is good. But sympathy cannot be the final answer to misconceptions, discouragement, and conflict. However a person might appreciate anyone who shares his pain, he still needs new insight for dealing with life in wisdom and faith.

All of this may well come down to the need for the preacher to be a real person himself. Preaching is strengthened by honesty, openness, understanding, and even vulnerability. Though the pastor is a shepherd, he is also one of the sheep. The people want him to be the shepherd; they expect him to have a role in the church no one else has. But they also need for him to be a fellow pilgrim, one who is engaged in the journey just as they are and so understands their needs. That dual role is a challenging one to play, but it is the only realistic and honest one.

Understanding the Need Element

The need element, as a factor in preaching, is the trouble experienced by those to whom we preach. Jesus said, "In this world you will have trouble" (John 16:33). As we indicated in the last chapter, every biblical concept should be thought of in plus or minus terms. A person has the moral and spiritual freedom to live on the positive or negative side of any biblical principle. In most cases what one does in response to the principle will determine the results in his experience. On any given Sunday more than half the people in your audience are experiencing some stress from personal needs. They want to hear an answer from God on how to deal with those troubles. The need element defines their negative experience.

William D. Thompson began with humankind in his hermeneutical method. In describing the need element, he wrote,

> What is the human need that forms the first ⋆ element of the model we are constructing? In the Scripture, it is portrayed in a staggering variety of ways: as sin, as transgression of the law, as conscious choice to defy the living God; as being under the judgment of God because of the alienation our ancestors chose and we continue; as question, revealing our lack of information about the will and purposes of God; as ambivalence in moral dilemmas; as sickness of the soul; as participation in tragedy; as fallen from grace.[2]

The need element is to be understood particularly with reference to the biblical concepts with which certain needs correspond. The biblical truth is an answer. It is a Word from God to address the need of man. It is to be embraced and applied by faith, with the assurance of a remedy in one's life by the grace of God. If the biblical truth is the solution, the need element is the problem. The preacher can approach his preaching from the need side and trace to answers in Scripture that can address that need. Or he can find biblical principles in his text and trace them to the needs they address in human nature.

If the biblical truth concerns love, the need element may be conflict or loneliness. If the message is faith, the need element may be uncertainty and doubt. If the answer is salvation, the need element is alienation and guilt. The need element is to biblical truth what hunger is to food, what a headache is to aspirin, what fatigue is to rest. The need element can be seen in the hearer's assumptions, his symptoms, and the consequences in his life.

The need element can take the form of your hearer's ~~assump-~~ ~~tions~~ *which run counter to the basic principles of Scripture.* This thinking is rooted in the nature of fallen humanity. He naturally operates out of the default system of his thinking, which comes equipped with understandings in harmony with the self-centeredness of that nature. "'For My thoughts are not your thoughts, Neither are your ways My ways,' declares the Lord" (Isa. 55:8). And the behavior is no different unless he intentionally chooses to adopt the thinking of biblical wisdom.

Def • i • ni´ tion: The Need Element

The Need Element refers to the human condition as a factor in interpretation and sermon planning. The premise is that every biblical concept has a corresponding need in the life of man which calls for its application. The need element does not refer to what is needed in the sense of a solution to some problem. The need element is rather the condition of the needy person—her lack, want, suffering, trouble, etc.

The need element is explicit in many texts and implicit in all. The gracious nature and activity of God is a constant in Scripture, as is the fallen nature of man. The causes, symptoms, and consequences of a failure to rightly respond to God all constitute the need element.

The preacher must understand his audience as carefully as he seeks to understand his text. He can then interpret his text with the needs of his people in mind. He can trace every biblical concept to its corresponding need in the life of man, not only for interpretation, but for more effective communication of the biblical truths.

In 2 Corinthians 10:5, Paul is discussing spiritual warfare. He has just mentioned "the destruction of fortresses." In this verse he says two defenses are raised against the knowledge of God. They are "speculations" and "every lofty thing." These terms may be understood as ideas and attitudes which are raised as defenses against the truth of God. This surely sounds familiar today. The truth of God is rejected on the basis of ideas, like "I don't believe in anything that can't be proved scientifically," or attitudes, like

"I feel I am the best one to decide what is best for me, not some religious system."

Ideas and attitudes similar to these are at the root of the thinking of the natural man. But he may never have heard them addressed and described in the context of alternative ideas in Scripture. He may not even realize what the basic roots of his own thinking are. When a biblical idea is presented, he finds himself rejecting it as impractical but he doesn't know why. When basic assumptions are uncovered as an expression of the need element, the hearer can look at them more objectively and see how they look in comparison to the wisdom of Scripture.

The need element can be seen as symptoms a person experiences which indicate a failure to live in harmony with the revelation of God. If we believe the truths of God's Word can make a difference in a person's experience, we must believe that difference will be observable. In fact we insist on it. An adult who puts her faith in Christ is a changed person, inside and out. Since that is so, we expect to see evidence in a person's life as to where she stands with those truths of biblical wisdom. God's wisdom makes a difference, and the difference shows.

The symptoms can be experienced by unbelievers or by believers, anyone who is ignorant of or rejects biblical principles. Like a fever or a rash or headache, these symptoms of disease can be identified. As the pastor describes them to his hearers, he makes contact with their needs in a direct way. He has moved the sermon to the here and now, to the you and me. Those who identify with the symptoms will pay attention to the remedy, but both must be presented in realworld terms.

Touch me at the point of my pain by describing my discouragement and weariness with life and I am ready to hear about the grace of God. But don't get philosophical with me. Keep the remedy on the practical, believable level with the symptoms. Tell me what's causing my emotional and spiritual burnout and what I can do about it. What I need is a prescription I can manage, not a religious slogan I don't really understand. What I need is a vision of faith, seeing the reality of God at the point of my need.

The need element can also take the form of consequences) in a person's experience. This differs from symptoms in that symptoms are particular aspects of one's suffering which indicate his disharmony with the truth of God. Consequences, on the other hand, are the results of wrong behavior and attitudes that naturally follow such an approach to life. Consequences include the effect on relationships, performance, responsibilities, and circumstances. The reasoning here is simple: wisdom (or lack of it) is reflected in one's assumptions about life; the application of that wisdom can be seen in the difference it makes in one's experience (peace or pain); then the changes will produce external results in our circumstances.

This entire approach rests on your assumption as a preacher that man's fallen nature means wrong thinking, but that right thinking is in the truth of Scripture. An obvious example is how one responds to the gospel in the first place. If his response is positive, he places his faith in Christ as his Savior. If his response is negative, he rejects the gospel. There are certain observable consequences in his present experience either way. The natural principle of cause and effect tells us that every effect has some cause and that causes can be identified by their effects. If this were not true a physician could never diagnose the cause of an ailment.

Addressing the Need

When we speak of "needs," the preacher may respond out of his normal tendency to address the weaknesses and failures in the lives of his parishioners. One of the most common phrases in preaching is "We need to . . ." The preacher sees needs as what needs to be done to be a better Christian. We need to live holier lives. We need to be more faithful in prayer. We need to be bolder witnesses. We need to study our Bibles. These common statements of need by preachers are not at all what we mean by the need element. It is actually the absence of what is needed that we want to notice, the point in human life where the hearer suffers because she does not have what God offers her.

108

The fundamental remedy for every need is to trust God. The overarching purpose for every sermon must be to call for faith. Most sermons, however, are do-better preaching rather than trust-God preaching. The preacher's aim is more often to call for a change in behavior than to encourage more confidence in God. It seems that most preachers would be satisfied with attitudinal and behavioral changes, whether they are rooted in faith or not. But moral reform is not our aim. Spiritual transformation by the power of God will bring moral reform, but moral reform cannot bring spiritual transformation. "Whatever is not from faith is sin" (Rom. 14:23).

When need is addressed, do not do so in terms of obligation or religious duty. The problems people face do not have "religious" solutions. Salvation is not a "religious" solution. It is a grace remedy. It is a faith remedy. Religious duties will not be an adequate answer to man's need because they are an attempt to gain God's acceptance rather than receive His grace. The Christian life is not just a better quality of life than that of an unbeliever. It is not merely morally superior. It is a different kind of life, with an entirely new orientation, from self to Christ. All we receive from God comes through faith in Him, not through religious obligations.

Faith is not ignited by concentrating on the duties of the believer. Faith comes by calling attention to the credibility of the object of faith. Confidence in God comes only by knowing more of Him—His character, His capabilities, His intentions, and His record. And faith never arises in the abstract. It comes in the midst of very particular needs. As one looks away from himself for help, calling out to God, it is then that he is open to a word of revelation. It is then that he can respond in faith. The human need is the point of contact in the individual, the fertile soil where faith can flourish if there is a word from God.

The remedy for man's need is in one sense conceptual. He suffers from being out of harmony with God because he does not know better. If he knew how to trust God, he could be delivered. But how can he if he does not believe in God? And how can he believe if he does not hear? And how can he hear unless someone tells him (Rom. 10:14)? Week by week the preacher presents the alternative—another viewpoint, another understanding, another option the hearer never knew or has forgotten. He can choose either the revelational alternative or the default system of his own thinking.

Preaching should provide basic insight into life. It should deal with a person's worldview, his philosophy of life, his values, his working strategies. The Bible provides all this, but the biblical view is shockingly out of step with the self-centered orientation of the natural man. Instead of clinging to your life, Jesus says give it away and you will keep it (Matt. 16:25). Instead of living for yourself, the Bible says we are to live for Christ by serving others (2 Cor. 5:15; Matt. 25:40). Instead of boasting in your good works, Jesus says to do them in secret (Matt. 6:1). Instead of hiding your sins from others, the Bible says to confess them (Jas. 5:16).

In another sense the remedy for man's need is volitional. Basic to the biblical revelation is the assumption that a faith response is necessary. Faith without works is dead (Jas. 2:17). But again let me emphasize that the actions called for are not religious in nature, aimed at satisfying God. They are relational, trusting God and receiving His grace for every need. The disciplines of the Christian life are expressions of one's confidence in God and a desire to honor Him. They are not for the purpose of appeasing Him and gaining His favor.

Every sermon should address the needs of the hearers with practical steps of action based on the wisdom of God. Real changes cannot come until a new truth is acted upon. Sometimes this action has to begin with a personal inventory of assumptions and attitudes at the point in question. The preacher can suggest what questions to raise and how to work through such an analysis on paper. But analysis must move on to changes in behavior. What the Bible tells me about my speech, for instance (Eph. 4:29), may challenge my unconscious motivations. But it must also direct my choices and actions in everyday conversation.

Sometimes the remedy for man's need is first interpretative. Some of the needs people experience arise from circumstances entirely outside their control. A lab report comes back: it's cancer. A loved one dies. The plant is closing, and pink slips have been issued. A child is born with a birth defect. How are we to make sense of what happened? Where is God in these new circumstances? "I am really hurting, Preacher. I am heartbroken and angry and frustrated. Do you have anything to say to me from God?"

The most trying needs of all are those that can't be fixed, those with no cause-effect pattern to them. And it is this kind of need that most tries one's faith. What are the resources of grace for this kind of suffering? On any given Sunday somebody in the congregation is experiencing this kind of trouble. The challenge to the preacher is to help his hearers interpret what is happening to them in the framework of faith, the basic world view of Scripture. Only with such a faith interpretation can they deal with the trouble by the grace of God.

Need-Oriented Interpretation

The need element is a vital factor for the entire work of sermon preparation. Without serious and insightful consideration of human need, sermon preparation is little more than a sterile academic exercise. It is not only in the development of the sermon ideas that the need element should be taken into account. If we wait until we have everything done but the application, we may well just tack on some bland suggestions just to keep in touch. The need element must be brought to bear throughout the interpretive process as well.

We have said that textual interpretation asks three questions of the text. The first is, "What do we have here?" Here we are examining the background, the structure, and the wording of the text in its original context. The second question is, "What does it mean?" Here we set forth the theological concepts as they unfold in the text. This reveals the meaning of the text for all humanity. The third question is, "What significance does it have for us?" In this question we probe the contemporary relevance of the text in its various possible applications to "us," the preacher and his congregation.

As he comes to the biblical world and approaches the sacred text, the preacher does not come alone. He comes as a messenger, a priest, a representative of his people. He comes with their personal concerns on his heart. He brings with him their needs, their hopes, their problems, their weaknesses. He does not come for himself but for them. But he is also one of them. He comes as priest and intercessor who is only able to serve as he identifies fully with his flock, entering into their pain, accepting their burden as his own, seeking grace in their behalf.

Frank Pollard describes going into the church worship center on Saturdays as he is finishing his sermon. He stands at the pulpit and thanks God for the people and the privilege of preaching to them. He continues,

> Then I go and sit in the pews. I will sit where a widow usually sits and think about her and what she may expect when she comes to worship. I sat for a long time one Saturday morning in the place a fifteen-year-old occupies on Sunday mornings at the eleven o'clock service. It changed me. It changed the way I thought about young people. . . . It made me want to preach sermons to which the young man would listen and be benefited.[3]

So when this intercessor, priest, preacher reverently searches the Scripture for its truth, he cannot but search with the needs of his hearers in mind. He asks the question, "What do we have here?" And he is like a medical researcher with a new compound before him. He focuses his attention on every detail of it, but in the back of his mind he cannot forget those who need this remedy. So he does not hear the text in a vacuum, not academically, not as a matter for scholarly fascination. In here somewhere is just the word someone needs, and he must find it.

The need element is often explicit in the text. The text may contain very direct descriptions of the needs of those whose story is told, or of the writer, or the readers. Who can forget the agony of David at the illness of a child who could not recover? Who can fail to see the many needs of the Corinthian believers? Who can miss the struggle of the disciples to understand Jesus and all He said and did? Who does not identify with the readers of Hebrews as their chastening is described?

The need element also can be implicit. In many texts the interpreter must read between the lines of the text writer's message to discern the need he is addressing. Often we can only guess. The evidence may be scarce. But our efforts to discover the needs being addressed on the occasion of the text's writing will often pay off in real insight into contemporary needs. God has not changed. Man has not changed. A word from God to that generation will speak to similar needs today.

Seeing the writer's original message in its context, we move to the next question, "What does it mean?" What are the universal theological truths which transcend the writer's time and speak to every generation? He identifies and writes those concepts carefully as his enthusiasm grows. Here is something with real possibilities. Here are truths the people need to hear. Here are principles of justice, grace, love, obedience, and faith. Here is a message from God Himself, an alternative view from heaven's vantage point.

The need element is also correspondent in nature. In tracing the correspondent need, the preacher asks the third question, "What is its significance for us?" By this I mean the principles revealed in the text can be traced to corresponding needs which they address. Those needs may or may not have been in the mind of the writer. The truth in the text will always have applications well beyond what the writer was thinking. Even though the original intention of the writer is our starting place for understanding, his message transcends that intention because of the universal and timeless concepts it contains. Discovering the correspondent need calls for a logical deduction from the theological principle to the problem in human experience it addresses.

As you think of your audience, focus your attention on individuals. Look beyond the group to the one, that unique, priceless person with a story to tell, a story not yet finished. Remember that the group has no life except here in the worship where they are gathered. At the close of the meeting they scatter as families and individuals. That does not mean they are not, as a church, one body. I mean, rather, that they do not experience this group life except in the meetings. And the real challenge of the Christian life is beyond the meetings, not in the gathered church, but in the scattered church.

The preacher thinks of his congregation. He sees faces. He recalls names. He sits among them in his mind and looks toward the pulpit as one of them. What will the messenger say? What does he bring us? What strength? What instructions? What reproof? The preacher begins to see how this Scripture passage speaks directly to us, to our needs. It is wisdom for that young father, encouragement for an elderly widow, direction for a confused youth, hope for a struggling victim. It is a Word from God to the Philippians, which became a Word from God to all mankind, and finally a Word from God to us, to this particular group in this place at this time.

The preacher asks, "Why does anyone need to hear this message? What difference does it make?" As he searches out the need element in his sermon preparation, he experiences at least three significant benefits. (1) He comes to a deeper understanding of the truth of the text. (2) He comes to a more sympathetic and understanding attitude toward his hearer. (3) He develops a more interesting and compelling presentation of the message in his sermon.

Completing the Exercise

Using the form at the end of this chapter, you can complete "The Need Element" exercise by following the directions step by step. At this point we are assuming you have already done the textual spade work of the earlier exercises. Remember, the aim now is to strengthen your skill in tracing from theological concepts in the text to corresponding needs in contemporary hearers. While the first steps in the exercise do not trace to the need element, they will set the stage for that logical deduction.

STEP 1: Identify the needs mentioned explicitly in the text. Remember, you are looking for the suffering, the trouble, the conflict that was being experienced by those associated with the original occasion of the text. Your structural diagram and observations will help, along with the interpretive questions you have answered.

STEP 2: Identify the needs suggested implicitly in the text. This means they are not stated openly, but only there by implication. Again, you are dealing at this point with the needs of those originally involved, not today's readers.

STEP 3: Summarize the writer's message by using your textual idea (subject / complement) and the aspects of it treated in the text. Your purpose here is to state clearly the universal truths contained in the text as a beginning point for discovering corresponding needs.

STEP 4: Describe the experience of a person who needs to hear the message of the text by logically tracing from the solution to the problem. This is the correspondent need. Describe his needs in terms of (1) his symptoms, (2) his assumptions, (3) the consequences of his approach, and (4) how he probably feels about his trouble. Use your imagination, but do not stray from the principles of the text.

STEP 5: Write a profile of the person needing the message of the text in concrete, descriptive terms. Think of one person. In fact you may think of someone you actually know. Be imaginative. Describe this person so realistically that those who need your message will see themselves in your description.

Summary

The preacher may fail to be attuned to the needs of his hearers because he is preoccupied with biblical studies and the institutional life of the church. The Need Element exercise helps trace biblical ideas to contemporary needs. The preacher needs to understand the realworld life of his people if he is to preach effectively. The need element is the trouble in human experience which corresponds to the principles in the message at hand. It can take the form of mistaken assumptions, negative symptoms, or normal results of being out of harmony with biblical wisdom.

The need element does not refer to religious duties one "needs to" perform. Nor does this emphasis on duty build faith. The biblical remedy for man's need may be conceptual (better understanding), volitional (wiser decisions), or interpretive (faith perspective). The need element helps the process of biblical interpretation get beyond sterile academics to human concern. The need element may be seen in the text as explicit in the writer's words, implicit in the problems he addresses, or correspondent as an application of theological concepts.

With the biblical text on the one hand and the needs of his hearers on the other, the preacher now continues the process of interpreting the text for his contemporary audience. We move next to the task of getting the biblical truth from the text to the sermon.

Study Questions

1. What are four ingredients in the preaching setting?
2. What is the purpose of the Need Element exercise?
3. Why do people need to hear biblical principles that challenge their root ideas and attitudes?
4. What are two underlying assumptions for the need element approach?
5. What, according to the author, is the over-arching purpose for every sermon?
6. What are three basic categories of remedy for man's needs?
7. How does the discussion of the need of the congregation affect your enthusiasm and commitment for preaching?

1. Edgar DeWitt Jones, *The Royalty of the Pulpit* (New York: Harper & Brothers, 1951), 55.

2. William D. Thompson, *Preaching Biblically* (Nashville: Abingdon, 1981), 80. The hermeneutical model Thompson presents is most helpful for seeing the vital role of the need element in biblical interpretation and homiletics.

3. Frank Pollard, "Preparing the Preacher" in *Handbook of Contemporary Preaching,* ed. by Michael Duduit (Nashville: Broadman, 1992), 135.

The Need Element

Text ___Psalm 1_____ Name __W. McDill___ Date_____

The need element is the human condition which corresponds to the truths that are presented in your text. The need may be described plainly in the text or only implied. The textual concepts can be traced to particular negative experiences, emotions, and circumstances common to human life which call for the message of the text.

1. Identify the needs mentioned directly in the text as they pertained to the original textual setting: ___hearing ungodly advice, influence; identifying with___ ungodly values, lifestyle

2. Identify the needs suggested in the text by implication as the writer addresses problems of his day: indifference to Word of God, unhappiness, no blessing, unfruitful, failure

3. Summarize the concepts from your text which will become the main ideas of the sermon. Use your subject/complement with whatever other explanation is needed to clarify the idea. ___The godly man is contrasted with the wicked in that he shuns the influence of the ungodly and delights in the Word of God.

4. Use the following categories to begin describing the likely experience of the person who needs to hear the message of the text as a remedy for his needs.

   (1) His symptoms of the trouble he is experiencing: be accepted by ungodly, little sense of fulfillment, unduly influenced by others, fruitless

   (2) His underlying assumptions about the issue: seems natural to want to be accepted by others, fits his own desires

   (3) Some of the consequences in his experience: unhappy, unfruitful, heading for destruction, no spiritual resource

   (4) How a person feels who is suffering at this point: frustrated, empty, angry, confused, disappointed his approach to life isn't working

5. Write a profile of the person needing your message in vivid, concrete terms as you sympathetically identify with his suffering and interest him in the good news you have for him. ___Depending on how far along he is on this path, he is becoming disillusioned, senses he has no moral compass, no firm convictions, sick of trying to please others, being corrupted by others. He may be open to a major change.

The Need Element

Text ___Ephesians 3:1–6___ Name ___W. McDill___ Date_____

The need element is the human condition which corresponds to the truths that are presented in your text. The need may be described plainly in the text or only implied. The textual concepts can be traced to particular negative experiences, emotions, and circumstances common to human life which call for the message of the text.

1. Identify the needs mentioned directly in the text as they pertained to the original textual setting: ___none___

2. Identify the needs suggested in the text by implication as the writer addresses problems of his day: ___no sense of destiny, purpose; unloved, not belonging___

3. Summarize the concepts from your text which will become the main ideas of the sermon. Use your subject/complement with whatever other explanation is needed to clarify the idea. ___God has blessed us with all we need in Christ, choosing us before creation for a holy life, adopting us as sons in Christ, giving us His grace freely___

4. Use the following categories to begin describing the likely experience of the person who needs to hear the message of the text as a remedy for his needs.

   (1) His symptoms of the trouble he is experiencing: ___sense of purposeless-ness, uncertain why he is here, lack of sense of belonging ultimately___

   (2) His underlying assumptions about the issue: ___not sure there is any destiny or purpose beyond what he creates___

   (3) Some of the consequences in his experience: ___does not know God, has no appreciation of his grace in Christ, no guiding purpose___

   (4) How a person feels who is suffering at this point: ___probably feels the need to keep busy, entertained; hasn't "found himself"___

5. Write a profile of the person needing your message in vivid, concrete terms as you sympathetically identify with his suffering and interest him in the good news you have for him. ___The person who does not know he is chosen by God is left to make his own purpose materially. He does the best he can, but knows something is missing. He may be restless, looking for something or someone who can finally give him a sense of being at home.___

The Need Element

Text _____ Name _____ Date_____

The need element is the human condition which corresponds to the truths that are presented in your text. The need may be described plainly in the text or only implied. The textual concepts can be traced to particular negative experiences, emotions, and circumstances common to human life which call for the message of the text.

1. Identify the needs mentioned directly in the text as they pertained to the

original textual setting: _____

_____

2. Identify the needs suggested in the text by implication as the writer addresses

problems of his day: _____

_____

3. Summarize the concepts from your text which will become the main ideas of the

sermon. Use your subject/complement with whatever other explanation is needed to

clarify the idea. _____

_____

4. Use the following categories to begin describing the likely experience of the

person who needs to hear the message of the text as a remedy for his needs.

(1) His symptoms of the trouble he is experiencing: _____

_____

(2) His underlying assumptions about the issue: _____

_____

(3) Some of the consequences in his experience: _____

_____

(4) How a person feels who is suffering at this point:_____

_____

5. Write a profile of the person needing your message in vivid, concrete terms as

you sympathetically identify with his suffering and interest him in the good news you

have for him. _____

_____

_____

_____

_____

_____

_____

_____

I have the conviction that no sermon is ready for preaching, not ready for writing out, until we can express its theme in a short, pregnant sentence as clear as crystal. I find the getting of that sentence is the hardest, the most exacting, and the most fruitful labor in my study. . . . I do not think any sermon ought to be preached, or even written, until that sentence has emerged, clear and lucid as a cloudless moon.[1]

J. H. Jowett, 1912

CHAPTER 6

BRIDGING FROM TEXT TO SERMON

It was a bad connection. Though the person on the other end could hear me fairly well, I could barely make out what he was saying. "You sound like you are a thousand miles away," I shouted. "Hang up and let me try it again." We started over with a new connection and were able to finish our conversation, even though we were a thousand miles away and more. What a wonder modern communication technology is! We are literally "brought together" over great distances.

We face an even greater communication challenge as preachers. We are to receive and proclaim a message from writers thousands of years and miles away, connected to us by just a thin line of print. We must hear them, though their languages were different. We must understand them, though their cultures are foreign to ours. We must faithfully report their message, though we have never seen their faces.

This understanding and reporting is what we mean by hermeneutics, biblical interpretation. This is one of the primary tasks of the preacher. Like an interpreter from one world translating the thoughts of another, he is to listen carefully and speak faithfully. He is to allow the message once delivered to speak again to this generation. But it must be the same message. The connection must be kept clear. This is done best with text-based preaching. Our aim is to have the primary message of the Scripture text come through as the primary message of the sermon.

In a way, every biblical writer is described in the words written about Abel in his faithfulness to God, "And by faith he still speaks, even though he is dead" (Heb. 11:4, NIV). And every one of us is called to fulfill the word of Jesus to Thomas, "Blessed are those who have not seen and yet have believed" (John 20:29, NIV). Those who wrote are dead, but they still live through their faithful report. We who read today have not seen what they describe, yet we believe through the message heard anew.

The exercises in previous chapters have concentrated on skills for examining the text inductively. Our aim was to discover the writer's main idea and its treatment in the passage. Now, after that study is completed, we must carefully make the connection between the textual idea and the sermon. The exercise for this chapter is *Text to Sermon*. The skill we want to strengthen is this: *constructing an interpretive bridge for bringing the truth of the text to its expression in the sermon.* That concept revealed in the text must be carried safely across the chasm of language, culture, and history so that it may be heard again today in its intended meaning.

Here is a series of steps you can take to bridge that chasm. ✳ These steps are the writing of four related sentences. The first is the statement of the *textual idea.* This is followed by the writing of the *sermon idea,* based on the textual idea. Look at the "Then and Now" chart to see how these sentences compare. The third sentence is called the *interrogative*, in which the sermon idea is written as a question. Finally, you will write a *transition* sentence as a statement designed to open the way into your sermon body and division statements.[2]

These four bridging sentences take you faithfully from the idea of the text to the preaching of it in the sermon. I realize that this process may seem like a rather mechanical approach to interpretation. You will find, however, that these sentences will keep you on track. They will provide a straight line of thought from text to sermon that allows you the confidence that you are preaching the intended theological message of the text.

The Textual Idea

The textual idea is a clear, precisely worded sentence which concisely states the idea of the text writer. It includes several elements in the historical situation from which the text comes. These are reference to the writer, speaker, or actors, any known occasion for its writing, and any special literary features. The statement provides a model to follow in the wording of the other sentences so that you can see at a glance whether you are allowing the text to speak its message.

The first step in writing the textual idea in a complete sentence is to discover the single subject of the text, as we have discussed in chapter 4. That subject is discovered, not by guessing, but by looking carefully at the evidence in the text. But the subject alone is not a complete idea yet. A complete idea must have two parts: a subject and a complement. The subject is "what the writer is talking about." The complement is "how the writer limits the scope of what he is talking about."

Text to Sermon: Four Sentences

The Textual Idea: the core idea of the text worded as subject/complement and stated as a complete, past-tense sentence. It contains reference to certain historical elements associated with the text—writer and readers, persons in a narrative account, circumstances or occasion of writing, special literary features.

The Sermon Idea: the same subject/complement as core of the textual idea, worded as a present-tense, universal statement, without the historical elements of the textual idea.

The Interrogative: the sermon idea translated into a question by the use of one of the following: who, what, when, where, why, how. Calls for the predicates revealed in the text writer's treatment of his theme.

The Transition Sentence: answers the interrogative by the introduction of a key word which categorizes the various predicates found in the text and introduces them as sermon divisions.

The textual idea should be characterized by brevity, as long as it contains the elements necessary to it. It should be a theological statement in that it contains the basic theological idea of the text. Every part of the biblical record is history as we discuss it today, so the textual idea is stated in past tense. This is not yet the sermon idea, which will be in present tense. It is rather a statement of what the text writer said in his own historical context.

In John 3:1–8 Jesus told Nicodemus he "must be born again." It seems clear that the subject is regeneration, meaning "new birth" or "birth from above" in this passage. Let me point out that "birth" is a metaphorical expression in this text. It may almost seem literal to us because new birth is commonly used as a theological expression for spiritual birth or conversion. It is best not to use figurative terms as your subject and complement, but to translate them into conceptual terms. The theological meaning contained in the figure is what you want as your subject or complement. In the sermon, however, you may want to clearly define and use the figurative language for its impact.

In this case the word *regeneration* is your theological subject even though it does not convey the strength of the figurative expression "born again" in English. At this point our aim is to identify the concept as clearly and precisely as possible. With that understanding in mind, let's say the subject for John 3:1–8 is regeneration. That is "what he is talking about" in the text. Now we need to find the complement, or "how he is limiting the scope of what he is talking about." These two elements will make a complete idea. If you look closely at the text you can see that Jesus is talking about the necessity of regeneration. This is the complement to the subject and makes a complete idea.

At this point you have The Necessity of Regeneration as a working title and the core idea of the text. Your aim is for this to be the idea of the sermon as well. It is the concept revealed in the dialogue recorded by John. Whatever the historical trappings of that late night meeting, the theological principle carried in the story is the necessity of regeneration. As best we can tell by the words in his report, John recounted this story to his readers to communicate something about the need for a radical spiritual transformation, a new birth from above.

To take that idea and write it as a statement, simply identify the actors or writers and state what you see as the idea originally intended in the passage. Since it is a narrative (actually a Gospel) account, we note the persons in the story, Jesus and Nicodemus. The occasion is not critical to the story. A special literary feature is the repeated mention of "the kingdom of God." With the core idea (as subject/complement) we include these historical elements. So our textual idea may be stated as follows: *Jesus explained to Nicodemus the necessity of regeneration in the kingdom of God.*

There are several ways to designate this sentence. We are calling it the textual idea. It is also called the exegetical idea or the central idea of the text. Be alert to the difference in terminology as you read from various writers. Be sure you understand that it simply means the theme or concept or idea the biblical writer had in mind when he wrote what he did. Whatever you call this statement, it is the first of a series of sentences you can write to take you faithfully from the text to your sermon, without losing the idea along the way.

As you encounter other ways of dealing with this textual idea under different names, also note that some writers do not distinguish between a statement of the writer's idea and the sermon idea. They may just call the sermon idea by one of the terms mentioned above, or perhaps thesis or proposition. The reason we distinguish the writer's idea from the preacher's here is to demonstrate that the writer's statement is bound up in his historical setting, as is every text in Scripture. Remember, our first task in interpretation is to discover the meaning of the text writer as he addressed his original audience. Out of that understanding we discern the timeless theological truth contained in that particular historical statement.

If we assume that the texts of Scripture are for us, as we often say, without being originally for someone else, we may overlook the significance of that original setting and miss the interpretation. We may neglect the research needed to span the distance to the biblical world. In one sense that would involve taking every text "out of context" historically and running the risk of perverting or missing its intended meaning. Remember that the text cannot mean now what it did not mean when it was originally written.

Back to our textual idea for John 3:1–8, *Jesus explained to Nicodemus the necessity of regeneration in the kingdom of God.* Though you might state it in somewhat different terms, you can see how the text itself determines this statement. This is what my text says, so it is what I want my sermon to say. Having this statement carefully written, we now move on to the next sentence in the series, the sermon idea.

The Sermon Idea

Every writer on speech or homiletics emphasizes the importance of a single idea as the theme for any address. The speaker is urged to write a carefully worded sentence which expresses that idea. Different terms are used to designate this sentence. As we have noted, some refer to it as the proposition. Others call it the thesis.

Discovering and writing the textual idea is the hard part. But when you have done a careful, inductive study of your text, it is not so difficult. Now you want to state the sermon idea. This will be a contemporary translation of the textual idea. For John 3:1–8, I stated the sermon idea this way: *Regeneration is necessary in the kingdom of God.* This simple and direct statement is the basic truth of the text and, therefore, the basic truth of my sermon. The key to keeping that truth intact across the hermeneutical distance is to use the exact words of the subject/complement for the textual idea and the sermon idea.

The sermon idea is a universal principle that applies to everyone who might hear it, instead of a particular message to the writer's audience. It is a timeless truth that can be stated confidently in any generation, instead of an historical statement for the biblical world. Thus it is stated in present tense language as a universal theological principle. You should be able to pull the sermon idea away from the rest of the sermon and state it as a complete idea of theological truth. It should stand on its own, without the sermon structure and development, as true and clear.

The Idea Then and Now

The Textual Idea	*The Sermon Idea*
What the writer said	What the preacher is saying
Based on subject/complement	Based on subject/complement
Written as complete sentence	Written as complete sentence
An historical statement	A timeless truth
Of a particular occasion	Of a universal principle
A theological concept	A theological concept

Once clearly stated, this sermon idea guides the preparation of the sermon. Notice that the kernel idea of the text, regeneration/necessity, is the kernel idea for the entire sermon. It may seem like an unnecessary task to write this sermon idea in such careful terms. But it may well be the most important task of sermon preparation. Until this statement is clear you are not sure what the sermon is to say and where it is going.

In Genesis 3:1–7 is the report of the encounter of Eve with Satan as she and Adam were deceived and took the forbidden fruit. Though the word temptation does not appear in the text, it is a good word to name the subject. For the complement we are looking for the limit the writer seems to put on his treatment of that subject as the story is told. Since this text is so clearly interpreted by James 1:14 ("But each one is tempted when he is carried away and enticed by his own lust"), perhaps we could use appeal as our complement. We then have temptation/appeal as our subject/complement. A working title is *The Appeal of Temptation.*

The textual idea always includes elements from the historical setting and writing of the text. Adding these elements to temptation/appeal, our textual idea may be stated: *Adam and Eve fell to the serpent's temptation through the appeal of forbidden fruit.* To translate that textual idea into a sermon idea, we exchange the historical features for the universal and timeless, while maintaining the theological concept. It can be stated, *Christians should beware of the appeal of temptation.* This is one way to state the lesson of the text for all time.

In dealing with a narrative passage, it is important to note that narrative does not teach in the same way as law or prophecy, or epistle. Whereas these other literary forms teach more directly, narratives teach by example or demonstration. Be careful not to read into a narrative some "teaching" not really there. Remember that a Bible passage is best interpreted by other biblical texts. Your security for theological truth is the clear confirmation of an idea in other texts.

Though different in expression, our first two bridging sentences, the sermon idea and the textual idea, are identical in concept. Now we come to the third of our bridging sentences, the interrogative.

The Interrogative

You will notice that we are attempting to establish a solid linkage from the text to the sermon and its development. Restating the sermon idea as an interrogative is simple: make a question of it.

Look at John 3:1–8 in light of the sermon idea and decide which of these questions fits best: who, what, when, where, why, or how. Which question does the text want to answer? How about this one: Who needs regeneration in the kingdom of God? If this is the right question, the text will give you a description of the one who needs regeneration, or perhaps various ones who need to be born again. Try this one: What is the regeneration that is necessary in the kingdom of God? These questions do not open the writer's treatment of the idea. Very simply, they do not work.

So we must try when, where, why, or how. I chose why: *Why is regeneration necessary in the kingdom of God?* That question seems to fit the main features of the dialogue between Jesus and Nicodemus. Jesus says in verse 5, "Unless one is born of water and the Spirit, he cannot enter into the kingdom of God." That is but one expression in the text about the necessity of regeneration, but it seems to answer the question why.

✴ Making a question of the sermon idea opens the way to the body of your sermon. Each of your sermon divisions will be an answer to the question you have raised. So you go to the text and look for answers. You have allowed the text to speak concerning its subject and complement and have stated that idea. Now you will add predicates to your subject and complement. Remember that the subject answers the question, "What is the writer talking about?"[3] The complement answers the question, "How does the writer limit the scope of what he is talking about?" Finally, the predicates answer the question, "What is the writer saying about what he is talking about?" In our next chapter we will deal with the predicates, and how to use them in the writing of your sermon divisions. At this point merely jot down the predicates as they appear verse by verse in the text.

The subject and complement together form the core of the sermon idea by making a complete theme. The multiple predicates express the features of the sermon idea as the text reveals them. The use of these predicates is the dividing of the sermon idea based on the writer's treatment of his subject. The idea is divided, so we call these predicates, our sermon points, divisions. So we have determined the subject, the limit of its scope, and the things said about that subject. All this together forms the conceptual skeleton of the sermon as it reflects the thinking revealed in the text. As the bridging sentences take the writer's idea to the sermon, the pattern may be diagrammed:

[subject/complement ——> predicates].

Now look again at Genesis 3:1–7. There we have named the idea temptation/appeal, or The Appeal of Temptation. The interrogative will probe the text for predicates, various aspects of the appeal of temptation. As the interrogative I chose what. So the question is this: *What is the appeal of temptation?* I looked closely at the text and ruled out who, when, where, why, or how. If I am reading it rightly, the text wants to tell me several things about what the appeal of temptation is.

The use of the interrogative is an effort to guide the unfolding structure of the sermon along a clear line of direction. The question you use will call for a certain kind of answer. But you do not choose the question arbitrarily. You have chosen the subject from the text, the complement from the text, and stated the textual idea based on the text. Now you will allow the text to determine the question you ask of its subject.

If you choose a question you think might work well, take it by the entire text, verse by verse, as a test. Does the text want to provide answers to the question you are raising? Can you look through the text and find, in the writer's treatment of his subject, specific answers to your question? If not, choose another question and reword the interrogative until you get it right. After that, we are ready for the final sentence in the series, the transition into the sermon body.

The Transition Sentence

The transition is the fourth of these bridging sentences designed to take the text idea safely from the text to the sermon. It answers the question raised in the interrogative and introduces the predicates of the sermon idea which will be found in the textual treatment of that idea. Those predicates are the answers to the question the interrogative raises and become your sermon divisions.

At this point we introduce a most helpful device, the key word. The key word is a plural, abstract noun which names a category to classify the predicates, your sermon divisions. The question you have attached to your sermon idea to make the interrogative will usually lead you easily to the appropriate key word. Since the question I have used for John 3:1–8 is why, I have chosen *reasons* as my key word. From a look at my text as I asked the question above, it seemed the answers were easily classified as reasons for the necessity of regeneration. So each of my division statements will be a reason found in the text that regeneration is necessary in the kingdom of God.

Def • i • ni´ tion: Key Word

The key word is a plural, abstract noun which classifies or delineates the character of the division statements of the sermon. In the method presented in this study, it is used in the transition sentence as a way to answer the question raised in the interrogative. The key word helps build a strong framework for the body of the sermon since all divisions must then conform to it.

The key word sends the preacher back to the text to find answers to his interrogative which can be characterized by the key word. The number of key words possible to use is almost unlimited. The right one for a text will follow the choice of question used with the interrogative.

There is almost an unlimited number of terms you can use as key words. A partial list is included in this chapter to show the variety.[4] Do not use "things" as a key word. It is too broad and nebulous to be useful. Neither should you use "points" as a key word, for the same reason. Remember, the key word is simply a device to identify the nature of your predicates or divisions as they emerge from the writer's treatment of his subject.

Sample Key Words

abuses	barriers	defenses	expressions	implications
accusations	beliefs	deficiencies	facets	impressions
acts	benefits	degrees	factors	improvements
admonitions	blessings	demands	facts	impulses
advantages	causes	devices	failures	incentives
affirmations	certainties	differences	faults	incidents
agreements	challenges	directives	fears	indictments
aims	changes	disciplines	features	insights
alternatives	commitments	discoveries	forces	instances
answers	comparisons	distinctions	functions	instructions
approaches	compromises	doctrines	fundamentals	invitations
areas	conditions	duties	gains	joys
arguments	consequences	elements	gifts	kinds
aspects	contrasts	encouragements	graces	lessons
aspirations	corrections	essentials	groups	loyalties
assertions	credentials	evidences	habits	losses
assumptions	criteria	evils	handicaps	marks
assurances	criticisms	examples	hopes	methods
attainments	customs	exhortations	hungers	mistakes
attitudes	dangers	expectations	ideas	motives
attributes	decisions	experiences	imperatives	mysteries

and more and more and more

At this point we have worded four key sentences to insure that the path from our text to our sermon is straight and true. In the actual preaching of the sermon you could state these sentences, but you may not. If you do so, they would come in the introduction and open the way to the body of the sermon. The discipline of writing them is important even if you never express them orally.

Completing the Exercise

Our purpose in this chapter has been to provide an exercise for strengthening the preacher's skill in constructing an interpretive bridge for bringing the truth of the text to its expression in the sermon. The exercise for practicing this skill is Text to Sermon. Here are the steps to take in completing the exercise.

STEP 1: Identify the subject of the text in one word. You will notice that this exercise goes back to overlap the end of the Naming the Textual Idea exercise. As we have said repeatedly, unless you accurately identify the subject of the text, nothing else in this method will work.

STEP 2: Identify the complement. This word represents the writer's way of limiting the scope of his treatment of the subject.

STEP 3: State your subject / complement together as a working title for the emerging sermon.

STEP 4: Write the textual idea statement as the first of the four bridging sentences. Remember the formula: the subject/complement plus elements of the historical setting and the literary context of the text.

STEP 5: Write the sermon idea by rewording the basic statement of the textual idea without the historical trappings. Test its validity by seeing whether it will stand alone as a timeless and universal statement of theological truth.

STEP 6: The third of the bridging sentences is the interrogative, a restatement of the sermon idea as a question. Choose one of the following to do this: who, what, when, where, why, how.

STEP 7: Answer the question raised above with the transition sentence. At this point you must choose a key word which best suits your question. The key word must be a plural, abstract noun which serves to classify your predicates as they become sermon division statements.

STEP 8: List the predicates in the text which indicate what the writer is saying about his subject. This final step provides a transition to our next exercise on wording the sermon divisions. You will word them as sermon divisions later.

Summary

The aim of biblical interpretation is to rightly discern the meaning of the text writer in his own historical context and to express the theological content of that meaning as timeless truths. The preacher, therefore, must construct a hermeneutical bridge to span the distance from the biblical world to his own. The method presented in this study calls for the wording of four sentences which carry the theological concept of the original writer to its expression in a contemporary sermon. Those four sentences are: the textual idea, the sermon idea, the interrogative, and the transition sentence.

The next step in preparing the sermon is to word the sermon divisions carefully as clear, theological statements. For that task we move on to the next chapter.

Study Questions

1. What are the four sentences in the Text to Sermon exercise?
2. What is the importance of stating the textual idea as an historical statement?
3. According to the author, what is probably the most important task of sermon preparation?
4. What is involved in restating the sermon idea as an interrogative?
5. What is the key word in the transition sentence?
6. Why do you think it is important to carefully bridge from text to sermon?

1. J. H. Jowett, *The Preacher: His Life and Work* (New York: Harper, 1912), 133–134.

2. These sentences are the heart of a traditional method for planning sermon structure described by a number of writers. Lloyd Perry and Faris Whitesell used this method in *Variety in Your Preaching* (Westwood, N.J.: Fleming H. Revell, 1954). Charles Koller used it as his "Basic Pattern" in *Expository Preaching Without Notes* (Grand Rapids: Baker, 1962). Lloyd M. Perry called it the "Foundational Pattern" in *A Manual for Biblical Preaching* (Grand Rapids: Baker, 1965). James Braga used it as his method in *How to Prepare Bible Messages* (Portland: Multnomah, 1969). Craig Skinner, in *The Teaching Ministry of the Pulpit* (Grand Rapids: Baker, 1973), 169, writes that in his examination of hundreds of preaching and speech books, he found nothing of the quality of this method. He writes, "This perspective is the finest developed for expository preaching and is in full accord with the best ideas in contemporary speech theory and educational psychology."

3. See H. Grady Davis on "predication," *Design for Preaching* (Philadelphia: Fortress, 1958), 22. He writes that it seems natural to use "subject for the thing talked about, predicate for the thing said about it, and predication for the process of saying or asserting something about the subject."

4. Extensive lists of possible key words appear in Koller, *Expository Preaching Without Notes*, 53–54; Perry and Whitesell, *Variety in Your Preaching*, 84–88; Perry, *A Manual for Biblical Preaching*, 67–69; Skinner, *The Teaching Ministry of the Pulpit*, 166–67; and Braga, *How to Prepare Bible Messages*, 128.

Text to Sermon

Text ___Psalm 1___ Name ___W. McDill___ Date_____

Bridging from text to sermon is a vital aspect of sermon preparation. The purpose is to construct an interpretive bridge for bringing the truth of the text to its expression in the sermon. This exercise overlaps the previous one, depending on the work already done to name the textual idea.

1. Identify the text subject in one word. This answers the question, "What is the text writer talking about?" This one word will be carried through the entire exercise for consistency of thought.

(the) ungodly

2. Identify the complement to your subject in one word. This answers the question, "How does the text writer limit the scope of his treatment of the subject?" This word completes naming the idea.

contrast

3. Using some form of the subject/complement words, write a working title for your emerging sermon.

The godly contrasted with the wicked

4. Write the textual idea statement as the first of the four bridging sentences. Use the subject and complement, plus elements of the historical setting and literary context of the text.

The psalmist used figures for life choices and stability to picture the godly man as he is contrasted with the wicked.

5. Write the sermon idea by adapting the wording of the textual idea. Omit the historical trappings and make it a present tense statement of a universal theological principle.

The life of the godly man is in sharp contrast with that of the wicked.

6. Write the interrogative by restating the sermon idea as a question. Choose one of the following questions: who, what, when, where, why, how. This question will seek answers in the text, the predicates.

How is the life of the godly sharply in contrast with that of the wicked?

7. The transition sentence responds to your interrogative by using a KEY WORD to categorize the predicates in the text which express the subject/complement. Include the KEY WORD with a rewording of the sermon idea.

Our text addresses three major differences as the godly are contrasted with the wicked.

5. List the predicates in the text which express what the writer is saying about his subject. These are specific answers to the question raised in your interrogative. They will become the basis for your sermon divisions.

1. ___how he orders his life___ 4. _____

2. ___his source of truth___ 5. _____

3. ___the consequences of his choices___ 6. _____

Text to Sermon

Text ___Ephesians 1:3–6___ Name ___W. McDill___ Date _____

Bridging from text to sermon is a vital aspect of sermon preparation. The purpose is to construct an interpretive bridge for bringing the truth of the text to its expression in the sermon. This exercise overlaps the previous one, depending on the work already done to name the textual idea.

1. Identify the text subject in one word. This answers the question, "What is the text writer talking about?" This one word will be carried through the entire exercise for consistency of thought.

chosen

2. Identify the complement to your subject in one word. This answers the question, "How does the text writer limit the scope of his treatment of the subject?" This word completes naming the idea.

grace

3. Using some form of the subject/complement words, write a working title for your emerging sermon.

Chosen by the grace of God

4. Write the textual idea statement as the first of the four bridging sentences. Use the subject and complement, plus elements of the historical setting and literary context of the text.

Paul used the figure of adoption to describe how believers are chosen by the grace of God to be His own.

5. Write the sermon idea by adapting the wording of the textual idea. Omit the historical trappings and make it a present tense statement of a universal theological principle.

Believers are chosen by God's grace to be His own.

6. Write the interrogative by restating the sermon idea as a question. Choose one of the following questions: who, what, when, where, why, how. This question will seek answers in the text, the predicates.

Why did God choose us by His grace to be His own?

7. The transition sentence responds to your interrogative by using a KEY WORD to categorize the predicates in the text which express the subject/complement. Include the KEY WORD with a rewording of the sermon idea.

Our text suggests five purposes of God as He chose believers by His grace.

5. List the predicates in the text which express what the writer is saying about his subject. These are specific answers to the question raised in your interrogative. They will become the basis for your sermon divisions.

1. bless with every spiritual blessing 4. fulfill His plan

2. be holy and blameless 5. to His praise

3. make us His sons 6. _____

Text to Sermon

Text _____ Name _____ Date _____

Bridging from text to sermon is a vital aspect of sermon preparation. The purpose is to construct an interpretive bridge for bringing the truth of the text to its expression in the sermon. This exercise overlaps the previous one, depending on the work already done to name the textual idea.

1. Identify the text subject in one word. This answers the question, "What is the text writer talking about?" This one word will be carried through the entire exercise for consistency of thought.

_____

2. Identify the complement to your subject in one word. This answers the question, "How does the text writer limit the scope of his treatment of the subject?" This word completes naming the idea.

_____

3. Using some form of the subject/complement words, write a working title for your emerging sermon.

_____

4. Write the textual idea statement as the first of the four bridging sentences. Use the subject and complement, plus elements of the historical setting and literary context of the text.

_____

_____

5. Write the sermon idea by adapting the wording of the textual idea. Omit the historical trappings and make it a present tense statement of a universal theological principle.

_____

_____

6. Write the interrogative by restating the sermon idea as a question. Choose one of the following questions: who, what, when, where, why, how. This question will seek answers in the text, the predicates.

_____

_____

7. The transition sentence responds to your interrogative by using a KEY WORD to categorize the predicates in the text which express the subject/complement. Include the KEY WORD with a rewording of the sermon idea.

_____

_____

5. List the predicates in the text which express what the writer is saying about his subject. These are specific answers to the question raised in your interrogative. They will become the basis for your sermon divisions.

1. _____   4. _____

2. _____   5. _____

3. _____   6. _____

> In the desire to make a sermon seem free and spontaneous there is a prevalent dislike to giving it its necessary formal structure and organism. . . . True liberty in writing comes by law, and the more thoroughly the outlines of your work are laid out, the more freely your work will flow, like an unwasted stream between its well-built banks.[1]
>
> Phillips Brooks, 1877

CHAPTER 7

WRITING SERMON DIVISIONS

Whatever the preacher has on his mind as he prepares his sermon, his chief goal will probably be to come up with a good outline. No matter what else the sermon has to commend it, it will likely flounder without a good outline to follow. Everybody knows that a sermon should have a few points to hang the preaching on. Most of us have laughed at the classic structure for a sermon—three points and a poem.

People think in orderly patterns, with logical connections and associations, with a reasonable sequence of ideas, with unity of thought. So there is an unspoken understanding that a sermon should be presented with a reasonable arrangement of its ideas. It must proceed in an organized fashion, for the sake of the preacher and the audience alike. Some sermons, however, have an order more like the essay on "Pigs" written by a grade school girl.

A pig is a funny animal, but it has some uses. (The uses are not mentioned.) Our dog don't like pigs—our dog's name is Nero. Our teacher read a piece one day about a wicked man called Nero. My Daddy is a good man. Men are very useful. Men are different than women and my Mom ain't like my Daddy. My Mom says that a ring around the sun means that a storm is coming. And that is all I know about pigs.[2]

Is it an exaggeration to say that some sermons actually wander about like this essay? Grady Davis asserts that sermon structure is an expansion of the basic thought. If that basic sermon idea is not clear, the structure will not be clear. He describes the preacher without a clear idea as his sermon unfolds in uncertainty and confusion.

Sometimes he proposes a subject and then wanders away from it. Sometimes he drags in many other things that do not belong to the subject. Sometimes he seems to be talking about several subjects at once, indiscriminately. Sometimes he just talks about this and that and the other in such a way as to create the suspicion that he either has no subject at all or, if he feels one looming at the back of his head, does not himself know for sure what it is.[3]

Sermon Outlining

Possibilities for outlining a sermon are almost unlimited. Broader categories of outlines include deductive, inductive, and narrative. Beyond that are specific outlines of every sort. Generally they follow the pattern of logical order such as: order of importance or climax, general to specific, cause to effect, effect to cause, question and answer, etc. Other patterns have been given creative names, such as the twin sermon, the chase technique, the ladder pattern, the surprise-package arrangement, etc.[4]

Recent emphasis on inductive and narrative sermon order has come from disenchantment with deductive methods. By deductive is meant a sermon in which the general ideas are stated first, and then the particulars of life application are given. Inductive preaching begins with particulars of experience and moves from there to the general truth of the sermon.[5] Narrative preaching follows a story-telling pattern.[6] Proponents of these approaches claim the audience is drawn into the thought of the sermon better with inductive or narrative as opposed to deductive patterns of organization.

For text-based preaching the aim of the preacher is to follow the text writer's treatment of his subject. his first task, then, is to discover the outline of the text itself. The approach we are taking in this study is designed to allow the writer's thinking to be expressed in the sermon as clearly as possible. Donald McDougall offers three guidelines for outlining the text: (1) Communicate the message; don't just outline it. (2) Find the outline; don't create it. (3) Let the passage dictate to you; don't dictate to it.[7] This is a good summary of our commitments in this task.

The method being presented in this study provides a straight line of thought from the text writer's idea to the preacher's sermon. Like a well-maintained track, the discipline of this method will keep the preacher's train of thought from wandering off and ultimately getting stuck in a bog of fuzzy thinking. That train of ideas is pulled by the core concept, the textual idea as subject/complement. Every other aspect of the sermon must follow that concept down the same track.

We will discuss two phases in the writing of sermon divisions in this chapter. First is a careful analysis of the writer's treatment of his subject. Second is the wording of the divisions as a contemporary expression of the sermon idea. The exercise introduced here is entitled *Writing Sermon Divisions*. The skill we aim to strengthen with the exercise is this: *wording the divisions clearly to state the teachings of the text on its subject.* Like a number of the other skills presented here, this one is centered in the conceptual link between text and sermon.

We will deal with sermon structure in two chapters. This is the first of the two, in which we will address only the task of identifying and writing sermon divisions. We move from the text writer's arrangement of his thought to our outlining of that same subject, guided by his structure. The next chapter will deal with structure in the broader sense of arranging the order of your sermon presentation. In that case we move beyond the main divisions to the design of the entire presentation, with special attention to the needs of the audience and the nature of oral communication.

The Text Writer's Treatment

The writing of sermon divisions must begin with the discovery of the various aspects of the writer's treatment of his subject. By the writer's "treatment" of his subject, we mean his handling of it, his approach to it in your text. We have assumed that the writer had a definite idea in mind as he wrote the text before us. We also assume that he had in mind certain aspects of that idea which he revealed in the text. Having discovered and named the writer's idea, we return to the text for what he is saying about it.

In this chapter we are dealing with the expression of that idea in its component parts. This is usually referred to as the body of the sermon, where the divisions of the sermon idea are presented, with their development. The interrogative in your bridging sentences will be answered by searching the text for predicates to give expression to the subject/complement. We have noted in the previous chapter that consistent thinking is maintained by use of the subject/complement——>predicates pattern.

The text has given us its subject. It has given us the limit placed on the scope of that subject, the complement. It has guided us in the writing of the four sentences which take that idea to the sermon. This will include, of course, the answer to the predicate question, "What is the writer saying about his subject?" Usually he will say several things about the subject; these are predicates. We have used the text as our reference point for the interrogative we raise about the subject. Now we look to the text for answers to that question. It is these answers, the predicates, which will form the divisions of our sermon idea.

Our first task in planning the sermon divisions will be to analyze the writer's treatment of his subject. Here are some guidelines to keep us on track.

Define primary conceptual terms for their theological content.
Key theological concepts in Scripture are directly associated with
the words used to name them. Look closely at the writer's
terminology for all such load-bearing terms. Justification is an
important teaching of Paul closely tied to the Greek word
dikaiōsis. As you study the word and its meaning you discover
that righteousness and justification are closely related concepts.
Do you understand the connection? Are the ideas associated with
these words clear?

One pastor preached on Romans 3:21–25, which has as a
primary word the term *dikaiosunē*, meaning "righteousness."
This is a vivid word that pictures legal acceptability at a court of
law. The preacher, however, talked throughout the sermon about
salvation, a very different idea related to rescue or deliverance.
The terminology for "salvation" does not appear in that text. His
failure to distinguish between these ideas made the sermon
confusing and out of step with the text.

Def • i • ni´ tion: Division Statements

The *divisions* of the sermon are the sections of the sermon body
where the main treatment of the sermon idea is presented. These
sections provide an orderly outline of the sermon idea. Each of
the divisions is related to the sermon idea as a logical aspect of
its truth.

The *division statements* are sentences which express the idea to be
treated in that section. These statements, like the sermon idea,
are complete sentences in the present tense which state theological truths as universally applicable principles.

Division statements reflect the text writer's treatment of his
subject. They complete the text-to-sermon bridge by expressing the predicates of the sermon idea as they are revealed in the
text. As the key elements of the sermon outline, division
statements are the focus of most sermon development.

Look at some of the concepts in Ephesians 1. Can you distinguish between "He chose us" and "predestined?" Do you know the
distinctive meaning of "redemption," "forgiveness," and "grace"?
Can you distinguish between "wisdom" and "understanding"?

What about God's "will" and his "good pleasure"? All of these terms are in the first ten verses of this chapter. It will be difficult to preach a sermon on good theological ground if you cannot distinguish between these concepts, some of which sound so similar at first reading.

Be alert to the theological basis for even the most practical instructions. A common error in the wording of sermon ideas and division statements is the failure to reflect the theological nature of the Bible's message. Your sermon idea and each of your division statements are essentially theological ideas. Theological means pertaining to theology. Theology is the study of God and the relations between God and the universe, the study of religious doctrines and matters of divinity. The essential concepts at the heart of the sermon are ideas related to God: His character, His purpose, His acts, His expectations, His wisdom for man, His grace.

Using the passage from 1 Corinthians 10:13, one preacher's outline followed the subject "Overcoming Temptation." The sermon idea was simple: *you can overcome temptation.* The divisions spelled out why you can overcome temptation. One point was that temptation is *predictable*, another that it is *limited*, and the third that it is *escapable*. That sounds pretty good, doesn't it? In fact, most of us could probably preach on that with enthusiasm. It even seems to be directly tied to the passage. The text says, after all, that temptations are common to man (predictable), that you will not be tempted beyond what you can bear (limited), and that you will be given a way of escape (escapable).

But there is one serious problem here. This sermon deals with the text only in terms of observations about the nature of temptation. It does not deal with it theologically. We learn nothing about God and His grace. We are not called to faith, but to self-confidence. I realize that the development of the sermon might help solve this problem. But this sermon focused more attention on individual effort.

So what is the theological concept here? It is simple. It is the faithfulness of God in your temptations. The key phrase is "God is faithful." So I suggested that we restate these ideas in different terms. The sermon idea was temptation/faithful, or *God is faithful when you are tempted.* The division statements answered the question, "How is God faithful when I am tempted?" The three statements were:

1. *God is faithful to make temptation predictable.*
2. *God is faithful to keep temptation limited.*
3. *God is faithful to provide a way out of temptation.*

This outline clearly goes to the basis for our faith as we deal with temptation. We are able to rejoice in God's faithfulness, rather than try to flex our own moral muscles. We are assured that we can trust Him. We are told what He is doing to help. The sermon therefore goes beyond positive thinking to theological assurance.

Watch for significance in the relationships between concepts in the text. One of the most common major errors I have observed in students' sermons is in confusing the relation of various concepts in the text. One student preached on Isaiah 6 under the title, "A Vision of God." His premise was that the Christian, like Isaiah, can have a vision of God if he will fulfill certain conditions. Among the conditions he named were: recognizing your sinfulness ("a man of unclean lips"), receiving cleansing ("touched my lips"), and being willing to answer the call of God ("Here am I, send me").

This sounded good to the class until the preacher was asked, "Do you think the attitude and actions of Isaiah caused the vision of God, or did the vision cause his response? Which was the cause and which was the effect?" At that point the student saw immediately what he had done. He had confused the relationship of the major concepts in the passage. He had reversed the cause and effect.

Beyond cause and effect relationships, look for primary ideas and dependent ideas as they are related. Watch for the progression of thought so as not to confuse sequences. One of the best exercises for this challenge is the structural diagram explained in chapter 1 as part of the inductive Bible study. As you write out the text in that diagram, you will see how various factors are related to each other.

A classic example of this challenge is Ephesians 2:8, "For by grace you have been saved through faith; and that not of yourselves, it is the gift of God." The question to be raised here concerning the various concepts in the verse focuses on the "that" which is the gift of God. What is the "that"? Is it grace? Is it salvation? Or is it faith? And if we can determine this, what difference will it make in our interpretation of the theology of this verse? I will let you figure this one out.

Translate figurative language in the text into conceptual terms. The Bible is full of figurative language. In text after text you must deal with metaphors, similes, and other more challenging figures of speech.[8] Preachers often fail to translate this picture language. Instead they just repeat it. Repeating Bible terminology is not interpreting it. The preacher must be an interpreter, not just a reporter. We often hear common figures like "new birth" used in sermons without any explanation of what this graphic analogy means. How is the radical spiritual transformation of conversion like being born?

One student preacher dealt with Matthew 5:13–16 by using two divisions in his sermon: (1) Christians must be like light. (2) Christians must be like salt. For his explanation of these metaphors he described scientifically how light dispels darkness and how salt preserves, flavors, etc. As we discussed the sermon, I asked him, "What is the conceptual meaning of salt and light? What did Jesus mean by these figures of speech?" He was not sure. He had not tried to state their meaning in conceptual terms. As a result his sermon was interesting, but not clear as to its theological meaning.

When we looked more closely at the text, I pointed out that there must be a conceptual theme behind Jesus' use of these figures of speech. Though He explained some parables and sayings, He did not explain these. The salt and light teachings seem to be a unit. As with the parables, there is a single idea at the heart of these metaphors. We were back to the need to name a subject, then a complement, then predicates. For the subject we chose influence. We said the complement was others. We interpreted the metaphors to mean *Christians are to influence others for Christ.*

Now our task was to translate the other figurative aspects of this text with reference to *influencing others for Christ.* There was the "flavor," the "trampling underfoot," the "city set on a hill," the "lamp," the "basket," the "lamp stand," and so on. If we were correct about the underlying theme of this text, these other figures would also make sense. The assertions with the various figures are the predicates, divisions of the overall thought.

Examine the writer's grammatical and rhetorical choices for the purpose and tone of his treatment. The way the writer intended to present his ideas can be discerned by a look at the grammatical mood and the rhetorical mode he employs. Mood has to do with the writer's use of verbs and reflects his attitude with reference to the subject. Mood includes the indicative (for primary statements and questions), the imperative (for commands), and the subjunctive (to express conditions contrary to fact). Rhetorical mode reveals the writer's purpose in how he deals with his subject, including narration, description, exposition, and argumentation.

Look at the words of Jesus in Matthew 6:25–34. The assertion of Jesus is simple: "Do not worry." We might state the textual idea: *Jesus argued that God's care for His creatures proves the foolishness of worrying about the necessities of life.* His assertion is a command based on the character of God. Though the qualities of God which make such worry unnecessary are not stated in a clear doctrinal formula, they are in the passage in the examples Jesus uses.

In planning your sermon divisions from this text, you will take into account that the writer uses the imperative (giving commands) and indicative (direct statements of fact) grammatical moods. He also uses the rhetorical modes of description (to make the hearers see, feel, or hear), and argumentation (to persuade the audience). Jesus vividly describes scenes with the lilies and birds to prove his point that worry is foolish because of God's care and provision. Since He uses indicative description and argumentation, it would be wise to consider the same approach for your divisions.

In this passage there are five arguments. First, Jesus uses a greater to lesser argument to ask whether the food and clothing they sought were as important as the life and bodies which God gave them. Since God gave life, will He not sustain it? Second, He argues from lesser to greater that if God feeds the trusting birds and dresses the lilies, surely He will feed and clothe you. His third argument reduces worry to the absurd by showing it to be a completely unproductive exercise since it cannot add a single hour to one's life. His fourth argument is from effect to cause, pointing out that these worries come from unbelief (like the Gentiles) instead of kingdom priority. His fifth argument is that worry is foolish because time is continually changing our circumstances.

These arguments are all used to demonstrate the foolishness of worry. So your interrogative will ask the question, "Why is worry foolish in light of the care and provision of God?" The answers to that question are your predicates. You look in the text for them: life is worth more than food; God, who feeds the birds, will feed you; worry is not productive; worry demonstrates unbelief; and tomorrow will bring its own conditions. These reasons not to worry can be carefully worded as divisions.

So this is the first phase of your work in writing sermon divisions: analyzing the writer's treatment of his subject. We have suggested you look at the text closely in an effort to understand the writer's approach to his subject and what he is saying about it. Now we will turn to the second phase of your task.

Guidelines for the Exercise

Here are guidelines for wording the division statements for the contemporary audience.

Use complete statements rather than phrases or single words. Most sermon outlines are sketchy lists of words or phrases. Very few are written as complete sentences. It is just easier to use a clever word or phrase than to craft a carefully worded statement. The problem with that, however, is that such one-word division statements do not contain a complete idea. For that reason they often do not really say anything. Consider this outline from Luke 18:6–8.

1. *The helpless*
2. *The helper*
3. *The appeal*
4. *The encouragements*[9]

It is only in the context of the sermon itself that this outline makes any sense. Otherwise it seems to be a code of some kind. Ask those who listen. What is there to write down? What is there to remember and share with another? Is it clear and complete, or simply clever? Not only does the hearer have trouble understanding precisely what you mean to say, but you will find that you are not so sure yourself until you write out the statement in clear language.

Use a key word to assure consistency in division statements. The concept of a key word is defined elsewhere in this study. It is simply a device to help you draw your division statements from the text in harmony with the sermon idea. It is a plural, abstract noun which serves as a descriptive category for the things you want to say in the sermon. You can allow your division statements to flow from the sermon idea, guided by the key word.

The four bridging sentences lead you from the text to your sermon outline. The fourth sentence, the transition sentence, contains the key word. For Genesis 3:1–10 we named the idea The Appeal of Temptation. For the interrogative we asked "What is the appeal of temptation of which the Christian should beware?" The transition sentence answers the question by introducing the key word and announcing the predicates stated as sermon divisions: "This account suggests three deceptions in the appeal of temptation." So each of the division statements will be a deception to beware of in the appeal of temptation.

1. *Beware the appeal of temptation when the moral instructions are questioned (vv. 1–3).*

2. *Beware the appeal of temptation when the consequences of sin are rationalized (vv. 4–5).*
3. *Beware the appeal of temptation when the satisfaction of your appetites is promised (vv. 6–7).*

Use statements which will stand alone as universal principles. The Bible reveals uncounted principles of universal application. These are timeless truths which are always valid, no matter what the circumstance or who is involved. As you outline your sermon in terms of the single sermon idea, word your division statements in such a way as to present guiding principles for the Christian life. Though the textual idea is an historical statement in the past tense, the sermon idea and the division statements are universal principles which are current and relevant for any people in any generation.

CHECKSHEET: Sermon Divisions

❏ I used complete statements for divisions rather than phrases or single words.

❏ I used a key word to assure consistency in my division statements.

❏ I made sure each of my division statements is distinct from the others.

❏ I avoided sub-points not explicit in the text.

❏ I used statements which will stand alone as universal principles.

❏ I used parallelism in phrasing, rhythm, or terminology.

❏ I arranged my divisions in a logical order of progression.

❏ I used present tense, contemporary language for my audience.

❏ I have written sound, theological principles to build faith.

A good test for sermon division statements is to pull them out of the sermon and see if they make sense standing alone. Ask, is this a clear statement of principle which is not covered with the trappings of cultural mores? Does it distill the essence of the idea from the text, even though that was written for another audience long ago? Does it make complete sense, even when separated from the rest of the sermon? Look at the division statements written above and ask these questions about each of them. Now ask the same questions of the outline on page 147.

Make sure your divisions are statements of ideas distinct from each other. As your outline begins to take shape, be alert for divisions which are very similar in concept. Answering the question raised by the interrogative from ideas in the text may lead you to state the same essential idea in two different ways. You may not notice you have done so until you begin to work on development. Then you will realize that you are explaining, arguing, illustrating, and applying the same concept twice.

Indistinct sermon divisions will also confuse the audience. Though they may appreciate your comments in support of similar points, they will not be quite able to grasp the ideas. It is a good exercise to look at each point for its essence. If the hearer were to write down only one or two words for the concept of your statement, what would she write? What do you think is the core of the idea? Make sure it is distinct from each of your other divisions.

Follow a logical progression of thought in the arrangement of the division statements. Most of the time the order of the ideas which make up your divisions will follow the text. You will find no need to make any change in the logical order of the writer's presentation. This is the best pattern to follow for your own delivery, since it is easier to remember your sermon points if they are in order in the text. It is also easier for your audience to follow if the divisions are in order with the text.

At times, however, you will want to rearrange the order to follow a logical form more in keeping with the sermon idea. Some forms of sermon structure require a specified order for the progression of thought to have its impact.

Avoid the use of subpoints in favor of balanced development for each division. Some preachers use subpoints and sub-subpoints to outline in an intricate and complex manner the audience cannot possibly follow. This seems to me to be an effort at development in the guise of outlining. Development is to be done by the use of explanation, illustration, argumentation, and application which elaborate on the specific idea of the division.

Development takes up where outlining leaves off, and outlining is best ended at the main division points. If you see in the text that there are sub-points in the writer's presentation, these may be used in the sermon. It is best, however, not to number these sub-points to avoid confusing the hearer with too many different levels of "secondly" and "thirdly."

Use parallelism in phrasing, rhythm, and terminology for poetic symmetry. To follow the key word and thus show the family relationship of your division statements, you will want to try to make them parallel. Be cautious, however, not to bend the truth to make it fit some clever outlining pattern you want to follow. Your aim is to let the text give you its outline, not to impose one on it.

There are several ways to write your division statements to be parallel. Phraseology can be parallel. The rhythm of the statements can be similar, like the lines of a poem. The choice of words can offer parallel terminology. All of this can help you to remember your outline and help the audience to grasp it. It can also force you to be more careful in your wording. But here is a caution. Do not work so hard on catchy parallelism that you lose sight of your purpose. Avoid trying to impress the audience and work for better communication. The idea is to achieve some poetic symmetry which gives your division statements a beauty and force of expression.

Look again at the outline from Genesis 3 on pages 147–148. Read it aloud and notice the rhythm. Notice that each statement begins with the main idea, "Beware the appeal of temptation . . ." There is obviously a parallelism, a family resemblance, between the statements. This will not only help you to remember them, it will help the audience to follow you. And since they are so closely tied to the text, you will probably be able to preach this without notes.

Use present tense, contemporary language suitable for the audience you will address. Your division statements are addressed to the contemporary audience. This brings us back to the two worlds the preacher has to deal with: the historical world of the biblical revelation and the contemporary world of the sermon audience. A Bible lesson focused in the biblical world can use historical, past tense language to state what the passage says. A sermon aimed at contemporary needs, however, will use contemporary, present tense wording.

I recently heard a sermon with the points all stated in historical observations about Simon Peter. The sermon would have been much more effective if those observations had been stated as universal principles of faith. I can assure you that the audience is much more interested in what you can say about their lives than in what you may observe about the life of Simon Peter.

State your division statements as sound theological principles which enhance faith in the hearer. Just as the sermon idea is a theological statement, so are each of the division statements theological. They are truths about God and His ways with men, His purpose, His attributes, His law, His redemption, etc. They are about His church, His people, and the nature of the Christian life. It is this clear word about God which builds faith.

If you aim for clear theological truths in your division statements, you will find it necessary at times to look behind the explicit ideas in the text to the basis in faith for them. Quite often we have to ask, "What did the writer believe about God in order to say what he said here?" Whatever was the basis for his faith can be the basis for the faith of your audience as well.

Let's review the process once more: (1) name the subject of the text; (2) add the complement for the idea; (3) word the four bridging sentences; (4) search the text for predicates which answer the interrogative in keeping with the key word; (5) write the sermon divisions as timeless truths. These last two steps in the process are the two phases of our present task.

Completing the Exercise

STEP 1: Make sure your sermon idea clearly reflects the writer's idea. Until you name the textual idea as subject/complement, the other steps in this method will not work.

STEP 2: Make sure your interrogative and transition sentences are compatible with the text and the writer's treatment of it. Do this by going through the text to see whether it answers your interrogative.

STEP 3: Analyze the writer's treatment for theological concepts, relation of ideas, figurative meanings, and grammatical and rhetorical patterns. Allow the writer's approach to be reflected in your sermon.

STEP 4: Identify the distinctive predicates you find in the writer's treatment of his subject. They will all fall into the category established by your key word. They will be the multiple expressions of your subject/complement.

STEP 5: Write your division statements as timeless truths, as universal theological principles. Work to word them in a parallel fashion, as concisely and precisely as you can.

Summary

Sermon divisions are the sections of the sermon body where the component parts of the sermon idea are presented. Division statements are sentences stating the theological principles which flow from the sermon idea. These statements complete the structural skeleton of the sermon idea. We have diagrammed it this way: subject/complement——>predicates.

Order in sermon outlining is needed because the human mind requires an orderly arrangement of thought. The possibilities for sermon outlining are almost unlimited. The method presented in this study requires you to follow the text in planning your outline. First, an analysis of the writer's treatment is needed, followed by a careful wording of divisions as contemporary statements.

The text writer's treatment of his subject should be analyzed in terms of the multiple theological concepts, implied theological ideas, relationships between concepts, meaning of figurative language, and grammatical and rhetorical features.

Guidelines for writing sermon divisions include the following: use complete sentences; follow the key word; write universal principles; keep statements distinct from all others; plan a logical progression; avoid sub-points; use parallelism in wording; use contemporary language; and state principles for faith.

In this chapter we have translated the writer's structural treatment of his subject into sermon division statements. Now we move to the overall design of the sermon as we aim for the most effective communication.

Study Questions

1. What is the relationship between the sermon idea and the division statements?

2. What is meant by "a straight line of thought from the writer's idea to the preacher's sermon"?

3. What skill is to be strengthened by the Writing Sermons Divisions exercise?

4. Explain the subject/complement——>predicates pattern.

5. What are some guidelines for analyzing the writer's treatment of his subject?

6. What is meant by division statements?

7. Why are sub-points to be avoided?

8. What qualities should the preacher use to test his divisions statements?

---

1. Phillips Brooks, *Lectures on Preaching* (New York: E. P. Dutton, 1891), 177–78.

2. M. R. DeHaan in *Daily Bread*, quoted by J. Daniel Baumann, *An Introduction to Contemporary Preaching* (Grand Rapids: Baker, 1972), 149.

3. H. Grady Davis, *Design for Preaching* (Philadelphia: Fortress, 1958) 26.

4. See H. C. Brown, Jr., Gordon Clinard, and Jesse J. Northcutt, *Steps to the Sermon* (Nashville: Broadman, 1963), 107–18 for a list of sixteen logical orders which may be used in sermon outlining. Donald Hamilton, in *Homiletical Handbook* (Nashville: Broadman, 1992), presents in detail eight kinds of organizational patterns for sermons.

5. See Fred B. Craddock, *As One Without Authority: Essays on Inductive Preaching* (Nashville: Abingdon, 1971), and Ralph L. Lewis and Greg Lewis *Inductive Preaching: Helping People Listen* (Westchester, Ill: Crossway, 1983) for inductive methods.

6. For a creative approach to narrative preaching, see Eugene L. Lowry, *The Homiletical Plot* (Atlanta: John Knox, 1980).

7. Donald G. McDougall, "Central Ideas, Outlines, and Titles" in *Rediscovering Expository Preaching,* Ed. by John MacArthur, Jr., (Dallas: Word, 1992), 233–34.

8. See Howard G. Hendricks and William D. Hendricks, *Living by the Book* (Chicago: Moody, 1991), 266–67, and Al Fasol, *Essentials for Biblical Preaching* (Grand Rapids: Baker, 1989), 84–85.

9. Faris D. Whitesell, *Power in Expository Preaching* (Old Tappan, N.J. Fleming H. Revell, 1963), 161.

Writing Sermon Divisions

Text ___Psalm 1_____ Name ___W. McDill___ Date_____

Sermon divisions are the sections of the sermon where the main treatment of the sermon idea is presented. The division statements express one subordinate concept each and divide the sermon idea logically. The sermon divisions are based on the predicates which are revealed in the text writer's treatment of his subject. Division statements (your sermon points) are best when the following qualities are present.

    ❏ They are complete statements rather than phrases or single words.
    ❏ Each is consistent with the KEY WORD you have chosen.
    ❏ Each division statement is distinct from the others.
    ❏ Each statement will stand alone as a biblical principle.
    ❏ The wording is parallel in rhythm and/or phrasing.
    ❏ They follow a logical order related to the sermon idea.
    ❏ They are worded in simple, contemporary language.
    ❏ They are stated in present tense, universal, theological principles.

After completing the text to sermon bridge, continue as follows:

1. State the sermon idea as subject/complement.
_____godly / contrast_____

2. Use the same subject/complement pattern to identify the concept of each of your divisions.

   (1) Subject ____choices_____ Complement ____lifestyle_____

   (2) Subject ____truth_____ Complement ____delight_____

   (3) Subject ____stability_____ Complement ____result_____

   (4) Subject _____ Complement _____

   (5) Subject _____ Complement _____

3. Use a KEY WORD _____differences_____, which sets a logical pattern for your divisions statements and guides you in the wording of them.

4. Word the division statements as complete sentences in as simple wording as you can to communicate the idea.

(1) __The godly and ungodly are contrasted in their lifestyle.____

(2) __The godly and ungodly are contrasted in their delight in truth.__

(3) __The godly and ungodly are contrasted in their resulting stability.__

(4) _____

(5) _____

5. Check your statements against the checklist above and reword them until you are satisfied with their clarity and consistency.

Writing Sermon Divisions

Text ___Ephesians 1:3–6___ Name ___W. McDill___ Date_____

Sermon divisions are the sections of the sermon where the main treatment of the sermon idea is presented. The division statements express one subordinate concept each and divide the sermon idea logically. The sermon divisions are based on the predicates which are revealed in the text writer's treatment of his subject. Division statements (your sermon points) are best when the following qualities are present.

❑ They are complete statements rather than phrases or single words.
❑ Each is consistent with the KEY WORD you have chosen.
❑ Each division statement is distinct from the others.
❑ Each statement will stand alone as a biblical principle.
❑ The wording is parallel in rhythm and/or phrasing.
❑ They follow a logical order related to the sermon idea.
❑ They are worded in simple, contemporary language.
❑ They are stated in present tense, universal, theological principles.

After completing the text to sermon bridge, continue as follows:

1. State the sermon idea as subject/complement.
____chosen / grace_____

2. Use the same subject/complement pattern to identify the concept of each of your divisions.

(1) Subject ___blessed___ Complement ___completely___

(2) Subject ___accepted___ Complement ___fully___

(3) Subject ___sons___ Complement ___adopted___

(4) Subject ___plan___ Complement ___fulfill___

(5) Subject ___God___ Complement ___glorify___

3. Use a KEY WORD ___reasons___, which sets a logical pattern for your divisions statements and guides you in the wording of them.

4. Word the division statements as complete sentences in as simple wording as you can to communicate the idea.

(1) ___We are chosen by God's grace to be completely blessed.___

(2) ___We are chosen by God's grace to be fully accepted.___

(3) ___We are chosen by God's grace to be adopted as sons.___

(4) ___We are chosen by God's grace to fulfill His plan.___

(5) ___We are chosen by God's grace to glorify God.___

5. Check your statements against the checklist above and reword them until you are satisfied with their clarity and consistency.

Writing Sermon Divisions

Text _____ Name _____ Date_____

Sermon divisions are the sections of the sermon where the main treatment of the sermon idea is presented. The division statements express one subordinate concept each and divide the sermon idea logically. The sermon divisions are based on the predicates which are revealed in the text writer's treatment of his subject. Division statements (your sermon points) are best when the following qualities are present.

❑ They are complete statements rather than phrases or single words.
❑ Each is consistent with the KEY WORD you have chosen.
❑ Each division statement is distinct from the others.
❑ Each statement will stand alone as a biblical principle.
❑ The wording is parallel in rhythm and/or phrasing.
❑ They follow a logical order related to the sermon idea.
❑ They are worded in simple, contemporary language.
❑ They are stated in present tense, universal, theological principles.

After completing the text to sermon bridge, continue as follows:

1. State the sermon idea as subject/complement.

_____

2. Use the same subject/complement pattern to identify the concept of each of your divisions.

(1) Subject _____ Complement _____

(2) Subject _____ Complement _____

(3) Subject _____ Complement _____

(4) Subject _____ Complement _____

(5) Subject _____ Complement _____

3. Use a KEY WORD _____,which sets a logical pattern for your divisions statements and guides you in the wording of them.

4. Word the division statements as complete sentences in as simple wording as you can to communicate the idea.

(1) _____

(2) _____

(3) _____

(4) _____

(5) _____

5. Check your statements against the checklist above and reword them until you are satisfied with their clarity and consistency.

The point is that the forms necessary in organizing a manuscript, the visible design, may betray the preacher, may make him think his design is clear when to the listener it is thoroughly jumbled. The only design useful to the listener is a design he can grasp through his ears, an audible movement of thought.[1]

Henry Grady Davis, 1958

CHAPTER 8

PLANNING SERMON DESIGN

I remember when the Edsel came out in 1957. It was Ford's wonder car. I was a teenager when my Dad and I went to look it over. It left an impression on me that lasts to this day. It was strange—that yawning grill, the push-button transmission controls in the center of the steering wheel. We had not seen anything like it before. But the final test of the Edsel was in the hands of the consumer, who said, "No, thank you." Instead of record sales as predicted, the Edsel was canceled after the '59 model. What looked good to the automobile professionals fell flat with the car-buying public.

Ford brought out another new car in the early sixties. This one, designed under the supervision of Lee Iacocca, was called the Mustang. It was sporty and economical. What a different story this was from the failure of the Edsel! The design appealed to the target market, and it was an instant success.

What was the difference in the two cars? One was an embarrassing failure and the other an overwhelming success. The difference was in the design. For a car, design refers to its concept, its shape, the feel of it to the driver, its power and responsiveness.

Good design works. It connects, functionally and aesthetically, striking a chord of response in the target audience. Poor design, on the other hand, does not have the same appeal. It does not fit the tastes, needs, or desires of those who must respond to it.

Design in preaching is much the same as design in anything else, including cars. *Design* in this sense means the *arrangement of parts, details, form, color, etc., especially so as to produce a complete and artistic unit.* Design for sermons is primarily a matter of arrangement. It has to do with how the various parts will be assembled, the order of details, the shape of the presentation, with its style and tone. This will include the selection of materials, balance in proportion, unity of thought throughout, and movement in the presentation order.

Some sermons are designed well. They connect with the audience, appealing to the hearer both functionally (according to their intended purpose) and aesthetically (according to a sense of beauty). Poorly designed sermons do not have the same effect. No matter how good it may look to the preacher, sermon design will ultimately be judged by the audience. Poor design receives its still and silent assessment—boredom, indifference, resentment, even embarrassment. No matter how sincere and earnest the preacher is about his message, poor design will cripple his presentation.

Effective sermon design must give equal attention to three points of reference. The first of these is the message of the biblical text. We have already discussed this at length. A second point of reference is the nature and needs of the audience. That was addressed in our discussion of the need element, but we will give it more attention in this chapter. The third reference point for good sermon design is the nature of oral communication. We will attempt to introduce the dynamics of oral communication and how to design your sermons for the ear of the hearer.

Def • i • ni ́ tion: Sermon Design

Sermon design is the selection and arrangement of the materials to be presented in the sermon. Sermon design must take into account the message of the text, the audience to be addressed, and the nature of oral communication.

Sermon design is not for the eye, but for the ear. Significant differences in written communication and oral communication call for sermon design specifically geared to the hearer. The task of sermon design should be approached from the viewpoint of the audience, not from the viewpoint of the preacher.

Sermon material must be arranged for a continuity in time, instead of a location in space. A sermon is a series of words used to convey the sermon idea a piece at a time. The order in which the pieces are presented is vital to the interest and understanding of the hearer.

In this chapter we are addressing the task of planning sermon design. This is not a discussion about outlining or sermon structure, though design includes those features. Design is the whole arrangement of the sermon material. The exercise is *Planning Sermon Design*. The skill we hope to strengthen is this: *determining the arrangement of sermon materials for the most effective communication.* First let's consider the functional aim of all preaching: communication.

Design for Communication

Sermon design, like the design of anything else, will follow the purpose of the designer. Without even realizing it, many preachers assume their purpose is to deal in an organized fashion with their sermon subject. So sermon structure usually follows the rhetorical patterns of an essay or speech—introduction, body, and conclusion. I believe that the pastor's greater concern, however, is communication. He wants to make a connection in the thinking of his people. He wants to have them understand and accept the principles that emerge in the sermon text.

Communication is the functional aim of preaching. By "functional aim" I mean the immediate, practical goal of the sermon delivery. Communication means making contact in the thinking of the hearer with the message preached. Unless genuine communication takes place, no other objectives can be met. It is easy for a preacher to think his aim is to present a sermon. That cannot be it! Presenting a sermon is a means to the goal of communication. But communication requires more than presentation. It requires that the message also be received and understood as intended.

If communication is our primary concern, let's not design our sermons solely around the treatment of a subject. Let's design them around the communication challenge of our audience. Let's deal with the subject not only in terms of the ideas we want to present, but also in terms of the needs of the audience. There does not have to be a conflict in these aims. The issue is focus. Is your sermon design subject-oriented or hearer-oriented? Is the arrangement of your material planned only for a well-rounded treatment of the subject, or for maximum communication contact with the hearer as well?

Since God has chosen to use human agency to communicate His revelation to man, the preacher becomes a partner in that divine endeavor. He has a great responsibility to do all that is humanly possible to bridge the communication gap and present the message in the most effective manner. The Word of God is alive and powerful, sharper than a two-edged sword, able to penetrate to the separating of soul and spirit, discerning the thoughts and intents of the heart (Heb. 4:12). The Spirit works to guide us into all truth (John 16:13). Paul described his communication strategy in these words, "I have become all things to all men so that by all possible means I might save some" (1 Cor. 9:22, NIV).

The preacher does well to begin with a realistic recognition of the communication gap he faces in every preaching situation. The audience may not be eager for his message. They may not even be passive and neutral. Their minds are on other matters. They are distracted and preoccupied with their own concerns. There is a distance to span between speaker and hearers; and that space is strewn with obstacles to overcome in the mind of the hearer—predispositions, biases, emotional baggage, ignorance, suspicion, indifference, hostility, defensiveness, etc.

The Word of God is too vital to the lives of the people for the preacher to give no attention to bridging that communication gap as best he can. Every sermon could well be a life-changing event. The audience is not likely to hear this message of truth anywhere else. It is an opportunity of unparalleled significance for the preacher. At no other time during his week does a pastor have the man-hours of influence with his congregation as in a single sermon. That potential calls for careful and prayerful planning.

You may want to respond to this problem as one preacher did. "Communication is a partnership," he said. "Both preacher and people have a responsibility in this matter. I can try to have something worthwhile to say, but I cannot force them to listen. Are they not Christian? Are they not responsible for their own spiritual growth? If I set the table, should they not at least feed themselves?"

This viewpoint may sound reasonable, but it is really not helpful in accomplishing the preacher's aims. It is never very wise to project a 50-50 partnership and then blame the other partner for failure in the effort. This is an especially doubtful strategy for a pastor or any other communicator. We all know that the burden of interest lies with the speaker in any communication situation. He must accept the greater responsibility and go as far as needed toward the audience in closing the communication gap. It could well be that our frustration as preachers lies mostly with our own uncertainty about how to bridge that gap.

Def • i • ni´ tion: Communication

Communication is the act of imparting, conferring, or delivering information from one to another. Communication is more than presentation, the mere announcing of a message. Presentation must be accompanied by reception of the message for communication to be complete.

Speech Communication involves a sender, a receiver, a medium, and a message. The sender encodes the message he has in his mind and sends it out in spoken words. The code for speech is the language we use, with words representing ideas. The receiver hears the words and decodes them by translating them into concepts in his mind. The goal of communication is to have the receiver understand the ideas precisely as the sender intended.

The preacher is wise to think through his own communication strategy. He can analyze his own approach using a basic communication formula: Who says What to Whom, When, and How, with what Effect. Though various preachers may place emphasis on different aspects of this formula, each factor must be taken into account. The preacher will make choices, consciously or unconsciously, concerning these six matters.[2] As those decisions are being made, he is reflecting the communication strategy which guides his preaching ministry.

Understanding Design

Design for anything man makes must involve four major factors. These aspects of design must be considered from the beginning stages of planning all the way to the final presentation of the product. So it is with the design for sermons. Let's examine these four factors as they affect your sermon designs.

The first consideration in making anything is function. The question asked to determine function is, "What is it supposed to do?" Unless we are clear about what a thing is to be used for, how can we know how to design it? In the manufacture of automobiles, this question of purpose is not taken for granted, even after a hundred years of experience. What is it supposed to do? It is supposed to carry you from one place to another. This intended function guides every decision made in the planning and construction of the car. The question of function is the first one to be asked, because nothing would be made without some reason to do so.

The function factor for preaching addresses the issue of purpose. What is preaching for? What is this particular sermon supposed to accomplish? We take for granted that preaching is good for something, and defining what that "something" is addresses the issue of function. The overarching purpose for preaching is to declare the biblical truth in such a way as to communicate effectively and thus contribute to a faith response in the hearer. The particular objective for each sermon depends on textual content and purpose, the audience and their needs, and the occasion or circumstances.

A number of apparent preaching purposes are mentioned in the Bible. Paul writes, "All Scripture is inspired by God and profitable for teaching, for reproof, for correction, for training in righteousness" (2 Tim. 3:16). He charges Timothy to "preach the word . . . reprove, rebuke, exhort" (2 Tim. 4:2). Sermons are to be designed, then, for purposes such as teaching, reproof, correction, training, and exhortation. All of these purposes depend on effective communication. All are to contribute to building faith in the hearer, for "whatever is not from faith is sin" (Rom. 14:23).

This leads us to the second factor in design, form. The question raised by the form issue is, "What shape should we make it?" This is, of course, the structure of the thing. The form of anything must follow its function. You don't know what shape to make it in unless you know what it is supposed to do. The shape of a shoe is determined by the function of it, to wear on the foot. No one would think of shaping a shoe in any form but that appropriate to a foot. So it is with a chair, or eyeglasses, or a telephone. Though some creativity can go into the design, the basic form is limited to the demands of function.

Form in preaching means the structure of the sermon, the outline, the organization. As we will see, oral communication structure is best conceived as the order of presentation for sermon material. What comes first, what is said next, how the ideas are related to one another—all this arrangement of sermon ideas must be planned. Since the function is communication, the form should be shaped to communicate. The sermon cannot do what it is supposed to do unless it is made to fit that function.

The preacher must be guided by three concerns as he plans the presentation arrangement for his sermon ideas. He must first consider the text from which he takes his sermon idea and its treatment. A second concern is the audience he will address. The nature of the audience and their needs, as we have already noted in chapter 5, is a major influence in planning preaching. The third factor is the nature of oral communication. We will address that in this chapter.

163

Design not only involves a consideration of function and form, but also of the fabric to be used. In most cases the material used in making something is already available. Shoes are made of leather, cars of steel and other materials, furniture of wood and cloth, vinyl, or leather. Suitable materials for one thing might not be suitable for another. Materials are chosen to suit the function and the form. A car cannot be made of paper because its function and form won't allow that. Neither is my writing pad made of steel. It wouldn't do what it is supposed to do.

The fabric of a sermon is the material it is made of—the ideas in the sermon and the words used to express them. That fabric must also serve the function and the form. The things you plan to say as sermon material will reveal what you think the sermon is supposed to do, its function. The arrangement of the sermon, its form, will also affect the choice of materials. Just as houses in different areas are made of different materials because of what is locally available, so a sermon begins with a given body of material, the biblical text. The word text comes from the Latin *textus*, meaning woven or fabric, from *textere*, to weave. The basic fabric of our sermons is to be the biblical text.

The fourth factor to consider in designing anything is the finish. Auto manufacturers have had much to say in recent years about "fit and finish." By "fit" they mean the close tolerances with which the various parts of the car are assembled. Finish has to do with the final look and feel of the product—the color, the smoothness of the surface, the care given to the details. The finish, along with the form, appeals to our aesthetic sense, that appreciation of and desire for beauty in the things around us.

In preaching, finish primarily means style. This is your characteristic way of expressing yourself. It is the clarity, force, and beauty with which you present the sermon ideas. The overall impression left by the sermon in its appeal to the audience is affected by all the factors we are mentioning, but the finish you put on it can make the difference between a good sermon and a great sermon.

As we plan the design of our sermons, it is important to take each of these factors into account. Remember that the factors are all interrelated. Function shapes the form by setting the purpose as the guiding principle. Form must also take the fabric, the available materials, into account. The text is a given. The preacher does not make up his own message. So the shape of the sermon must reflect the shape of the text. The form of the sermon is also affected by the finish, the style of the preacher and the creativity he brings to the communication task.

Understanding Oral Communication

Oral communication is presenting a spoken message for aural reception. "Oral" simply means by mouth. "Aural" has to do with hearing. Oral communication, then, is speaking by mouth to be received by ear. Sermons are oral communication. A text is not a sermon. An idea is not a sermon. An outline is not a sermon. Even a manuscript is not a sermon. A sermon is an oral presentation of theological truths to a particular audience at a particular time. The sermon does not come into existence until it is preached. It is only finished when the final word is said.

Sermon preparation, however, normally involves writing. This means the preacher is working on paper to plan a design which will be presented orally. He is recording his ideas in writing, even though they will be presented in speech. He goes over his written thoughts visually even though they will be received aurally. This normal process can be a hazard to effective oral design. The preacher may have a sermon design that looks good to the eye, but will not work for the ear. He must think of his sermon from the hearing side if his design is to be effective.

Communication for the eye calls for different design techniques than does communication for the ear. Some of the same principles apply, but they have different meanings in print and speech. The principle of unity means that the dominant theme must prevail in the details. In print that means avoiding clutter; in speech it means staying on the subject. The principle of proportion means there should be a balance among various parts of the presentation. In print that means space on the page, size, and position; in speech it means the amount of time given to a part. Clarity has to do with precise and simple presentation. In print that calls for the right fonts and a sharp image; in speech it calls for good articulation.

Written communication can be designed differently from oral communication in several ways. Take this book as an example. I have used bold print, italics, large chapter titles, boxes of auxiliary material, footnotes, summaries, study questions, exercise forms, sample exercises, and so on. How could I do all that in a lecture? I could use visual aids, but I would no longer be using strictly oral communication.

When you preach, your audience has no perception of titles, paragraphs, italics or bold print, reference material, punctuation marks, boxes, or any such features of visual design. All they have to go on is the sounds you make and the body movements you associate with them. Your sermon comes at them as a long string of words which starts at a particular time and stops at a particular time. Everything you communicate must be done with those words and any physical movements, gestures, or facial expressions you use to enhance them.

A sermon is not like a painting. A painting stands before you at once as a completed presentation. In a single instant you see the whole—the color, the style, the relationship of the parts. As visual design it is complete and static. A sermon, on the other hand, is like music which is heard note by note, chord by chord. It is experienced a tone at a time and only makes sense as the hearer assembles the whole in his mind.[3]

The preacher, like a musician or an actor or a storyteller, parcels his material out a piece at time. His hearer cannot go back and rehear something he missed. He cannot look up a word he doesn't understand. He cannot skip ahead to see where the presentation is going. He does not see the total picture in the preacher's mind. He must allow it to develop in his own thoughts as he receives it part by part. The problem of sermon design must be solved from the point of view of the audience, not the preacher.

Think of the common sermon structure, with introduction, body, and conclusion. Does the hearer experience the sermon in those three segments? Is he aware of the introduction and what it is accomplishing? Does he think of the body and the conclusion? What about a complex outline of the divisions, with subpoints and even sub-subpoints? What about all the things you will say in support of each point? It may look logical and clever on paper. But how will it work as a string of words received by the ear?

Since the hearer receives the sermon as a flow of ideas in time, he must assemble it in his own mind. Like a puzzle received a piece at a time, he must put it together, watching it take shape until the last piece is received. The hearer is dependent on his memory for the record of all he has already heard at any point in the sermon. If the preacher designs his sermon with this in mind, he will be careful to plan the order in which he hands the pieces to his audience. If they have to wonder where each piece "fits in," they will not be able to assemble the idea properly.

So design for oral communication is basically arranging the sequence in which your material is to be presented. You will begin at a particular moment and finish at a particular moment. You may want to think of your sermon as a row of three-minute segments which must be lined up in just the right order for the hearer to put the idea together in his mind. The order in which you present these segments will make all the difference in the effectiveness of the communication. Whatever your logical outline looks like, you are still not able to give your audience more than one word at a time.

I have heard many a sermon with good material which was, unfortunately, afflicted with poor aural design. Good things were said, but in the wrong order. Let's consider now an order of presentation designed for bringing the audience with you, step by step, through the sermon.

The Motivated Sequence Outline

Every preacher needs an understanding of the preaching situation from the viewpoint of the audience. It is not the sermon material alone which should occupy the mind of the preacher. He must be aware of the attitudes, personal concerns, spiritual alertness, and other qualities of his hearers. Beyond that, he must arrange his presentation in such an order and utilize such material as will meet them where they are, rather then requiring them to overcome any and all the communication obstacles on their own.

Part of the problem is in the attitude of the preacher. Unless he is willing to accept the whole burden of communication, he is not likely to present his sermon in terms of the congregation's viewpoint. It is always a challenge to move beyond our normal subjectivity and get into the mental framework of another person or group. It takes intention, imagination, and hard work.

When the preacher does decide to take the communication task seriously, however, he will need to understand how to proceed. Let me suggest you use Alan Monroe's motivated sequence outline. He defines it as "the sequence of ideas which, by following the normal process of human thinking, motivates the audience to respond to the speaker's purpose."[4] This is not intended to replace other kinds of sermon structure, but to serve as an overlay for your normal outline. In other words, use the motivated sequence outline to check the communication value of your plan for presenting the sermon. The motivated sequence outline involves a series of five steps designed to bring the hearer along on the basis of his interests.

Rhetorical Outline	Motivated Sequence
Introduction	Attention
	Need
Body	Satisfaction
Conclusion	Visualization
	Action

The first step is attention. The preacher must not assume as he steps to the pulpit that his audience is alert and eager to hear what he has to say. As we have noted, they are probably preoccupied with personal concerns, tired, bored, and suspicious that the preacher is about to make it worse. Those of us who have preached know this well. We have seen their faces. We have seen that vacant stare, that absent expression. We have known that they were definitely not with us. And we have felt frustration and discouragement.

From the first words of the presentation, the preacher aims to bring the attention of the audience to his sermon idea. This can be done by the use of a natural analogy as an illustration. That was Jesus' method in much of His teaching, especially in His parables. There are other ways to get attention as well. Remember that the key here is the order of your material. In your sermon design, your first segment would be something to get the attention of the audience to the subject. If you are thinking of introduction, body, and conclusion, the attention step is the first thing in your introduction.

The second step is need. Getting their attention is just the beginning. The audience must have their interest in the subject awakened. They are interested in whatever touches their personal concerns. So the preacher must show how his subject is relevant to the life of the hearer. This step is called the need step because the way to gain interest is to discuss some need in the hearer that you might help to meet. The common expression for this appeal is "scratching where they itch." In the chapter on the need element we dealt with this aspect of the sermon and how to address the needs of the audience.

The third step in the motivated sequence outline goes into the body of the sermon material. It has been called satisfaction because the need described in step two is directly tied to the sermon idea. The sermon idea satisfies the need as the believer puts that truth to work in his life. Notice that we do not begin with the answer, the satisfaction of the need. We begin with getting attention. We do not even present the answer next. We demon-

169

strate the need in human life that calls for the answer. Only then do we come to the satisfaction step and present the substance of the sermon idea in its divisions. In this sequence the hearer is with you step for step because you have begun where he is in his normal thinking.

Step four in the plan is visualization. The purpose of this section is to appeal to the imagination with a picture of the hearer applying the truth of the sermon. This step answers the question, "How would this work in real life?" It is a graphic description of the listener actually living out the main principle of the sermon. The preacher is saying, "Imagine with me what it will be like when you put this faith principle to work in your own life." Using visualization in this strictest form is a challenge when the preacher must preach two or three sermons a week. The preacher can also seek to visualize and apply with the use of natural analogy which appeals to the imagination of the hearer without putting him in the picture. Either way, the point is to illustrate and apply the key idea graphically.

The final step in the motivated sequence outline is action. The purpose in this step is to describe specific and concrete steps of action the hearer might take as she puts the faith principle of the sermon to work. It is here that the preacher seeks to give the audience real handles on the concept of the sermon. You could use a practical summary of applications you have made with your divisions. Or you can suggest two or three specific ways to respond in faith to the message. Most sermons fail at this point, leaving the audience with much about what they should do and very little about how they should do it.

Planning for communication is a complex and challenging task. These suggestions will help as you begin to do something specific about that challenge. The key may well be to think from the pew side. We preachers are so occupied with our sermon material and how to get it said that we are often oblivious to the preaching experience from the vantage point of the audience. As we have said before, a good exercise would be to imagine yourself in the pew and see what that viewpoint might suggest about your preaching.

Guidelines for Sermon Design

Let me suggest some of the principles you can follow as guidelines for planning the design of your sermons. If you will keep these suggestions in mind, your design will come closer to the goal of making real communication contact.

Design a dynamic format rather than a static one. Dynamic means forceful, alive, moving. Static means set, complete, still. Plan your sermon design to be moving and alive as you interact with your audience. Do not plan everything you will say down to the last word and then present what was already complete in the study. Remember that a sermon is an oral presentation which does not come into existence until it is preached.

Keep your outline clear and simple. Writing your sermon idea and division statements for the ear will make a difference in the way you word them. These statements of your main ideas should be clear in concept and wording. What you write may look good on paper. But read these statements aloud. How do they sound? Are they immediately understandable? Is there a rhythm and symmetry to their wording? Do they roll off the tongue without a stutter?

Sermon design should be oriented to time rather than space. The amount of weight you give to a particular section will depend on the time you spend with it. To declare your bridging sentences, read your text, and state your divisions will all take only two or three minutes. The rest of a twenty-five minute sermon is support material, or development. Written notes may be misleading when you jot down only a word or two to indicate a long illustration, argument, or application. Take care to orient your design to time rather than space, planning carefully but remaining flexible.

CHECKSHEET: Sermon Design

❏ I have planned a dynamic rather than static format.
❏ I have kept my outline simple in wording and concept.
❏ I have oriented my design to time rather than space.
❏ I emphasized main ideas by placement and reiteration.
❏ I have planned careful transitions at shift points.
❏ I have used appropriate inductive and deductive movement.
❏ I have used language for the ear, not the eye.
❏ I have carefully planned the introductory segments.
❏ I have carefully planned the concluding segments.

Emphasize main ideas by placement and reiteration. Remember that the audience can tell that a statement is a main idea only by how you say it. They don't see the bold print or underlining. Place your division statements in prominent positions, first and last in a section. What you say first and last is remembered. As you repeat your division statements in the same words, the hearer will grasp their significance. Also announce and number them, using your key word.

Use carefully worded transitions as you move through the presentation. If you begin with a natural analogy, make the point clear as it relates to your sermon idea. This will smooth the way to your next segment. Plan a transition from the need element into the introduction of the text. Use the bridging sentences and let the transition sentence with the key word usher your audience into the divisions. Wrap up each division with a restatement of previous points and introduction of the next one. Think of transitions like a hand-off in football. If they are not done well, you will probably drop the ball.

Plan carefully for a combination of inductive and deductive movement. Remember that inductive thinking begins with particulars. Start the sermon inductively by talking about something familiar to the audience which parallels your subject and gets their attention. From there you will move toward your general concept, the main idea of the sermon. The movement is the key, from particular to general. Use deductive movement when you give the division statement and then move to particulars of development. We will deal with this in the chapter on Natural Analogy.

Use language best suited to the ear, not the eye. Choose words that will be easily understood in passing. You only get one opportunity to say something. Even though you repeat main ideas, keep them simple and direct. Avoid vocabulary beyond the audience's understanding. Use "people talk" but not poor grammar or pronunciation. Do not assume people know what historical biblical references mean. Explain them. Do not use technical theological terms without defining them. Use language for the ear.

Plan the introductory segments carefully. What we call the sermon introduction is as important as anything you do to communicate effectively. Unfortunately, most preachers just stand up and wander into their subject. There are five purposes of the introduction: (1) arrest the attention of the hearer; (2) awaken interest in your subject; (3) introduce your subject; (4) introduce the text; and (4) make a smooth transition into the body of the sermon. Each of these aims calls for careful planning. The introduction is so important because it is the beginning. If you do not get off to a good start with real communication contact, you may never achieve it.

Plan the closing segments of the design carefully. What we usually call the conclusion is as important as the introduction. In the motivated sequence outline the conclusion will include the visualization and action steps. This is development which returns to your sermon idea. For the visualization step use illustration and application to picture the experience of the sermon idea for the hearer. The action step calls for the specific changes which are needed to apply the sermon idea. This step leads into a time of prayer, reflection, or invitation to allow the hearer to respond to the message.

Plan the whole design from the audience's point of view. Try to get beyond the narrow viewpoint of your expository material and how to organize it. Think of the audience. Who will be there? How do they think? What do they understand? What do they need to know? If you do not communicate your material effectively, it is of no value to your hearer.

173

Completing the Exercise

The exercise for this chapter is Planning Sermon Design. The purpose is to arrange the order of your presentation for the most effective communication.

STEP 1: Survey the two-page exercise form. Notice that it provides a format for your sermon design in segments. It is a time arrangement to indicate the order of your presentation.

STEP 2: Insert your bridging sentences and division statements in the proper places in the design. Write them out word for word.

STEP 3: Place words or phrases as needed to indicate your developmental material for each division. (Chapters 9–11 will deal with development.) Plan for a balance of the four kinds of development.

STEP 4: Complete the development for the introduction (the attention and need steps), and for the conclusion (visualization and action steps).

STEP 5: Go over the sermon design CHECKSHEET to determine whether your design honors these principles.

STEP 6: Estimate the time allotted to each section in the design and make adjustments as needed to keep the proportion you want.

Summary

This chapter is about sermon design, particularly as it applies to the preparation of sermons. Sermon design involves the selection and arrangement of sermon material to achieve the preacher's aim, effective communication of a biblical truth to enhance a faith response. The sermon should be designed around the message of the text, the needs of the audience, and the nature of oral communication.

The preacher must accept full responsibility for bridging the communication gap. Any design must take function, form, fabric, and finish into account. Since preaching is oral communication, sermons must be designed to be heard. Sermon designs pleasing to the eye may be jumbled and confusing to the ear. Design decisions should be made from the viewpoint of the hearer, not the preacher.

The normal processes of human thought should be taken into account in planning sermon design. Monroe's motivated sequence uses five steps to accomplish this: attention, need, satisfaction, visualization, and action. Effective preaching calls for a dynamic format, a simple outline, orientation to time rather than space, emphasis by placement and reiteration, careful use of inductive and deductive movement, language for the ear, and well planned introductory and concluding segments.

Study Questions

1. What is meant by design for sermons?
2. What three points of reference must be considered in planning sermon design?
3. Explain: "Sermon design is not for the eye, but for the ear."
4. What skill is the sermon design exercise aimed to strengthen?
5. What is the functional aim of preaching? Explain.
6. Explain what takes place in speech communication.
7. What four factors are involved in any design?
8. How does design for oral communication differ from that for written communication?
9. Describe the five steps in the motivated sequence outline.
10. What is the role of transitions in sermon design?
11. What should the introduction and conclusion accomplish?

---

1. H. Grady Davis, *Design for Preaching* (Philadelphia: Fortress, 1958), 165. I am indebted for the ideas in this chapter to *Design for Preaching* as a whole, and particularly to chapter 10.

2. This communication formula is fairly standard among speech educators. For an emphasis on the importance of the audience see Theodore Clevenger, Jr., *Audience Analysis* (Indianapolis: Bobbs-Merrill, 1966).

3. Davis, *Design for Preaching*, 163.

4. Alan H. Monroe, *Principles and Types of Speech,* 4th ed. (Chicago: Scott, Foresman, 1949), 307–57.

Planning Sermon Design

Text ___Ephesians 1:3–6___ Name ___W. McDill___ Date_____

Sermon design is critical to effective communication of sermon ideas. It involves the arrangement of structural and developmental material in a planned order of presentation. In the diagram below you will find the various features of sermon design which have been described in this study. In the space provided write abbreviated notes to indicate your handling of each segment. Remember to think in terms of time instead of space in the material devoted to each segment. The segments are not of equal value.

Introduction:	Attention Chldhood experience of being "chosen" for games
	Need Belonging, acceptance, affirmation? Left out, unwanted?
	Bridging Sentences
	Textual Idea: Paul uses the figure of adoption to show how believers are chosen by God's grace
	Sermon Idea: We are chosen by God's grace.
	Interrogative: Why did God choose us by His grace?
	Transition: Our text suggests five reasons why God chose us by His grace.
Body:	Satisfaction
	Division 1 Statement We are chosen by God's grace to be completely blessed. (v. 3)
	Explanation "every spiritual blessing"
	Illustration Analogy: a trust or endowment unseen and untouched
	Argumentation Romans 8:32 greater to lesser argument
	Application What "blessing" are you missing? Can you trust Him?
	Transition (Div. 1 to Div. 2) Not only completely blessed, but also fully accepted
	Division 2 Statement We are chosen by God's grace to be fully accepted. (v. 4)
	Explanation "holy" and "blameless" "before Him"
	Illustration Child bathed and dressed for church won't stay that way.
	Argumentation Only God could make us blameless in His sight: in Christ.
	Application Recognize God's view of you in Christ.

	Transition (Div. 2 to Div. 3) We have seen that we are completely blessed and fully accepted...
	Division 3 Statement We are chosen by God's grace to be adopted as sons. (Vs. 5)
	Explanation "adoption" —customs of that day
	Illustration Story of Mike and Jane choosing adoption
	Argumentation Romans 8:17 "if children, then heirs..."
	Application You have the full privileges of sonship.
	Transition (Div. 3 to Div. 4) Not only blessed, accepted, and adopted, but also...
	Division 4 Statement We are chosen by God's grace to fulfill His plan. (v. 5)
	Explanation "kind intention" "His will"
	Illustration Parents delighting in planning for their children
	Argumentation If parents plan carefully for children, God much more
	Application What does God have planned for
	Transition (Div. 4 to Div. 5) reiterate
	Division 5 Statement We are chosen by God's grace to glorify God. (v. 6)
	Explanation "praise" "glory" "grace"
	Illustration Children a reflection of parent's character
	Argumentation Matthew 5:16—Your deeds bring glory to God
	Application concious of turning praise to Him?
	Transition (Div. 5 to Concl.)
Conclusion:	**Visualization** Family that adopted handicapped children
	Reiteration [go over five reasons]
	Action Acknowledge what God has done and thank Him.
	Appeal Trust your needs to Him now.

Planning Sermon Design

Text _____ Name _____ Date _____

Sermon design is critical to effective communication of sermon ideas. It involves the arrangement of structural and developmental material in a planned order of presentation. In the diagram below you will find the various features of sermon design which have been described in this study. In the space provided write abbreviated notes to indicate your handling of each segment. Remember to think in terms of time instead of space in the material devoted to each segment. The segments are not of equal value.

Introduction:	Attention
	Need
	Bridging Sentences
	Textual Idea:
	Sermon Idea:
	Interrogative:
	Transition:
Body:	Satisfaction
	Division 1 Statement
	Explanation
	Illustration
	Argumentation
	Application
	Transition (Div. 1 to Div. 2)
	Division 2 Statement
	Explanation
	Illustration
	Argumentation
	Application

	Transition (Div. 2 to Div. 3)
	Division 3 Statement
	Explanation
	Illustration
	Argumentation
	Application
	Transition (Div. 3 to Div. 4)
	Division 4 Statement
	Explanation
	Illustration
	Argumentation
	Application
	Transition (Div. 4 to Div. 5)
	Division 5 Statement
	Explanation
	Illustration
	Argumentation
	Application
	Transition (Div. 5 to Concl.)
Conclusion:	Visualization
	Reiteration
	Action
	Appeal

In this sense, the work of development is the composition of the sermon as distinct from the planning of it. It is the doing of the thing proposed in the plan. It is the clothing of the skeleton of the sermon with the elements of effective discourse.[1]

Austin Phelps, 1898

CHAPTER 9

DEVELOPING SERMON IDEAS

Watching a Polaroid picture "develop" right before your eyes is fascinating. At first all you see is a dim outline of the scene. Then shapes begin to emerge as the image you captured appears on the paper. But the details—the clarity, the contrast, the color, the recognizable features—are all awaiting development. Finally the picture is clear, with not only the outline but the details of your subject.

The ideas in your sermons must be "developed" the same way. When your outline is finished, the development is what you do to complete the picture: the color, the contrast, the images, the details—all that is required for the effective communication of those ideas.

Since your outline and your text would only take a minute or two to read, it is obvious that most of your sermon will be development.

Understanding Development

Very simply, sermon development is the "preaching" you hang on your outline. Sermon development is an important element in your sermon design. It is what you say to amplify and unfold the meaning of the truths you state in your sermon idea and division statements. If your outline is the skeleton, sermon development is the muscle and skin which makes a body of it.

Some preachers prepare a detailed outline when they are actually working on development. They add to the main sermon points a clutter of subpoints and sub-subpoints. This is often an effort to plan all they want to say without knowing when outlining leaves off and development begins. I recommend that you do no outlining beyond your main divisions. The ideas which would go "under" your main points should be considered sermon development and not outlining. Your audience will not easily be able to follow you into sub-points. They have trouble enough clearly grasping your main ideas. Occasionally a text will call for sub-points—contrasts, comparisons, or other obvious divisions in the thought. Unless these natural sub-points are called for by the text, it is best to avoid them.

In normal conversation you use four basic kinds of discussion for elaborating on your ideas. These are also the elements you will employ in your sermon development. This simply means that everything you might say to develop your points will fall under the heading of one of these: explanation, illustration, argumentation, and application.[2]

Let's say you declared that Ford is making a better automobile these days than Chrysler or GM. You might immediately get a difference of opinion from others. So you would want to support your assertion with development material designed to make your point.

For one thing you might explain what you mean by a better car. You might also illustrate your assertion by giving examples of technology and design you think are superior. You may want to bring out an article from *Car and Driver* magazine to argue your point. Then you might apply your assertion to your audience by urging them to test drive a Ford.

Just as you want to support your contention that Ford builds a better car, you want to support the sermon idea your text has given you. While dealing with a biblical truth from a text is not the same as defending your opinion, the ways you support the idea will be much the same. You will explain, illustrate, argue and apply.

Def • i • ni´ tion: Development

The word *development* comes from a verb which means to cause to grow gradually in some way: to cause to become gradually fuller, larger, better, etc. The French source of our English word means to unfold, or unwrap. Sermon development, then, means the unfolding of the sermon ideas in a fuller, larger, better way.

Sermon development takes up where outlining leaves off. It is the discussion which elaborates on the assertions made in the outline of sermon ideas. The purpose is to take the sermon ideas and guide them into the thinking of the hearer for understanding, acceptance, and action.

A variety of material can be used for sermon development, anything which contributes to the unfolding of the sermon ideas. Four forms of development have been identified in the actual use of sermon development. They are explanation, illustration, argumentation, and application.

So sermon development is the unfolding, the expansion, the enlargement of the ideas expressed in the sermon idea and division statements. In this chapter we will introduce the exercise called *Planning Sermon Development*. It is designed to help strengthen the skill of *enlarging on sermon ideas for the understanding, acceptance, and response of the hearer.* Let's consider development now in terms of the material you will use and the four basic kinds of development.

Material for Sermon Development

You will be working on your sermon development from the time you open your Bible to the text. When your outline is finished, you will then sort out all the development ideas you have noted and add more as needed for each section of the sermon. There is an almost unlimited variety of material you can use to develop your sermon ideas. There are word studies, quotations, cross references, stories, examples, personal experiences, reasons, challenges, admonitions, poems, and so on. The more attentive and wider read the preacher is, the richer the material he can use.

Even with this unlimited variety of materials, each item will function primarily as one of the four elements we have already identified: *explanation*, *illustration*, *argumentation*, and *application*. The preacher who understands these four elements can monitor his development for balance. Each form of development plays a significant and distinct role in fleshing out the sermon outline. Each makes a special appeal to the hearer. Each has a part to play in effective communication. If they are in balance, sermon development is much more effective. If they are not balanced, weaknesses will limit the impact of the sermon. Understanding what each of the elements does to develop your sermon ideas will help you to think of the supporting material you need.

Effective development depends on clear thinking and precise wording in your sermon idea and division statements. If your sermon division statements are fuzzy or overlap each other you will have a difficult time figuring out what to say as supporting material. Your sermon will seem repetitious and lacking in direction.

As you plan sermon development, you will want supporting material for each of your sermon divisions. This means you will be explaining, illustrating, arguing, and applying each of these main points. You may discover that some of your illustrations or applications will fit in more than one place, depending on the slant you give them. Your precisely worded outline will allow you to "plug in" each of the supporting ideas in the right place.

Much of your sermon development will come from the text itself. Just as the text has given you its subject and complement, just as it has given you its predicates for your divisions, now it will give you its development. Your inductive Bible study will uncover observations, definitions, historical background, and other material. You will also see reasons in the text to support sermon ideas. There will be figures of speech you can use to illustrate division points. Applications used by the writer will be effective for the sermon as well.

Some of your material will be better suited to develop the main idea of the sermon rather than sermon divisions. Development for the sermon idea itself will be used in the introduction and the conclusion. As you open the sermon, you will want something to gain attention and create interest. This will require introductory material that is precisely in line with the sermon idea. Then, in the conclusion, as you draw the hearer back to the main idea of the sermon, you will want to use illustration and application material to call for a response.

Forms of Development

Each of the forms of development has a distinctive role to play as you enlarge on your sermon points. The better you understand what each kind of material contributes, the better you will be able to prepare the balanced development which gives real impact to your sermon ideas. So let's look at the "science" of sermon development. By that I mean we will examine the kinds of material which can be used to support your outline and discuss what contribution each of these elements makes for good preaching.

Your division statement needs explaining. You need to explain how your text is the basis for the principle you stated in your outline. You may also need to explain further what you mean by your statement. You will go to the text and point to significant words and phrases. You will give historical background and other fruit of your textual study. You may resketch the narrative of your text. All of this is explanation. It is aimed at establishing the basic concept in the mind of your hearer.

Explanation bridges the gap between the historical world in which the text was written and the world of the contemporary audience. It ties your sermon point firmly to the text and confirms to the hearer that you are preaching from biblical authority and not just opinion. To do this you must go back and explain that biblical world so that your audience better understands it. You explain how what God said then is what He is saying to us now in the timeless principle you have stated in your outline division.

Def • i • ni´ tion: Forms of Development

Sermon development takes on four forms, each with its particular contribution to the support of sermon ideas.

Explanation is sermon development which aims for an understanding of the biblical and homiletical concepts by using background and interpretation material.

Illustration is the function of sermon development which illuminates the sermon idea for the imagination of the hearer; it is any word picture that gives the biblical truth a familiar enough image that the listener can see it in his mind.

Argumentation functions in sermon development to guide sermon ideas through the rational barriers in the thinking of the hearer by giving him reasons to accept those ideas as valid and relevant.

Application is that form of development which presents the implications of sermon ideas for human experience. It can be descriptive in analyzing contemporary life or prescriptive in advocating certain behavior.

If it is weak in explanation, your sermon will seem to have slipped its moorings and drifted away from your text. The biblical authority you want for your preaching will be eroded. On the other hand, too much time given to explanation will turn the sermon into a history lesson, or a lecture on biblical backgrounds and word studies. As interesting as that may be, the goal of preaching is not usually academic.

Illustration serves to clarify the textual truth in the mind of the hearer with images which appeal to his imagination. The word illustration is from the Latin *lustrare*, to illuminate. It means to throw light on an idea, to illuminate it. A sermon illustration is any word picture that gives the biblical truth a familiar enough image that the listener can see it in his mind.

A clear understanding of any idea requires that your hearer be able to visualize it. The most common kinds of illustration are examples, like testimonials, of people applying or denying the point, and analogies, using parallel images from outside the religious dimension. Like opening a window to let light into a dark room, illustrations shed light on your sermon ideas so that the hearer can "see" what you mean. Illustration demands imagery; no imagery means no illustration. Test every illustration for specific, concrete imagery.

Illustration has a special role in that it can serve each of the other elements. It can help to explain, argue, or apply the truths of the text. Or it can be devoted to picturing the sermon truth solely for the purpose of clarity and vividness. Strive to keep your illustrative material concrete, vivid, and believable. Make sure that each of your key sermon ideas is adequately illustrated.

If your development is weak in the area of illustrative material, it will tend to be dull and dry. It will not sparkle with the life and vividness which is so needed for attention and impact. On the other hand, too much illustrative material will make the sermon seem showy and lacking in substance.

Sermons are designed to persuade. But if you are to be persuasive, you will have to make a case for your ideas. You will have to demonstrate that your point is reasonable and worthy of belief, that what you are saying "makes sense." Argument is always that part of your development in which you give reasons for accepting the principle you are presenting. If there are no reasons, you are using some other form of development.

A persistent problem of preachers is that we are usually speaking to an "in-house" crowd, to those who are already convinced. Our hearers, however, may not be as convinced as they seem. They live in a secular world where conflicting ideas constantly challenge their Christian faith. They need evidence to support their convictions. They need to see where these ideas help with ordinary living. They need to know how common criticisms and accusations can be answered.

Since a sermon is not a debate or a philosophy seminar, you will want to avoid complex and abstract arguments. A simple, direct, "common sense" approach will be much more convincing. You can appeal to biblical authority by citing passages in addition to your text. You can argue your point from common knowledge about human nature and real people. You can argue from analogy. You can make a case by taking the truth of your principle and its opposite worldly idea to their logical conclusions. You can offer statistics and the testimony of various authorities. You can show how the principle makes sense for everyday experience.

Weakness in the area of argumentation will tend to make you sound narrow and presumptuous because you are not inviting your audience to see how reasonable the sermon ideas are. Too much argument, however, can make your sermon seem belligerent and adversarial. The proper balance will depend on your subject, the audience, and the occasion.

The most commonly used kind of support for sermon points is application. Most preaching simply jumps from the biblical truth to the application of it for the audience. Preachers seem to have an interest in application more than other kinds of development. We want to make sure the audience responds, that they know what to do about the sermon truth.

Application is more than just taking the sermon truth and attacking the congregation with it. Application presents the implications of biblical truth for the contemporary audience. It is a call for action, for putting the principles of Scripture to work in our lives. It deals with attitudes, behavior, speech, lifestyle, and personal identity. It appeals to conscience, to values, to conviction, to commitment to Christ.

Application can be descriptive. In this we apply the principles of Scripture to the contemporary scene and point out the instances and results of violation or obedience. The implications of biblical truth are thus used as a measure for life, not to tell the hearer what he should do but to show him what is actually taking place. The principles of God's revelation are the means for interpreting what is going on in the world and in the lives of people.

Application is also prescriptive. By this we mean that the truths of the Bible can be applied as guidelines and instructions for living. Our hearers want to know in concrete terms how they are to live out the implications of Bible truth. This may be what the audience wants most from your preaching—clear instructions, steps for action, principles to live by, guidelines for dealing with the challenges and conflicts they face in normal experience.

If application is weak, the sermon seems to be more or less irrelevant to everyday life. If there is too much application, the preacher may appear to "stretch the point" in order to harangue the congregation. They may become oppressed with too heavy a dose of obligation and turn him off, or chalk his comments up to "just preaching."

Balance is the key, then, in sermon development. But this does not mean that equal weight must be given to explanation, illustration, argumentation, and application. The preacher should rather seek to understand the task of each of these elements and work for the balance and order that will make the sermon most effective.

As you complete the careful wording of your sermon divisions, make a place under each of the division statements for the four kinds of support. (Remember to avoid the use of sub-points.) Then, as you add your supporting material you will be able to see at a glance where your development might be weak. Also look at your introduction and conclusion for balance. This simple technique will help you round out your support of each point and thus communicate the sermon truths in a more effective way.

The four forms of sermon development are separated and distinguished here so that you may understand the role each can play. In the sermon itself these four kinds of material will be intermingled. Some sentences and paragraphs will serve double duty. It is important, however, that you have clearly in mind the distinct role each of these elements can play. Consider the four in terms of their appeal, their aim, and the desired response in the hearer.

Appealing to the Whole Person

In the first place you will want your preaching to have a broad-based appeal to the audience. Since a person has a number of capacities for considering ideas, you want to appeal to her in as many ways as is appropriate to her nature. Preaching is too often narrow and limited in its appeal, overlooking the varied dimensions of the whole person. A full response to the biblical message, however, will require a full appeal. Look at the diagram below for the four kinds of appeal you will make.

The Work of Development			
	Appeal	**Aim**	**Response**
Explanation	intellect	clarity	understand
Illustration	imagination	vividness	imagine
Argumentation	reason	plausibility	accept
Application	volition	practicality	intend

You appeal with explanation to the intellect. This word is from the Latin *intellectus*, a perceiving, understanding. It means the ability to reason, perceive, or understand. As we have already indicated, explanation is your effort to interpret the ideas of the sermon so that the hearer may understand. The human capacity to perceive ideas in their relations and differences is the beginning point for hearing the Word of God. This intellectual function is also called cognition, the process of knowing or perceiving, the act of acquiring an idea.

The fact that human beings can "acquire an idea" makes preaching possible. The ideas of Scripture can be passed along from one person to another, just as any idea can. As you preach, the idea in the mind of the original writer is (hopefully) the idea you have discerned from his words and are now proclaiming to the audience so that they can perceive it. Preaching, then, is about ideas or concepts, not just a loosely connected series of thoughts.

Beyond appealing to intellect, you will appeal with *illustration* to the *imagination*. This capacity in man is the act or power of forming mental images of what is not actually present. This ability to picture in the mind what is only suggested by words or other impressions is another wonderful capacity of humankind.

As you appeal to the imagination, you seek to draw pictures on the screen of the mind so that the spiritual, abstract, theological ideas of the Bible can be "seen" as concrete, tangible, real.

Your appeal to imagination in your preaching calls on you to be imaginative. You will never be able to project pictures in the minds of your hearers if you do not see them yourself. The images you see will take the form of what is common in human experiences. This is why analogy of one sort or another is so vital to preaching. You draw pictures of heavenly truth in earthly images so that earthbound man can grasp what is beyond him. So with illustration your appeal is to imagination.

The third element, argumentation, appeals to the reason of the hearer. Though reason is an aspect of man's intellectual ability, I am distinguishing intellect and reason here. Intellect is our ability to perceive and understand, while reason is our ability to analyze, to think logically and systematically. In your appeal to reason, you attempt to give such evidence that the reasoning hearer will come to the same conclusions you have about the biblical ideas you preach.

Appealing to reason does not mean you are placing reason over faith. Reason must be engaged if faith is to be valid. God never calls on us to believe what does not make sense. He has made Himself known in the experience of man in a logical and systematic way. He has involved Himself in history purposefully, not whimsically. He has revealed Himself within the stuff of creation, not in some fantasy realm outside the range of man's familiar world. So you appeal to reason by appealing to the common experience of man with cause and effect, logical relationships, the natural ways that work in this created order.

With application you appeal to the volition of your hearer. Volition means the exercise of the will, the settlement of vacillation or determination by a decision or choice. This is another of the wonderful capacities God has given mankind, the power of the will. Never forget that your audience can choose, decide. Effective preaching will call for decision, for choice. It is so throughout Scripture.

In appealing to volition, you are presenting new possibilities for attitude and action. Your audience may have forgotten, or may have never known, that they have such an alternative as you present. In this sense you are bringing news. You are offering a different approach. But the choice is left to the hearer. You spell out the alternatives clearly and call for decision, but then you have done all you can do. Each person must make a personal decision.

Aiming for Impact

Look again at The Work of Development chart. After the appeal of each of the developmental elements, there is a column with the aim of the development material in each case. By aim I do not mean what you hope will be the outcome of the sermon. I mean rather your own aim for the material you are preparing for your sermon. Each form of development aims to present the sermon ideas in a certain way and with a certain impact. Each makes a certain contribution to the effective communication of the ideas.

The aim of explanation is clarity. You simply want to plan your explanatory material in such a way as to interpret the sermon ideas as clearly as possible. "Clear" means easily seen or comprehended, free from obscurity, easily intelligible. Not only do you want the historical record of the message to be clearly understood, you want the timeless truths of the text to be clear. Unless the ideas are clear, other kinds of development are of little use.

Illustration aims for vividness. Your best way to appeal to the imagination of your audience is to use vivid language, to draw pictures. Your material is vivid when it brings strikingly real or lifelike images to the mind of the hearer. These images give life to the ideas of your text. They make them striking and real. They leave an impact on the imagination so that the concepts will not be easily forgotten.

Assess your argumentation for plausibility. It may seem at first that this is a rather weak aim for this part of your development. You may rather want to aim for undeniable proof. Though that would be a great thing to achieve, I doubt you will ever produce material which cannot be challenged at all. "Plausible" means seemingly true, acceptable. If your argumentation achieves that level of effectiveness, you will have removed the logical barriers and opened the way to faith. That is enough.

Application in your development aims for practicality. The most common failure of application is that it is too general, too religious, too vague. The vague and general applications of most preachers do not really connect with the hearer's sense of what real life is about. Avoid sweeping criticisms. Aim rather for your application to be practical. Deal with real life. Give concrete suggestions as to changes which might be appropriate in response to the ideas of the text. Show how one's emerging faith can be expressed in such a way as to experience the grace of God.

The Response You Seek

Refer again to the chart. Notice that the last column traces the response hoped for with the use of each of the four kinds of development. The sermon ideas cannot just be stated and left to stand there without the elaboration which calls for a response from the hearer. Those ideas must be clothed in appealing support which moves carefully from the hearing to the doing of the Word.

Notice that the response moves progressively from the mere understanding of the idea, to the picturing of the idea in concrete terms, to accepting the idea as credible and relevant, to intending to act on the idea personally. This progression demonstrates the importance of effective development in preaching. It shows also how the four forms of development work in harmony for good communication.

Explanation hopes for the simple response of understanding. Appeal to the intellect with clear thinking and your ideas will be understood. This understanding does not necessarily include the grasp of every detail in the text, nor of the larger theological and philosophical implications of the ideas there. You are hoping only for an understanding of the subject of the text (and sermon) and the divisions of that subject.

The response you seek with illustration is that the hearers imagine the ideas. The power of imagination is great indeed in learning. Unless a person can "see" a concept in some symbolic or real image in his mind, he does not really grasp it or remember it. Since you are preaching about theological ideas, you will picture them in natural analogies so that your audience can form mental images of the concepts. You want only that they see it. If your illustrative material accomplishes that, it is effective.

Argumentation seeks acceptance of the ideas of the sermon. No idea can make a difference in the life of your audience until it is accepted. Up to this point the idea may be understood and imagined, but until it is accepted it can do no work in the hearer. Acceptance means the person receives the idea as credible (seems to be true) and relevant (seems to apply to me). She is willing to give the idea a place with what she thinks she already knows. This does not mean you have overwhelmed her with your logic. It simply means she sees that the ideas are valid and will receive them on that basis.

The chart indicates that the response sought by application is intention. This may again seem like a weak goal for response to your preaching. Why not hope for decision or action? It could very well be that your sermon will result in a clear decision on the part of the hearer. That decision could be expressed in some action in the meeting, such as coming forward to express commitment when an altar call is given. Most of the time, however, the change desired in the lives of the people cannot be lived out in the church building. They need to make changes in their lives beyond the church. If the response to your preaching week after week is an intention to trust God with concrete changes, you have accomplished a great deal.

Guidelines for Development

Now that we have surveyed the appeal, the aim, and the response sought by sermon development, let's consider some specific guidelines for planning your development. Remember that sermon development is a major aspect of sermon design. No sermon is fully prepared until development is carefully planned. The following guidelines can serve as a checklist for insuring that your development is effective.

Make sure your sermon ideas are clearly and precisely worded. The wording of your bridging sentences and sermon divisions is not directly a part of planning development. Having these concepts precisely stated is so necessary to development, however, that you cannot plan well without it. You are never sure exactly what you are talking about if your concept statements are fuzzy and imprecise. If you have trouble with development planning, look first to see whether additional work should be done on the wording of your sermon ideas.

Check each development segment for precise consistency with the idea it supports. It is at this point that development is often weak or strong. If your audience is not sure how your development supports the point you are making, they become confused and frustrated. The introduction should be developed precisely to support the sermon idea, not just to "break the ice." Each division should be supported with development which is perfectly in line with the concept.

Plan for a balance of the four forms of development for each division. One key to effective development is balance. Only as you make a broad appeal to intellect, imagination, reason, and volition will you communicate your ideas effectively. Notice the place in the sermon design form for each of the four elements so that you can see at a glance where your presentation is weak and needs more support.

CHECKSHEET: Sermon Development

❑ I have clearly and precisely worded my sermon ideas.
❑ I have checked all development for precise support of the idea.
❑ I have planned a balance of the four elements in each division.
❑ I have tested each part of development for its intended func
tion.
❑ I have avoided my own tendencies toward certain development.
❑ I have carefully planned development for the introduction and
conclusion.
❑ I have designed development order for the most effective appeal.
❑ I have planned my development in specific and concrete language.

Test each of the four elements for the essence of its function in your development. It is one thing to put something down in your notes for some aspect of development. It is quite another to have that material function well in the role you have assigned it. Remember, explanation wants understanding—exegesis, definitions, clarification, background, restatement. Illustration calls for imagery; without imagery there can be no illustration. Argument means specific reasons to accept your sermon ideas. Application is about measuring attitudes and behavior by the principles you are presenting, and calling for change.

Avoid following your own tendencies to favor one kind of development over others. I have observed that the "teacher" types usually spend too much time in explanation. The creative personality may overdo illustration. The analytical mind likes argument. The exhorter favors application. Whatever one emphasizes tends to edge out the other forms and leave development out of balance. Because good illustrations are such hard work, some just try to do without them. Students have asked, "Do we have to have an illustration for every point?" "No," I answer, "you only need illustrations for the points you want to be understood and remembered." That same quip applies in differing ways to each of the development forms.

Carefully plan development for your introduction and conclusion. Development in the introduction and conclusion supports the sermon idea itself, not one of the divisions. The introduction should (1) arrest attention, (2) awaken interest, (3) introduce the subject, (4) introduce the text, and (5) make a smooth transition to the sermon body. These purposes will require illustrative material (attention), application (the need step), and explanation (subject and text background, transition). The conclusion needs to restate the sermon idea and divisions, illustrate the sermon idea vividly, and call for a response, with specific applications.

Note the sequence of development material for the most effective appeal. We have consistently listed the four forms of development in the same order: explanation, illustration, argumentation, application. Though these elements will be intermingled in the sermon presentation, the general sequence should be noted. The order of these elements moves from understanding through imagining and accepting to intending to act. It is obvious that you could not work in the reverse order; that just doesn't fit the way people think. Other orders are confusing as well. So be aware of the order for your development in your sermon design.

Present development in specific and concrete language. We will address this principle at length in chapter 11. Just make sure you do not throw out general and vague references the audience will not understand. Nothing is really dynamic until it is specific. Make everything as down to earth and specific as possible.

Completing the Exercise

The exercise sheet for Planning Sermon Development is designed to deal with only one concept. In your sermon planning you will want the entire outline before you. If you are preparing development for the introduction or conclusion, write the sermon idea. Development for each division relates directly to that concept.

STEP 1: Write out your division statement or sermon idea in complete form. Remember, your planning of development is directly dependent on the clarity and precision of your concept statements.

STEP 2: Circle the word or words in your statement which carry the central concept you are developing. I prefer to capture the essence of each idea in the subject/complement pattern for the best precision and clarity.

STEP 3: Begin with explanation and write an abbreviated set of notes as to what needs to be explained from the text and its background for your idea. Also note explanation you mean to give to define and clarify the principle involved.

STEP 4: Plan an illustration which relates directly to the point you are making. Be sure it is exactly on target with the concept and contains vivid imagery. Note figurative or other illustrative material in the text itself. You may also use illustration to support the other elements.

STEP 5: Make notes as to argument which will support your point. Remember, it is only argument if you are offering reasons to accept the idea. Make use of arguments in the text.

STEP 6: Plan application, both descriptive and prescriptive. Keep the application concrete and specific. Avoid general, religious "preacher talk" which does not touch real life.

STEP 7: Check the development plan again for balance and for the time which will be required to present the material. Remember that written notes can deceive you as to the time needed.

Summary

Sermon development means to enlarge, unfold, and elaborate on the ideas in your sermon. Four kinds of development are: explanation, illustration, argumentation, and application. Each of these has its distinctive function. There is an unlimited variety of material to use for development, and much more will come from the text.

Explanation seeks to have the hearer understand the meaning of the sermon concept. Illustration wants the hearer to picture the idea in his imagination. Argument wants the hearer to accept the idea as valid and relevant. Application seeks to have him determine to do something about the idea. The four forms of development can be analyzed in terms of their appeal, their aim, and the response sought in the hearer.

In planning sermon development, the preacher should make sure his concept statements are clear and precise. He should work for balance of the distinct roles played by the four elements. His introduction and conclusion require development which supports the sermon idea, not one of the divisions. Development should be planned with the logical order of the elements in mind, using specific and concrete language.

Study Questions

1. Define what is meant by *sermon development.*
2. What is the distinctive role of each of the forms of development?
3. Why is balance so important in planning for development?
4. Describe the appeal of the four elements used in development.
5. What is the aim of each of the elements of development?
6. What response does the preacher seek with the use of each element?
7. Explain the natural order of the four elements of development.

---

1. Austin Phelps, *The Theory of Preaching* (New York: Charles Scribner's Sons, 1898), 426.

2. These elements or forms of development were presented by John A. Broadus, *A Treatise on the Preparation and Delivery of Sermons,* revised 1898 by Edwin Charles Dargan (New York: George H. Doran, 1926), chapters 5–8. More contemporary writers have continued to use these categories of development.

Planning Sermon Development

Text _____ Ephesians 1:3–6 _____ Name _____ W. McDill _ Date _____

Sermon development is the enlargement, the elaboration of the concepts you present in your sermon. It is the step beyond outlining in which you offer support for sermon ideas. Development is particularizing the general statement of sermon concepts. It purposes to have the hearer understand, visualize, accept, and determine to act on the truths of the sermon.

1. Write the division statement you are developing. You may use the sermon idea for planning development for the introduction and conclusion.

Division 1 We are chosen by God's grace to be completely blessed. (v. 3)

2. Circle the word or two in your statement which carry the central concept of your idea. You may want to use the subject/complement pattern. Write your core terms here:

blessed / completely

3. Write the ideas you have for development as explanation. Note developmental material used by the text writer which you can adapt. Then add explanation needed by your particular audience. Explanation aims for an understanding of the biblical and homiletical concepts by using background and interpretation material.

Define "blessed," "heavenlies." Emphasize "in Christ." Note "spiritual"

nature of the blessings. A focal word is "every" (Phil. 4:19).

4. Note the development as illustration you will use. Begin again with any illustrative material in the text. Then add your own for contemporary needs. Remember to use natural analogies. Illustration seeks to illuminate the idea through the use of imagery and narrative to appeal to the imagination of the hearer.

"Heavenlies" like a bank holding a trust fund, like an endowment which pays

dividends but is not the less. School endowment.

5. Write your ideas for development as argumentation. Use any arguments in the text. Plan arguments you know can be effective with your audience. Argument uses reasons to show how an idea makes sense and to guide it around the rational barriers in the mind of the hearer.

"Blessed" is past tense. Would it make sense to write no checks if your rich

cousin had already put a vast sum in your account?

6. Plan your development as application. Note any application in the text, then plan what is needed for the contemporary audience. Application spells out the implications of the biblical idea and calls for change and action in a faith response.

Where are you not completely blessed? Can you trust God's complete blessing

in that area? The resource is already there.

7. Look back over your development notes and check for balance. Be careful about the amount of time a particular segment will take in delivery. Make changes as needed.

Planning Sermon Development

Text _____ Name _____ Date_____

Sermon development is the enlargement, the elaboration of the concepts you present in your sermon. It is the step beyond outlining in which you offer support for sermon ideas. Development is particularizing the general statement of sermon concepts. It purposes to have the hearer understand, visualize, accept, and determine to act on the truths of the sermon.

1. Write the division statement you are developing. You may use the sermon idea for planning development for the introduction and conclusion.

_____

_____

2. Circle the word or two in your statement which carry the central concept of your idea. You may want to use the subject/complement pattern. Write your core terms here:

_____

3. Write the ideas you have for development as explanation. Note developmental material used by the text writer which you can adapt. Then add explanation needed by your particular audience. Explanation aims for an understanding of the biblical and homiletical concepts by using background and interpretation material.

_____

_____

_____

4. Note the development as illustration you will use. Begin again with any illustrative material in the text. Then add your own for contemporary needs. Remember to use natural analogies. Illustration seeks to illuminate the idea through the use of imagery and narrative to appeal to the imagination of the hearer.

_____

_____

_____

5. Write your ideas for development as argumentation. Use any arguments in the text. Plan arguments you know can be effective with your audience. Argument uses reasons to show how an idea makes sense and to guide it around the rational barriers in the mind of the hearer.

_____

_____

_____

6. Plan your development as application. Note any application in the text, then plan what is needed for the contemporary audience. Application spells out the implications of the biblical idea and calls for change and action in a faith response.

_____

_____

_____

7. Look back over your development notes and check for balance. Be careful about the amount of time a particular segment will take in delivery. Make changes as needed.

All mental and spiritual states and operations are expressed by terms borrowed, by analogy, from the physical; all that we know of the future life, by terms derived from analogous objects or relations in this life.[1]

John A. Broadus, 1870

CHAPTER 10

EXPLORING NATURAL ANALOGIES

Maybe you could call it "preacher's block." Like writer's block, you draw a blank as you try to plan your sermon development. You want to explain your first point more clearly, but you just cannot think of a way to do it. You want to illustrate the idea more vividly, but the images just won't appear. You want to argue your concept, but you cannot think of any credible reasons. You want to apply it in a practical way, but you cannot make the logical connection between idea and action.

This block of your creative powers can be caused by a number of factors. For one thing, poor textual study leaves you with little substantive material to draw upon. Or you may be suffering from fuzzy thinking and need to clarify your ideas more precisely. You may just be tired and need to leave your unfinished sermon to simmer while you give attention to something else. Or you may be under the pressure of last minute preparation. These causes for a creative block can all be remedied by better preparation habits and time management.

Sometimes you will experience this blank wall in your creative thinking because of spiritual dryness. There is no substitute for the soul nourishment of personal Bible reading and prayer.

Preaching is a supernatural enterprise. It is the very work of God. It is fully beyond your natural abilities to prepare a life-changing, spiritually effective sermon. The solution to creative blockage may be a spiritual refreshing. But do not expect a spiritual bailout for poor planning and laziness.

Devising Illustrations

Much of your development material will be gleaned from your inductive study of the text. You will probably have much more material than you can use. The challenge will come when you need contemporary development for specific ideas. Though the text will provide some material and suggest more, you want your sermon to be a present-day interpretation, with contemporary explanations, illustrations, arguments, and application. That is the creative challenge.

How do you come up with the needed developmental materials for your sermons? For the most part you just "think them up," without even examining the process you use to do it. As you ponder a sermon point and go over your notes, the ideas just seem to come. They are personal experiences, observations, anecdotes, examples, analogies, and so on.

What is happening is that you are tapping into your own store of information, your knowledge of the world around you, the world of human experience. Your own memory, programmed like a computer, is full of great ideas for every sort of sermon development. The problem you often face is coming against that blank wall. Try as you might, sometimes you cannot come up with appropriate contemporary support for the sermon idea.

Most of us have heard admonitions about preparing files of developmental material to draw from. Few of us do that, however. Even if you have a very good file, you still face the challenge of finding precisely what you want when you need it. Books of illustrations are also disappointing. Though some of the material may be good, finding the right picture for a specific sermon idea is pretty difficult.

Specifically, we are talking about what we generally call "illustrations." Though illustration is but one of the four functional elements of sermon development, it has a unique roll to play. Illustration can serve each of the other elements. Illustrative material can be used to explain, argue, and apply, as well as to illustrate the concept directly. In one sense all development should be illustrative; it should be vivid, clear, and picturesque.

In this chapter we are discussing the use of analogy in sermon development. The exercise is Exploring Natural Analogies. You will find this technique one of the most dynamic and valuable of all your sermon preparation methods. The skill we aim to strengthen is *devising specific natural analogies for illustrating sermon ideas*. We will discuss a step-by-step approach for tapping into your own memory bank of natural analogies from human experience.

The Language of Man

Human nature is such that effective communication demands illustrative material. A concept does not impact our thinking unless we can see it. Abstract ideas elude us unless they are attached to concrete symbols. This is especially true of spiritual truth. Jesus pointed this out when He told Nicodemus, "If I told you earthly things and you do not believe, how shall you believe if I tell you heavenly things?" (John 3:12).

Whatever his dialect, the language of man is the language of human experience, of "earthly things." He can comprehend ideas only when they fit somewhere into that vast store of common knowledge. He knows little or nothing beyond the range of human observation. He is bound by the limits of human history and earth's geography. He cannot grasp eternal truth unless it is clothed in earthly images.

This is why God uses human means to make Himself known to man. Our language is the language of human experience, so God speaks to us in our own language. Jesus came as man so we would understand God. "He who has seen Me," He said, "has seen the Father" (John 14:9). Seeing the Father would be entirely beyond us unless He had come to us in human form.

This incarnational (in human form) principle must guide us today as we seek, through preaching, to be channels of God's ongoing revelation. "The Word became flesh, and dwelt among us," John wrote, "and we beheld His glory" (John 1:14). God's method is "the Word become flesh," not only for the Son, but for the preaching which declares Him. The only way the hearer will "see" the reality of God in our preaching is that in it the Word becomes flesh. We must declare eternal truth in terms of human experience.

As the record of God's revelation, the Bible is written in the language of human experience. It is not a book of mysterious philosophies and abstractions. It is concrete, vivid, experiential, very human. It has to be in that format or the common man would never understand. Look at the way the great truths of the Bible are given. God is not presented in Scripture as the Ultimate Mind or the Ground of Being. He is rather the Shepherd of Israel, the Covenant King, the Rock and Fortress. These figures and many others communicate the eternal God to us in terms of earthly images.

So it is with the miracle God works in the lives of men. It is salvation, rescue from peril and death. It is reconciliation, the renewal of a broken relationship. It is regeneration, the new birth of resurrection life. It is redemption, the restoration of what was lost, freedom from bondage. Every one of these biblical metaphors pictures God's miracle in man's life in terms drawn from human experience and familiar to us.

Preaching is a part of the ongoing process of God's revelation to man. The preacher must, therefore, speak the language of man, the language of human experience. Every biblical truth he wants to communicate can be clothed in a form familiar to the people to whom he speaks. This is the essence of illustration by analogy. It is not an optional element to add pizazz to our sermons. It is a function of human communication necessary to God's revelational process.

Natural and Spiritual Reality

Everything other than God Himself was created by God. It is all one creation, wherever it lies along the continuum of spiritual and natural. Though we cannot see the spiritual dimension, we know something about it by the revelation of God. What we know has been made known to us in terms of what we can see in the natural dimension. Heaven, unseen to our eyes and inconceivable to our minds, is nonetheless known to us as a royal city, a living garden.

This understanding of what we cannot see is possible because there is a oneness and consistency in all of God's creation, whether natural or spiritual. The same patterns and principles are in operation throughout the full dimensions of reality. "For since the creation of the world His invisible attributes, His eternal power and divine nature, have been clearly seen, being understood through what has been made" (Rom. 1:20).

Could we ever understand, for example, how human beings respond to the eternal Word of God? We could not, except for the parallel of those spiritual concepts in the natural dimension. Jesus explained it simply in our own language when He told the parable of the sower and the seed. Here is the constancy of the Word of God and the variety of reception in the simple imagery of a farmer scattering seed in his field. In the four kinds of soil, we can understand something of the various human responses to the revelation of God's truth. Natural reality, the receptivity of the soils, corresponds to spiritual reality, the receptivity of the hearts of men.

This continuity of natural and spiritual reality is a tremendous source of encouragement to the preacher. He can be sure that the powerful spiritual truths he wants to communicate can be couched in language his hearers will understand. There is a parallel picture in human experience for every concept God intends to make known to man. This does not mean we can know all about God. It does mean that those truths God wants us to know can be pictured in earthly images we can comprehend.

Not all the imagery you might use to support sermon ideas is analogy. Make a clear distinction between example and analogy. An example is like testimony. It presents support from experience in the religious dimension. Analogy, however, is a nonreligious parallel image. For the John 3:1–8 sermon our first point was "Regeneration is necessary to see the kingdom of God." An *example* to develop this point would be a story about someone who experienced new insight into spiritual matters upon his conversion. An *analogy* would involve some nonreligious experience of seeing what was otherwise unseen. Exploring natural analogies will lead you to both analogies and examples.

It is obvious that the teachings of the Bible are not all otherworldly. Most of them concern our interaction with other people in this world. Even in these ethical teachings, however, there is the dimension of faith which calls for a supernatural response. Good illustrations are needed to show the believer the faith dimension of the most mundane Bible admonitions.

Spiritual Enlightenment

Paul prays for the Ephesians "that the eyes of your heart may be enlightened, so that you may know what is the hope of His calling, what are the riches of the glory of His inheritance in the saints, and what is the surpassing greatness of His power toward us who believe" (Eph. 1:18–19). He wants for them the inner illumination of the Spirit which will impress these grand concepts on their understanding. In the task of preaching, we can be confident that the "spirit of wisdom and of revelation" (v. 17) is at work in the hearts of our hearers.

This role of the Holy Spirit is a vital necessity in the awakening of faith. Faith comes from hearing, and hearing by the word (Rom. 10:17). That "hearing" is spiritual understanding. It is the "seeing" Paul desires in the passage above. We can be sure that the Spirit of Truth is always at work to enable men to grasp the truth of God which can only be known by this supernatural revelation.

The role of the preacher, as modeled by Jesus Himself, is to present those truths from God in the language of man's own experience. We must not presume on the Holy Spirit to do what we are to do. "How shall they believe in Him whom they have not heard? And how shall they hear without a preacher?" (Rom. 10:14).

Producing the "seeing" and "hearing" which awakens faith is a divine/human process. Faith is spiritual sight. It requires seeing in the imagination what is unseen in the natural world. But because of the limitations of man's experience, that picture in the imagination must be sketched in terms of the familiar images of the world around us.

The preacher, then, must draw the picture of spiritual reality which the imagination can present to the "eyes of the heart." The Holy Spirit then spiritually "enlightens" that picture as truth so that faith is awakened and the believer is able to "see" what is otherwise unseen. He can then act on what he sees to be true; he can "walk by faith, not by sight" (2 Cor. 5:7).

Let me suggest a simple step-by-step method for tapping into your own computer for developmental sermon material through the use of natural analogies. *Natural* refers to the fact that our development materials are drawn from the natural dimension, the familiar experience of man on earth. *Analogy* means that the continuity between the spiritual and natural dimensions will allow us to find earthly images to portray spiritual truth.

Def • i • ni´ tion: Natural Analogy

Analogy: A relation of likeness between two things, consisting in the resemblance, not of the things themselves, but of two or more attributes, effects, or circumstances.

Natural: Of or pertaining to the physical universe or the study of it.

Natural analogies are relationships, circumstances, events, or other factors observed in the natural dimension that may serve as parallel images for theological concepts. These are analogous, having points of likeness that make them useful in better understanding, visualizing, accepting, and practicing biblical concepts. They are natural, a familiar part of human experience.

There is really nothing mysterious about this method. It is actually the process you automatically use without realizing it. When you draw a blank, however, you can take these logical steps to tap into your own file of common experience for the developmental material needed for the sermon.

Clearly State the Idea

The first step in the process is to make sure you have a clear grasp of the idea. This is best accomplished by carefully wording precisely what you want to say. We have addressed this at length in earlier chapters. If you cannot state your sermon idea or division statement in a clear sentence, you are still not sure what you are saying.

Explanation aims at understanding. You want your audience to comprehend sermon ideas. Illustrations are for the purpose of picturing the idea for your audience. You want them to "see" it as vividly as possible to grasp it in graphic terms. Argument hopes to have them accept those ideas as credible and relevant. Application is to present practical faith actions in response to the ideas in the text. If your thinking is not precise, you will have difficulty finding developmental material to achieve these goals.

The revelation of God in Scripture is written in the language of man, the language of human experience. The world of creation serves as a rich source of images that make the abstract and spiritual ideas concrete and visual enough to grasp. The parables of Jesus, along with other figurative material in the Bible, aid the reader in grasping the meaning of theological concepts.

In seeking to develop textual ideas in his sermon, the preacher can explore these natural analogies. He wants to vividly illustrate each sermon idea for the hearer. He will find help in the text in this task of development, but he will also want to elaborate on sermon ideas with images and parallels from the contemporary world. Clearly identifying the theological concept, he can look for natural manifestations of the same concept to use as analogies.

So the first step is to craft carefully the wording of your idea. One-word sermon "points" do not really say anything. Complete ideas require a subject and a complement. Your division statements, like your sermon idea, need to state universal principles that can stand alone as biblical truth. Until each idea you want to communicate is spelled out this way, you will have trouble planning effective development.

Generalize the Concept

Once you state your idea clearly, you may find yourself automatically thinking of developmental material. To intentionally explore natural analogies, however, the next step is to generalize the idea. Here you are moving from the specific idea in your sermon text to the general idea. Every teaching of Scripture is a particular expression of a general concept normal to God's creation. So the general idea includes the sermon truth and all other expressions of that same concept. Very simply, you are moving from the particular idea to the general idea.

In a sermon from Matthew 9:35–37, my sermon idea was *There aren't enough workers for the harvest.* Each division statement answered the question "Why aren't there?" The first point was "Too few Christians see the condition of the multitudes." To illustrate this idea, I moved to the general concept of *seeing need.* Whereas Jesus saw the multitudes in their need, there is no indication the disciples saw them that way. We often fail in the same way.

Moving to the general concept of seeing need opened a whole channel of input from my own memory bank of information. I could think of a number of instances in which this concept shows up in life. So I illustrated the point by talking about how people are aware of the needs of others according to their point of view. Barbers notice shaggy hair, while auto salesmen see worn out cars. I made this concrete by telling of walking into a barber shop and seeing the barber check out my haircut. I told of the car salesman who sized up every customer's car for replacement. The point was, of course, that we may not see the spiritual needs of others because we are not thinking in those terms.

By going from the specific sermon idea of our failure to see the spiritual needs of people to the general idea of seeing needs, I was able to go to the third step and recall particular instances where that general concept emerges in life. These became pictures for my sermon idea from the familiar experience of my hearers.

The key to this step, generalizing the concept, is to identify the specific idea and make sure you are clear about it. Remember, the concept is generic, nontheological, nonreligious. It helps me to circle one or two of the focus words in each of my division statements so as to distinguish each from the others and to isolate each idea. The subject/complement pattern is helpful at this point. Notice how this works in the Genesis 3 outline, with the concepts identified as subject/complement.

The Appeal of Temptation, Genesis 3:1–8

1. Beware the appeal of temptation when the moral instructions are *questioned* (vv. 1–3).
2. Beware the appeal of temptation when the consequences of sin are *rationalized* (vv. 4–5).
3. Beware the appeal of temptation when the satisfaction of your appetites is *promised* (vv. 6–7).

From this outline we have three distinct concepts: instructions/questioned, consequences/rationalized, and satisfaction/promised. Each of them carries an implication of deceit (temptation). Each of them has a certain appeal to the carnal nature. But the concept in each division goes beyond the religious dimension. It is common to human experience.

As we identify that general concept we are ready then to think of natural analogies (in nonreligious areas) that could be used to communicate the idea effectively. This brings us to the next step in exploring natural analogies, discovering as many specific manifestations of the concept as we can.

Brainstorm Natural Analogies

This is the third step in this process of pulling developmental material out of what you already know. Notice the pattern in the example above. First, you precisely state your idea. Second, you identify the general concept as subject/complement. Now you look for specific expressions of that concept in areas other than the spiritual dimension. These expressions can be natural analogies. You will also think of examples.

Once the general idea is in hand, search for it in arenas of life other than the religious. You will find that the concept will show up repeatedly. Some of these other arenas are science, politics, business, nature, family, children, history, athletics, current events, friendship, working world, and so on. There is really no limit to the arenas of human interaction where you might find an analogy for your sermon idea.

Notice what happens when we explore for analogies in these arenas using the points in the outline above. Can you think of examples of instructions questioned?

❑ Science—contractor for space shuttle not following design exactly
❑ Politics—lawyers reinterpreting the Constitution to accommodate contemporary trends
❑ Business—new employee not agreeing with company policy at some point
❑ Family—children questioning instructions brought by a brother or sister
❑ Animals—trained dog ignoring his master's instructions
❑ Athletics—quarterback questioning the play sent in by his coach

As you can see, the point is to come up with instances in which the same concept appears in normal human experience. The list above could go on for more than the few I have identified. It is best to write more than you need so that your selection of the few you use will be better. Your selection will depend on the sermon itself, the audience, and the ability to state the analogy in concrete terms. You will notice in your list certain analogies which will serve best in one or another developmental function.

If you are looking for explanation material to make the concept clear to the contemporary audience, look for analogies that will help your hearer understand the idea. For the example given above, questioning instructions, I would look for instances which make it clear in everyday terms that this questioning is normal to human nature. If we are so prone in other arenas of life to question instructions, we can understand what a temptation that is in moral and spiritual matters. It is a part of the human nature not to like being told what to do, to think we have a better idea than the instructions of some authority.

For argumentation you are looking for analogies that will

prove your idea to be credible and relevant to the audience. In the above example, the political analogy might be useful for argument. The relationship of contemporary law to the Constitution is much like that of current Christian ethics to the teachings of Scripture. In both cases there is a natural appeal to question the fundamental instructions in favor of our own desires. Where this has led in constitutional law shows where it leads in biblical ethics.

Sermons need concrete and practical application. Most preachers exercise little creativity at this point, reverting inevitably to church-related actions of commitment like attendance, personal witnessing, and tithing. Exploring natural analogies will open a world of application for any sermon idea. Think of all the arenas of life in which the Christian functions and ask whether faith can act on this idea in that arena. Take the example of questioning instructions. You can think of situations when a Christian might be tempted to question, to his own apparent advantage, the plain teachings of the Bible.

Exploring Natural Analogies

1. Clearly identify the biblical concept with as precise wording as possible.
   Regeneration is necessary to see the kingdom of God.
2. Using the subject/complement pattern, generalize the concept in nontheological terms.
   Special qualifications for seeing the unseen.
3. Explore modern life and experience for appearances of that concept, listing all you can think of.
   Astronomer sees constellations
   Engineer sees circuitry
   Fisherman sees good spot
   Lover sees facial expressions
4. Choose from the list of natural analogies you have named those which can be most effective for your sermon and particularize them as specific anecdotes, situations, events, or conditions.

Particularize the Analogy

The fourth step for exploring natural analogies calls for particularizing your analogies by tailoring them for specific use in the sermon. To be effective for development, your analogies will need to be true to life, concrete, and believable. You cannot just say, "like a child receiving instructions from his sister." Though some may get your point, it certainly has little imagery to it. Tell a story. Draw a picture. Make it live. Tell of the time you questioned your mother's instructions brought by your sister.

Particularizing your analogies for use in the sermon is really a matter of packaging them best for communication. The vivid and concrete language you use will make a big difference. That skill will be addressed in chapter 11.

Another aspect of packaging your analogies for use in the sermon is tailoring them to the congregation. As we have said, your selection of development material should take your audience into account. There can be a great difference between preaching audiences. Background, region, local community, education level, vocational mix, ages, and other factors cause a uniqueness for each audience.

Packaging your analogies requires clearly drawing the analogy. This means clearly indicating the point at which the analogy compares to your sermon idea. Illustrations can be effective or useless depending on the "twist" you give them. Do not assume everyone "gets" it. Go ahead and state clearly what the point is. To demonstrate the point that *God can help us fully only as we trust Him,* I told of an incident with my wife's cat. The cat ran up a pine tree to escape the neighborhood dogs. Then he started to slip on the flaky bark. When I called him to come down, he just climbed higher. He finally fell some twenty feet to the ground. My point? If the cat had trusted me, I might have helped him. Here is how I drew the analogy with my audience.

> Does some threatening trouble have you up a tree? You are losing your grip. You are tired. But you are afraid to face your trouble. You are like that kitten in the poster hanging with one paw, with the

caption, "Hang in there, baby." But listen. God cannot help you if you won't let go and trust Him. Just let go. He will always be there to catch you. You can trust Him.

In a sermon about the implications of the return of Christ, one point was, *God has set a point of no return in human affairs.* To find an illustration for this idea, I moved to the general idea, point of no return. From there I did a memory search for expressions of that concept. What I came up with was a novel about nuclear war I had read called *Fail Safe.* A second picture was the common idea of going over a waterfall in a canoe after passing the last chance to get ashore. For both analogies, their effectiveness depended on how realistic and concrete I made them.

In the same sermon I also needed an opening illustration to get attention and create interest in my subject, the return of Christ. At this point, as always in the introduction, I wanted to illustrate the sermon idea itself. My sermon idea was, *The return of Christ gives urgency to the demands of the Christian life.* The general idea was life urgency. Using this generalized concept, I searched for a graphic, contemporary picture.

Quickly coming to mind was the Challenger disaster in which seven astronauts died. I described how I felt, that somehow we couldn't do enough to acknowledge that tragedy, but that even then "life goes on." From there I described other historic events after which "life goes on." Then I moved into the text by indicating that one day it would all be over and we could no longer say, "Life goes on." The use of these analogies depended on their being particularized to be specific and concrete, and upon making the point clearly.

Exploring natural analogies is basically a method for manually operating the normal creative process in planning development. The steps are simple: clearly state your idea, generalize the concept, brainstorm natural analogies, then carefully particularize them for communication. After you get the feel of it, you will never run out of illustrative material again. I can assure you that there is an ample supply of vivid images, striking arguments, and practical applications to be called to mind by this systematic look at the world around you.

Guidelines for the Exercise

Natural analogies are a normal part of Christian preaching. We have only touched on the subject lightly in this chapter. Our purpose is to give you handles on a method for using analogy in your sermon development. Here are some summary guidelines for their use.

We have said repeatedly that the common fault of most preaching is fuzzy thinking. Using analogies as illustrative development calls for the same precision and clarity of thought as the rest of your sermon design. Be insistent on having all your development follow that straight line of thought you have established in the structural skeleton.

Become an expert about the distinctive role played by each of the functional elements of development: explanation, illustration, argumentation, and application. Natural analogies are effective for each form of development. But the analogy will serve a somewhat different function in each of the four forms: clarity, imagery, reasons, and action.

Remember that analogy is essentially illustrative, whatever your intended function in the sermon. Make sure that you present your natural analogies in vivid, down-to-earth, imaginative language. This is what we mean by particularizing the analogy.

Always draw the analogy. This simply means to make your point directly. Some of the most effective and striking preaching you do will be when you bring the point of an analogy home to your audience. Plan carefully to use the imagery of the analogy for the best impact.

Completing the Exercise

The Exploring Natural Analogies exercise is designed for use with one specific idea from your sermon. This can be either the sermon idea itself or one of the divisions. You will notice that two of the basic steps for exploring natural analogies have been divided in the exercise for more clarity in spelling out the task.

STEP 1: Write your sermon idea or division statement in a precisely worded, complete sentence. Remember, you cannot plan good support for an idea that is not clear.

STEP 2: Identify the generic concept in your idea and state it in one or two words. Using the subject/complement pattern is best and most precise. This generalization of the concept should be in nontheological terminology.

STEP 3: Brainstorm the arenas of life listed on the exercise form for analogies which reflect the generic concept. Do not second-guess yourself as to the value of the analogies. The more you list, the better your final choices for use in the sermon. Also make use of any examples you discover.

STEP 4: Choose the best analogies from your list on the basis of your subject, your audience, and your own ability to make them work in the sermon. Your background and knowledge will make some analogies more usable for you than others.

STEP 5: Particularize the analogies you choose by presenting them in concrete, specific terms. For the exercise, describe how you will present each analogy in realistic terms.

STEP 6: Write out how you would present one of the analogies in your sermon. Also draw the analogy, bringing its point home clearly and directly for your audience.

Summary

The language of man is the language of human experience. Effective communication of any kind calls for reference to the common experiences of man in the natural dimension. Jesus and the biblical writers used figurative language to communicate spiritual truths. All of creation, natural and spiritual, is on one continuum and operates according to the same principles.

God has made Himself known to man in terms of the created order. There is a natural image for every spiritual truth God wants us to know. Otherwise man would never grasp the revelation of God. The Holy Spirit works with the preacher to enlighten the minds of the hearers to the truth of the biblical message.

Our experience in the natural world makes it normal for us to discuss abstract ideas in concrete natural images. This normal process of thinking can be followed intentionally for sermon preparation by exploring natural analogies. Beginning with a clear statement of the sermon truth, the preacher identifies the concept as a general idea, brainstorms it for natural analogies, and particularizes the most promising ones for preaching.

Study Questions

1. Explain, "The language of man is the language of human experience."
2. Define natural analogy.
3. What is the incarnational principle?
4. What is meant by "a continuum of natural and spiritual creation"?
5. What are the four steps for exploring natural analogies?
6. What arenas of life should be explored for natural analogies?
7. What does "drawing the analogy" mean?
8. How do you "particularize" an analogy?
9. What is the difference between analogies and examples?

---

1. John A. Broadus, *A Treatise on the Preparation and Delivery of Sermons,* revised 1898 by Edwin Charles Dargan (New York: George H. Doran, 1926), 179.

Exploring Natural Analogies

Text _____Ephesians 1:3–6_____ Name _____W. McDill_____ Date_____

Natural Analogies are parallel images from the experience of man in the created order, which may be used to communicate spiritual and theological truths. These analogies can be used as development for your sermon ideas. Though you will think of them without much concentration, you may also use the following method to devise illustrations by exploring natural analogies.

1. Write the division statement you are to illustrate. You may use the sermon idea for exploring analogies for the introduction and conclusion.

Sermon Idea: We are chosen by God's grace. (i.e., chosen apart from any

merit or qualifications on our part.)

2. Circle the word or two in your statement which can be used to identify the generic idea in nontheological terms. Write it here in the subject/complement pattern:

chosen / grace

3. Brainstorm the arenas of life listed below for analogies which are natural expressions of your generic idea. Write as many as you can. Do not evaluate them now or second-guess your ideas.

❑ Family   ❑ Nature

❑ Business   ❑ Children

❑ Animals   ❑ Education

❑ Athletics   ❑ History

❑ Common Objects   ❑ Travel

❑ World Affairs   ❑ Friendships

❑ Other   ❑ Other

4. Circle the best analogies from the list above on the basis of your subject, your audience, and your own ability to make particular ones work in the sermon.

5. Plan here how you will particularize the analogies you have chosen. You will want to present them in concrete, specific, imaginative language. Describe how you will make them your own in this way.

Family adopting handicapped children: find article in *Reader's Digest* and give

the details.

David and Mephibosheth—tell this story

Children choosing sides: tell experience of my little brother.

6. On the back of this sheet, write out one of the analogies as you might present it. Show how you will particularize it and how you will bring its point home to your audience.

When I was a boy my brother Bobby always wanted to do everything I did, even though he was three years younger. He was little and skinny. He couldn't really keep up with the bigger boys. When we would play softball in the pasture, two captains would choose players for their teams, taking turns. No one would choose Bobby even though he would jump up and down and wave his arms, calling, "Me, Me, Me." He would be so disappointed when the last choice would be him and the captain would take him because he had to.

When I was a team captain I would choose Bobby early on. After all, he was my brother, even if he was little and skinny and couldn't play well. God has chosen you and me, not because we are the best, but because of His goodness and grace.

Exploring Natural Analogies

Text _____ Name _____ Date_____

Natural Analogies are parallel images from the experience of man in the created order, which may be used to communicate spiritual and theological truths. These analogies can be used as development for your sermon ideas. Though you will think of them without much concentration, you may also use the following method to devise illustrations by exploring natural analogies.

1. Write the division statement you are to illustrate. You may use the sermon idea for exploring analogies for the introduction and conclusion.

_____

_____

2. Circle the word or two in your statement which can be used to identify the generic idea in nontheological terms. Write it here in the subject/complement pattern:

_____

3. Brainstorm the arenas of life listed below for analogies which are natural expressions of your generic idea. Write as many as you can. Do not evaluate them now or second-guess your ideas.

❏ Family—story of family who adopted handicapped children
❏ Business—hiring based on ability and experience
❏ Animals—stray puppy gets to stay

❏ Athletics—making the cut

❏ Common Objects—buying useless and ugly lamp
❏ World Affairs—feeding famine-stricken populations
❏ Other—David and Mephibosheth

❏ Nature—tooth and claw, natural selection
❏ Children—choosing sides for a game
❏ Education—children in honors program
❏ History

❏ Travel

❏ Friendships—non-reciprocal friendship
❏ Other

4. Circle the best analogies from the list above on the basis of your subject, your audience, and your own ability to make particular ones work in the sermon.

5. Plan here how you will particularize the analogies you have chosen. You will want to present them in concrete, specific, imaginative language. Describe how you will make them your own in this way.

_____

_____

_____

_____

6. On the back of this sheet, write out one of the analogies as you might present it. Show how you will particularize it and how you will bring its point home to your audience.

He who would hold the ear of the people, must either tell stories, or paint pictures.[1]

H. W. Beecher, ca. 1880

CHAPTER 11

DRAWING PICTURES, TELLING STORIES

It is a miracle. At least it seems miraculous to the preacher. He is preaching along, struggling through the apathy like wading in two feet of muddy water. He can see it in the faces of the audience. They are not with him. What he is saying is just not of interest to them. Then the miracle occurs. They suddenly look his way. They become very still. Some lean a little to the side to see around the person in the next pew. An older man cups his hand to his ear. Children who have been drawing look up in anticipation.

What has happened? Has the preacher suddenly become a great communicator? In a sense, he has. All he has done is to begin telling a story or vividly describing a scene. And for no other reason than that, the communication connection is suddenly complete. The attention of the audience is riveted on him as they strain to hear his every word. The preacher loves it. The congregation loves it. Suddenly they are really interested in what is being said by the preacher. There is a sense of exhilaration about connecting with your audience. Nothing can compare to it.

Unfortunately those marvelous moments of connecting are all too rare. Preachers learn to preach on, in spite of the fact that few are really listening. I have even heard preachers complain because the people only remember the stories they tell and forget the points that were made. The congregation should be more interested in the truths from the Bible. They are too shallow and childish. Most preachers have felt this way once in a while. But

222

the fact remains that effective communication is largely dependent on the speaker, not the audience.

Not only are word pictures and stories essential to good speech communication, they are inherent to the revelation of God in Scripture. Ours is a historical faith. What we believe has been made known in history—in particular events, specific places, the lives and sayings of real people who have encountered God. Our faith has not come to us in philosophical pronouncements, mysteries, secrets, or theological formulas. God has rather revealed Himself through the experiences of ordinary people made extraordinary by His special involvement in their lives.

Our faith comes to us in their stories. God speaks in the language of human experience. In the stories and scenes of their lives, we learn who He is and what He is doing. We meet Him ourselves in their stories as He awakens our understanding to the meaning of what happened there. Ultimately we come face to face with the God of creation in the story of Jesus Christ. In the life of Jesus we see Him as never before. He meets us there, in that "gospel," that story of the life of one man who was actually God Himself.

If the revelation of God comes to us in scenes and stories, the preaching of that revelation should be given to the audience in the same form. This does not mean, of course, that the preacher is a storyteller only. He is an interpreter as well. He must not only draw the pictures and tell the stories, he must interpret their meaning for his audience. And he must tell new stories and draw new pictures for this generation. In them they will see the truths of the biblical stories replayed in contemporary places and lives.

In this chapter we will deal with the preacher's skill at *vividly and imaginatively portraying biblical and contemporary scenes and stories*. The exercise aimed at strengthening this skill is *Scenes and Stories*. This is the third chapter devoted essentially to sermon development. We have surveyed the idea of development in chapter 9. In chapter 10 we introduced a method for exploring natural analogies. Now we will consider how to use narrative and word pictures to develop sermon ideas. First, let's consider the place of scenes and stories in sermon design.

Generals and Particulars

Effective design for your sermon must include a balance of *generals* and *particulars*.[2] By generals we mean statements which present a whole idea at once, in its full scope and meaning. Your sermon idea and division statements are generals. Generals are more abstract, conceptual, and universal. Particulars, on the other hand, are more specific and concrete fragments of some general idea. Your sermon development will be made up largely of particulars. In one sense all development is a matter of particularizing a thought, bringing it down to earth in real human terms.

Generalizations have the advantage of presenting a whole thought in one statement. Crafting that one statement, whether the sermon idea or a division, is challenging mental work. These generalizations, however, can only communicate the *essence* of the concept. They do not convey the *experience* of it. The attitude, the emotion, the behavior, the benefit of a biblical concept can only be carried in the particulars you use as development. "God answers prayer" is a general statement which presents the audience with the essence of an idea. A story about a specific answer to prayer is a particular which allows the audience to experience the idea.

While generals are interpretations of reality, the particulars aim to have the hearer experience the principles of Scripture in his imagination. The generals set the concept forth in principle. The particulars drive it home in the understanding, imagination, reason, and volition of the hearer. They connect the concept to his experience, either remembered or imagined. Without this connection to experience, the principles are remote, irrelevant, not credible.

You have experienced the need for a balance of generals and particulars in everyday conversation. When they are not in balance, the hearer becomes frustrated, even irritable. Have you heard comments like this? "What is the point?" "What are you trying to say?" "What is your meaning?" These questions call for you to state the general concept which interprets your particular facts or examples. Particulars are confusing and trivial without the meaning given by a general principle which ties them together. A similar frustration is experienced when the hearer is given an overdose of generals without the needed particulars. He may complain, "What does this have to do with anything?" "How is this relevant to the present situation?" "Can you give me an example?"

The human mind cannot take a steady diet of generals. It craves particulars, those down-to-earth, specific, true-to-experience details which give the sermon its sparkle and credibility. This is why the attention of your hearers is suddenly arrested when you begin to draw a picture or tell a story. There is an automatic control mechanism in the mind which shuts down attention when the hearer gets an overload of generals. You can see it in the eyes, that faraway look that tells you they're not listening.

Development is not all particulars, however. As you enlarge on your sermon divisions, you will make some general assertions. These complementary assertions are still general, even though they seek to enlarge on your sermon points. In our outline on Genesis 3:1–8, the third point was *beware the appeal of temptation when the satisfaction of your appetites is promised.* As you explain it you might say, "Temptation appeals to us at the point of our own desires." That is a complementary assertion, a general statement in support of your main idea. But it is not a particular. You might use an analogy and say, "When I'm on a diet, broccoli is no temptation; it's the cheesecake and the hot fudge sundaes I crave." That is particular.

A serious mistake made by preachers is developing sermon ideas by the use of complementary assertions, with little or no particulars. If the sermon doesn't have the particulars, with specifics like broccoli and cheesecake, it seems abstract and dull. It is too heavy with generals. These rather generic attempts at development are often announced with preacher talk like "We live in a world that . . ." Or "Oftentimes . . ." Or "Many times. . . ." What follows is usually a bland, flat generalization instead of a specific, concrete particular which makes the concept come alive.

It is important in your sermon design to keep the relationship clear between your generals and particulars. Clusters of support of various kinds should be carefully matched with the concepts they develop. This is where your skill at planning development is important. As you sketch scenes and stories from the text or from today, make sure they are exactly on target with the idea you are developing. Otherwise the audience may become confused. This precise development is only possible if your sermon ideas and division statements are carefully worded so as to precisely present the concepts you have in mind.

One of the most important skills you can develop for preaching is recognizing the level of generalization or particularization in your material. If you are not aware of what makes a general statement general and particular material particular, how can you plan your sermon design with balance and appeal? Let's consider the kinds of language which provide the interest and impact only particulars can give.

Language with Appeal

If you are to draw pictures and tell stories effectively, you will need to use certain kinds of language. These words and phrases particularize your concepts. They create in the hearer's imagination a personal involvement and experience with the truth you are presenting. Generalizations cannot do this. Language which particularizes has some of the following qualities: *figurative, descriptive, sensate, concrete,* and *specific.* Though these categories will overlap in actual use, let's consider them separately.

Figurative language portrays one thing in terms of another to create a more exact and vivid image. Figurative language helps your hearer understand your ideas by seeing them more clearly. Most figurative language is based on the comparison or association of two things which are essentially different, but really alike in some way. Notice how James 3:5–6 describes the tongue, "Behold, how great a forest is set aflame by such a small fire! And the tongue is a fire, the very world of iniquity." What a vivid way to present the destructive power of so small a member.

The most common figures of speech are the simile and metaphor. Similes make direct and explicit comparisons, usually introduced by like, as, as if, or as when. In Psalm 1:3 an extended simile is used, "And he will be like a tree firmly planted by streams of water, Which yields its fruit in its season, And its leaf does not wither." Metaphors present the comparison less directly, but just as vividly. Jesus used metaphorical language when He said, "I am the vine, you are the branches" (John 15:5).

Figurative language can be most effective if it is fresh and creative. This will take some thought and planning. Worn out and overused figures become so familiar that their impact is lost. They are nothing more than clichés or hackneyed expressions that no longer carry their original impact. Have you ever heard these? "Flat as a pancake," "strong as an ox," "the big gorilla," "hard as nails," "sings like a bird," "we'll cross that bridge when we come to it." The hearer probably no longer sees the imagery of these figures of speech.

Descriptive language uses modifiers to add color and precision to the picture. The figurative language we discussed above can be descriptive, of course. But here I am talking about nonfigurative description to add vividness to your narratives. Adjectives describe nouns or pronouns; they are descriptions of persons, places, or things. Adverbs modify verbs, adjectives, and other adverbs. Either of these modifiers can be single words or word groups.

A single word of description can change the scene dramatically. "Paul and Silas were led to the jail." Now add one word. "Paul and Silas were led, stumbling, to the jail." With one word you see them beaten, weak, abused. "David moved toward the giant, stopping to pick up several stones as he went." Try this: "David moved warily toward the giant." What a difference in the scene. You see David as cautious but unafraid, keeping his eyes on his foe, knowing the danger.

Use descriptive language carefully. Flowery language designed to impress or appeal to emotion is best avoided. Choose words and phrases that exactly capture the scene as you want to present it. Your work as a wordcrafter is involved here. Never settle for the almost right word to say what you want to say. Use description sparingly. One of the marks of novice writers and speakers is an overuse of adjectives and adverbs. As we noted above, one word will color a whole scene, so do not use more where it is not necessary.

Sensate language identifies qualities particularly perceived by the senses. As you describe a scene, always survey it for what the senses would pick up in it. What are the sights? What sounds would be heard? What are the odors which one would notice? How would objects feel to the touch? What about tastes? Then, of course, there is that sixth sense, the emotional. It is often represented as a visceral sense as emotions are physically perceived.

A survey of the scene with the senses in mind will allow you to describe it much more realistically. Consider, for instance, the Philippian jail where Paul and Silas were imprisoned that night. They had been severely beaten. Then they were placed in the inner dungeon, a maximum-security cell. What did they see? Maybe nothing but the dense darkness. What did they hear? A drip of water. A rat scurrying across the floor. The moans and curses of other prisoners. What did they feel? The stocks about their ankles. The throbbing pain of their bloody backs. The cold and dampness. What did they smell? The stench of human waste. The musty, stale air.

Can you describe that scene? With just the right sensate language you can help your audience experience that cell with Paul and Silas. They will never forget the Philippian jail because they have been there in their imagination. You may also describe how the two men felt at the time—angry, discouraged, tired, etc. But be very careful in describing emotions not to overdo it. Just telling what they did in that dungeon will reveal their attitudes about the situation.

Concrete language brings ideas and principles down to earth for clarity and understanding. Concrete means those things which can be perceived by the senses as actual and particular. The opposite is abstract, which means conceptual, transcendent. Abstract words identify qualities, ideas, and concepts, like love, honesty, wisdom, sincerity, authority, weakness. Concrete things, perceived by the senses, are like roast beef, apple pie, yeast rolls, all concrete expressions of the abstract idea delicious.

Sermons present abstract ideas, as in the sermon idea and division statements. As we have said, all development is particularizing these general ideas. One way to particularize is to use concrete language. You may talk for some time about love. But a few concrete examples of love will really bring it home to your audience: "She always could tell when he had had a particularly hard day." "He never forgot the anniversary of their first date." "They listened patiently while he shouted at them angrily."

There are many levels along the way from abstract to concrete. Your aim is to recognize when you need to use abstract language and when concrete is needed. Good communication calls for both, used in the right balance and at the appropriate times. Similar to the abstract/concrete distinction in words is the general/specific difference. Notice the diagram on the next page for some clarification. Though these classes overlap and are relative, there is a useful distinction to be made as you aim for particularizing terms.

Specific language refers to individual members of a larger class of things. The opposite term, general, refers to all members of a class or group. As we have said, there is some overlapping in our discussion of general and specific with abstract and concrete. To distinguish them, think of abstract and concrete as referring to the degree to which something can be perceived with the senses. Think of general and specific in terms of the degree of individuality of something.

"Weapon" is general. "Sword" is specific. "Two-edged sword" is even more specific. You can see that "weapon" refers to a large class of things, while "two-edged sword" is a very specific individual weapon. Use the most specific term you can in drawing pictures and telling stories. One specific word will call up an entire segment of the scene. When Martha spoke to Jesus about Mary helping her with the chores, Luke 10:40 says "she rebuked him." This is much more specific than "she spoke to him." "Speak" is general, while "whispered," "yelled," "rebuked," "whined," or "growled" are all specific.

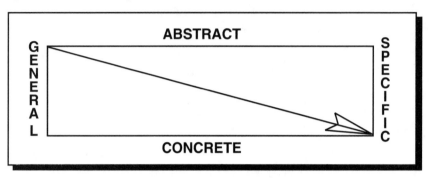

The goal in using *concrete* and *specific* language is to come "down to earth," as the diagram indicates. To the left is the broad category of things, the general. To the right are the individual things, the specific. For words and phrases which speak to the imagination, move to the right. The upper line represents abstract ideas, the lower line concrete objects, actions, etc. Again, move down for more concrete language. So overall you want to move to the right and downward for more particular and vivid pictures.

Now that we have considered the kinds of language you will use in drawing pictures and telling stories, let's move on to discuss the usual outline of a story.

Story and Plot

A large portion of the Bible is narrative of one kind or another. When you preach a passage that carries a story line, you will want to make sure that story lives again in the sermon. The narrative passages of Scripture are not fairy tales or Disney fantasies. They are actual accounts of historical events. The people and places and happenings are real. Unfortunately, however, many preachers retell these stories in such a manner as to make them seem remote, dull, and hardly believable.

Though most Christians would claim to believe the biblical

accounts, they may believe them in a different way than they do secular history. These are stories they have heard since childhood. They know them by heart—Adam and Eve, Jonah and the whale, David and Goliath, Daniel in the lion's den. But they do not seem real in the same way other historical accounts do. I can remember as a boy going to a church camp and hearing for the first time a Bible story told as though it actually happened. It was the story of Naaman and his healing in the river. The preacher described the chariots and the dust they raised as they approached the home of the prophet. I have never forgotten it. I saw it. I was there.

Some preachers may be reluctant to tell biblical stories with such realism. It may seem to be adding to Scripture to tell more than is there. There is no violation of the sacredness of Scripture to retell its stories imaginatively. It may be a violation of biblical intent to tell them in such a way that nobody can believe them. Preachers may fear being thought of as showy by their congregations. They may fear making a fool of themselves. They may not be sure how to draw pictures and tell stories. I can understand each of these concerns, but I think the desire for effective communication overshadows each of them for preaching.

Story Outline

Stories ordinarily follow a pattern of five phases. These phases may not be in balance or of equal weight in the story. Some aspects of the account may be unstated or only implied. The preacher may use the normal story pattern to analyze his narrative texts and to plan narrative as sermon development.

Phase 1: *Situation.* The setting, background, characters, etc.

Phase 2: *Stress.* The trouble which gives the story its dynamic.

Phase 3: *Search.* The various solutions explored as the story unfolds.

Phase 4: *Solution.* The solution discovered, resolving the stress.

Phase 5: *(New) Situation.* The new circumstances which prevail.

Stories follow certain patterns as they unfold. For a novel we call that pattern the plot. This means that the story is told in such a way as to make its point or accomplish its purpose. Eugene

Lowry has used the idea of a plot to describe a sermon form like a story. He writes, "In whatever type of narrative plot, the event of the story moves from a bind, a felt discrepancy, an itch born of ambiguity, and moves toward the solution, a release from the ambiguous mystery, the scratch that makes it right."[3] I am not suggesting that you plan your sermon in this form. If you wish to read about how to preach that way, read Lowry and others on narrative preaching. For now I want to point out the pattern he sees in the plot, the movement from a "bind" to a "solution."

Let's consider how stories normally unfold. Here are five phases you will see in stories: *situation, stress, search, solution, (new) situation.* I have worded these in alliterative form for easy recall. Each story in the Bible can be analyzed according to this pattern. Analyzing a narrative text in this way will help you to notice insights into the meaning of the account, to outline the writer's structure, and to prepare your retelling of the story.

A story begins with the situation. This is the background, circumstances, persons, etc., which set the scene for the narrative. In the parable of the good Samaritan the situation is established very briefly, "A certain man was going down from Jerusalem to Jericho" (Luke 10:30). We are used to this phase of the story in the classic formula, "Once upon a time." As you analyze biblical accounts, look for this setting of the scene. If it is understood or presented in an earlier chapter, you will want to check the context for the details.

In using stories in your sermon, do not spend too much time on this phase. In a few sentences you can let the audience know the setting of your story. Use only the information which is relevant to the story. Remember, a story is told with a specific aim in mind. Whatever does not contribute to that goal is not needed. As you set the situation, use specific and concrete information, like names, places, and dates. When retelling a biblical account, dig into your research to get at these details.

The second phase of a story is the stress of some problem which occurs. This phase creates interest and draws the audience into the struggle. In the Good Samaritan parable, Jesus presents the stress phase in these words, "and he fell among robbers, and they stripped him and beat him, and went off leaving him half dead" (Luke 10:30). Here is a graphic picture of the man in his pitiable condition. This phase of the story demands resolution. It cries out for a satisfaction of this terrible situation. Remember that this story is designed to address the question, "Who is my neighbor?" The condition of the traveler leaves the hearer most curious as to where the drama is going.

In retelling biblical accounts, make sure the stress phase is credible. Sometimes biblical stories are a bit too farfetched for the modern hearer. It is important for the preacher to fill in the information necessary to understand the human struggle involved in the story. Explanation is needed, for instance, to understand why Abraham would take seriously God's command to offer Isaac as a sacrifice. Otherwise your modern audience may have a hard time relating. Work to make the biblical characters human, as much like us as they really were. Do not labor the stress phase. State it clearly and quickly. It will have its own impact.

A story moves from the stress phase into a search for the solution to the problem. The parable describes in Luke 10:31–33 the three men who came by on the same road and saw the wounded traveler. The search phase is explicit here. The priest saw the man and passed by on the other side. The Levite took a look and passed by also. Then Jesus says, "But a certain Samaritan. . . ." He is here announcing a possible solution with the Samaritan. He came upon him, saw him, and felt compassion. The solution is not presented yet, but the search seems to be over. The search is simply that phase in which the possible solutions are explored. Always take some time here to explore alternatives.

Sometimes the search is not spelled out, as in Abraham's sacrifice. As you retell that story you will want to fill in some of the struggle Abraham went through as he explored what might be done to deal with God's demand for the sacrifice. You might imagine him going over alternative solutions as he traveled to the dreaded mountain of sacrifice. I have pictured him sitting by the fire on the second night while the servants and the boy Isaac slept. He prays silently to God for any answer but the one he fears. He watches the boy sleep and remembers God's promises and the miracle of his birth. Make it live for your hearers.

After the search comes the solution to the trouble at the heart of the story. In the parable we are following, the solution is given in detail as the Samaritan treats the man's wounds and takes him to an inn for further care. Jesus obviously intends to have his hero go beyond the normal call of duty. Remember that his aim is to answer the question, "Who is my neighbor?" In reality Jesus is changing the question to "Who is neighbor to those in need?" The solution is more dramatic and surprising because of the racial element; the Samaritan is but a "dog" to the Jewish audience.

The solution is the second turning point in the story. The first, of course, is the stress. Sometimes the solution will be a surprise, as with the Samaritan. Sometimes it will be a return to what was lost or forgotten. In the biblical accounts it often involves the intervention of God Himself. The exodus from Egypt involves many stories. Analyze the Red Sea episode with the formula. Situation: they are leaving Egypt. Stress: the Egyptians again pursue them. Search: there seems no escape as they face the sea. Solution: God intervenes mightily through Moses.

The final phase of a story is the (new) situation. The story has come full circle to a resetting of the scene. But it is a new scene, a new situation. The events in the story have altered circumstances. Nothing is quite the same. For the Red Sea experience, the (new) situation sees the Israelites continue their journey, with the Egyptian army drowned in the sea. The wounded traveler is restored to his health by the care of the Samaritan. The prodigal son returns home and is restored with a grand celebration. Abraham receives Isaac back, having proved his faith and obedience.

The (new) situation is to be sketched quickly. Once the solution is found and applied, the problem is essentially resolved. The (new) situation merely brings a closure which settles and delights the audience. This phase represents the classic statement,

"And they all lived happily ever after." Of course, it is possible that the story does not end happily. The parable of the rich fool is resolved with a surprise solution, the announcement of his death. The (new) situation is "and now who will own what you have prepared?" (Luke 12:20).

So these are the five phases of a story. As you analyze a biblical narrative, look for these elements. Your retelling of it will be much more effective if you plan for the five phases. Think through contemporary stories as well and plan them with this outline. For practice, think of any testimony from your personal experience about God's blessing and plot the story with the five phases. Now let's consider some guidelines for scenes and stories.

Guidelines for the Exercise

There is tremendous communication power in scenes and stories. Plan to use them in your sermon, not only in the retelling of biblical accounts, but in contemporary illustrations as well. Before we work on the exercise with this chapter, Scenes and Stories, consider some guidelines for making the most effective use of word pictures and stories.

Distinguish between the inner story and the outer story. In every word picture you draw and every story you tell, two different realms are involved. The outer story or the outer scene is the objective events and circumstances in the situation. They include whatever action takes place, whatever dialogue is included. The inner story is the interpretation and response taking place within the actors in the story. The inner story may include the purposes of God which are not apparent in the objective facts. Give most of your attention to the outer story. Only present the inner story as it is necessary to understand what is taking place. You may speculate about the inner responses in biblical accounts, but do so carefully.

Report the scene or tell the story as if you are an eyewitness. This does not mean you refer to yourself. It means you tell what would be seen by any eye witness. Remember, you are a reporter. Notice the details—names, places, times, events. Describe what you see.

To do this, you will have to place yourself in the situation. For contemporary scenes and stories, try to get the specifics down so you do not sound like your story is only rumor. The details will add greatly to your presentation.

CHECKSHEET: Scenes and Stories

❏ I am distinguishing between the inner story and the outer story.

❏ I am reporting as an eyewitness to the events.

❏ I have carefully researched the setting for details I need.

❏ I have kept my presentation simple in language.

❏ I have used language which particularizes the scene.

❏ I am presenting the scenes and stories with flair.

Do the research necessary for getting the information you need. Biblical narratives have historical settings you may not be familiar with. Who are these people—Amalekites, Philistines, Moabites? What were their origins, culture, dress? Find out. Where is this place? What was the terrain like? Details like these will make your sermon alive with interest. As you tell contemporary stories, go to the trouble to find out the details. You cannot use concrete and specific language if you do not know the particulars.

Keep your presentation simple in language. Clarity calls for simplicity. Avoid elaborate terminology. A sure sign of inexperience is the attempted use of poetic or impressive words. Do not try to be dramatic. Let the drama of the scene or story come through. Do not try to manipulate the response of the audience. There is emotional impact built into stories and word pictures. You need not try to create an emotional response. Avoid technical terms unless you explain them. Use people talk.

Use language which particularizes the scene for the hearer. The use of language which particularizes will keep the scenes and stories interesting and vivid. This requires using figurative language, with similes and metaphors. Descriptive language is needed, with careful use of adjectives and adverbs. Use sensate language which can evoke experience of the scene. Use concrete language as opposed to abstract. Use specific language rather than general.

Present scenes and stories with enough flair to compel attention. Let me balance the call for simplicity above by urging you to put something into your presentation of scenes and stories. Do not let inhibitions keep you from telling the story or sketching the scene with some drama. Notice how parents tell stories to their children. They do not use a monotone voice and listless expression. A story or word picture calls for vitality and involvement in the presentation.

Completing the Scenes and Stories Exercise

The exercise, Scenes and Stories, is designed to strengthen your skills in drawing pictures and telling stories. In order to practice this skill, we will analyze and retell a biblical story. The exercise form helps with your analysis and the planning of your presentation.

STEP 1: Read the biblical narrative or scene over several times, perhaps using several translations. Watch for details as you read. Discern the theological purpose.

STEP 2: Note the descriptive details of the scene and jot them down on the form. Look for figures, descriptions, sensate language, concrete and specific details. Relax, close your eyes, and walk through the scene in your imagination.

STEP 3: Look for the dynamics of the situation and note them as well. Here you are watching for characters, relationships, motives, changes, divine involvement, incongruities, and surprises.

STEP 4: Sketch the story by using the five phases: situation, stress, search, solution, and (new) situation. Jot down features of the story under each section.

STEP 5: Make notes for your presentation, filling in where the textual account gives little or no information. Add descriptive details. Use the five phases to plan your presentation.

Chapter Summary

Word pictures and stories have a dynamic effect on the attention and interest of your preaching audience. They are essential to effective speech communication. They are also a key element in the revelation of God in Scripture. The exercise for this chapter, Scenes and Stories, will strengthen the skill of vividly and imaginatively portraying biblical and contemporary scenes and stories. Effective development calls for an understanding of the respective roles of generals and particulars in sermon design. All development is particularization.

Drawing word pictures calls for certain kinds of language: figurative, descriptive, sensate, concrete, and specific. Each of these qualities for language focuses on the particular for clarity and exactness of communication. Stories usually follow a pattern as they unfold. Understanding this pattern will help in analyzing biblical narratives and in retelling them. It also helps in planning the presentation of contemporary stories. The usual pattern for a story is: situation, stress, search, solution, (new) situation. Guidelines for the use of scenes and stories include an eyewitness perspective, distinguishing action from interpretation, necessary research, simple language, and dramatic presentation.

Study Questions

1. Why does a scene or story seem magical in a sermon?
2. What does "Ours is an historical faith" mean?
3. Explain five qualities of language needed for scenes and stories.
4. What phases do stories usually follow?
5. Why is research necessary to scenes and stories?
6. What is the outer story and the inner story?

1. John A. Broadus, *A Treatise on the Preparation and Delivery of Sermons,* revised 1898 by Edwin Charles Dargan (New York: George H. Doran, 1926), 160.
2. This section draws on H. Grady Davis, *Design for Preaching* (Philadelphia: Fortress, 1958), chapter 14, "Forms of Development."
3. For a creative approach to narrative preaching, see Eugene L. Lowry, *The Homiletical Plot* (Atlanta: John Knox, 1980), 23.

Scenes and Stories

Text _2 Kings 4:1–7_ _____ Name _W. McDill_____ Date _____

Scenes and stories refers to the use of word pictures and narrative for illustration in sermon development. These are some of the most effective developmental materials you will use. Scenes refers to the setting and its details. Stories means the unfolding of the narrative. In order to practice this skill, we will analyze and retell a biblical story.

1. Read the biblical narrative over several times in different translations. Note here the theological purpose of the story as best you can discern it.

_____ To demonstrate God's power in providing for His own in their need _____

2. Notice the descriptive details in the scene and jot them down here. Look for the kinds of language used to present these details. From research and imagination, fill in where no description is given.

Figurative language: ___ (none) _____

Descriptive language: ___ various vessels they found, boys going house to house ___

Sensate language: _____ (none) weight of vessels full, quiet and secretive ___

Concrete language: _____ her desperation, what was being done to her ___

Specific language: _____ kind of oil, quality, price _____

3. Analyze the dynamics of the situation and note them here. Look for characters, relationships, motives, divine involvement, and surprises.

Characters: _____ Widow, two sons, Elisha, (departed prophet) ___

Relationships: Preacher not provide for family, Mother and sons, Elisha caring ___

Motives: _____ Hers to protect her sons. Elisha not to dishonor God, provide ___

Divine involvement God multiplied the oil using what she had ___

Surprises: _____ Perhaps the solution, as her own doing. ___

4. Sketch the story by using the five phrases: situation, stress, search, solution, and (new) situation.

Situation: _____ Prophet dies leaving his family in debt _____

Stress: _____ Creditors threaten to take the two boys as payment ___

Search: _____ "What shall I do for you?" "What do you have in the house?" ___

Solution: _____ Oil to fill every vessel, then stops _____

(New) Situation: Oil to be sold for debt, with also enough to live on ___

5. Fill in from background research and imagination the phases not given in the text.

Scenes and Stories

Text ___Acts 16:23–34___ Name ___W. McDill___ Date_____

Scenes and stories refers to the use of word pictures and narrative for illustration in sermon development. These are some of the most effective developmental materials you will use. Scenes refers to the setting and its details. Stories means the unfolding of the narrative. In order to practice this skill, we will analyze and retell a biblical story.

1. Read the biblical narrative over several times in different translations. Note here the theological purpose of the story as best you can discern it.

___To show God will deliver His servants / trouble can turn to ministry___

2. Notice the descriptive details in the scene and jot them down here. Look for the kinds of language used to present these details. From research and imagination, fill in where no description is given.

Figurative language: ___none___

Descriptive language: ___inner prison, great earthquake___

Sensate language: ___blows, feet in stocks___

Concrete language: ___about midnight, foundations shaken, everyone's chains___

Specific language: ___out of sleep, washed their wounds___

3. Analyze the dynamics of the situation and note them here. Look for characters, relationships, motives, divine involvement, and surprises.

Characters: ___Paul, Silas, Jailer, prisoners___

Relationships: ___two missionary partners, jailer an adversary___

Motives: ___Jailer to protect himself, Paul & Silas to glorify God___

Divine involvement: ___midnight earthquake, doors opened, family saved___

Surprises: ___praises in prison, earthquake___

4. Sketch the story by using the five phrases: situation, stress, search, solution, and (new) situation.

Situation: ___Paul and Silas ministering___

Stress: ___Arrested, beaten, jailed___

Search: ___How to respond to this trouble___

Solution: ___Sing hymns of praise___

(New) Situation: ___God delivers the preachers, saves the jailer___

5. Fill in from background research and imagination the phases not given in the text.

Scenes and Stories

Text _____ Name _____ Date_____

   Scenes and stories refers to the use of word pictures and narrative for illustration in sermon development. These are some of the most effective developmental materials you will use. Scenes refers to the setting and its details. Stories means the unfolding of the narrative. In order to practice this skill, we will analyze and retell a biblical story.

   1. Read the biblical narrative over several times in different translations. Note here the theological purpose of the story as best you can discern it.

_____

   2. Notice the descriptive details in the scene and jot them down here. Look for the kinds of language used to present these details. From research and imagination, fill in where no description is given.

   Figurative language: _____

   Descriptive language:_____

   Sensate language: _____

   Concrete language: _____

   Specific language: _____

   3. Analyze the dynamics of the situation and note them here. Look for characters, relationships, motives, divine involvement, and surprises.

   Characters: _____

   Relationships: _____

   Motives: _____

   Divine involvement: _____

   Surprises: _____

   4. Sketch the story by using the five phrases: situation, stress, search, solution, and (new) situation.

   Situation: _____

   Stress: _____

   Search: _____

   Solution: _____

   (New) Situation: _____

   5. Fill in from background research and imagination the phases not given in the text.

Deal much with the promises; . . . there is a rich perfume in every promise of God; take it, it is an alabaster box, break it by meditation, and the sweet scent of faith shall be shed abroad in your house.[1]

Charles Haddon Spurgeon, ca. 1880

CHAPTER 12

PREACHING FOR FAITH

The frustration and discouragement were clear on his face and in his voice. We sat in the cafeteria with our coffee between us discussing his ministry. "They're really not interested in the work of the church," he said. "I have challenged them, encouraged them, tried to motivate them, really preached hard at them. But they don't really care. They are not listening anymore. They haven't listened to me for some time now. I could see it coming. Now there is a real wall between us. I guess I don't care, either. The Lord is obviously through with me there."

We talked quite a bit that day about preaching. My friend assured me he had done everything he could to "light a fire" under his apathetic congregation. His unspoken aim in the preaching was to get them moving in some fashion. And now it was obvious he had failed. "I've been told I'm a pretty good preacher," he said. "If that's the case, why have five years of my preaching and leadership only alienated the congregation from me?" Within months he resigned.

Preaching and Purpose

Why do we preach? That may be such an obvious question that it seldom is asked. We assume that preaching is a purposeful task, something God wants done by His servants. But if preaching is purposeful, we must clearly identify that purpose. If our preaching is to be as effective as it can be, we will have to relate each sermon and the whole preaching ministry to that purpose.

Books on preaching sometimes suggest sermon objectives such as teaching, inspiration, devotion, evangelism, consecration, etc. These objectives indicate what the preacher wants to see take place in the hearer as a result of the sermon. Long-term aims for preaching are also of special concern to the pastor who hopes to see his people grow. He realizes that no one sermon will get the job done and result in the growth he wants to see.

Preaching results are often a serious source of frustration for the pastor. Those who study the problem tell us that most pastoral burnout is due largely to unfulfilled expectations. And there is little doubt that preachers have high expectation for their sermons. Preaching is close to the heart of their calling and their relationship with God. But zeal in the study is often squelched in the sanctuary.

I confess that for many years my aim in preaching was to "tell it like it is." I hoped to straighten out the people in the pews. If they would just do what I told them (from God, of course) we would all be happy and fruitful Christians and the church would be a roaring success. While my goal was to straighten out God's people, their hope was to hear some word to meet their need, and God's purpose for my preaching was simply that the people trust Him.

I have since come to the conclusion that the fundamental objective of preaching is faith. That is the one response over all others we want to see in our hearers. Most of us, however, take such an idea for granted. While we may agree that faith is the desired response, we really do not plan our sermons for faith. We aim at other responses more likely to produce immediate and outward results, or at no particular purpose at all. Much preaching has as its aim to unload a sermon without making a fool of the preacher.

In this chapter we are dealing with the practical biblical aim of preaching, to enhance faith in God at the particular point of the sermon subject. The exercise for this chapter is *Aiming for Faith.*

The skill for sermon preparation we hope to strengthen is this: *conforming every aspect of sermon design to the aim of a faith response in the hearer.* As the preacher plans with this purpose in mind, his preaching will take on a different tone, involve different content, and will receive a different response.

Let's consider first whether it makes sense to plan all our preaching for one aim, namely faith.

God's Plan for Preaching

Preaching is a part of the plan of God for giving His revelation to man. Look again at Romans 10:14, "How then shall they call on Him in whom they have not believed? And how shall they believe in Him of whom they have not heard? And how shall they hear without a preacher?" In this series of questions, Paul makes clear that God's intention for preaching is that the people may hear, believe, and call on the Lord.

Def • i • ni´ tion: Preaching for Faith

The overarching aim of preaching is to call for faith in the hearer. Thus, *preaching for faith* means planning every element of sermon design to achieve that aim. This will include the interpretation of the text, the statement of the sermon idea and division statements, and the planning of development.

Since biblical faith is objective, the focus of preaching must be the object of faith, the person of God. The preacher enhances faith by pointing his hearers to God, to His character, His capabilities, His intentions, and His record.

Not only does the preacher plan his sermons for faith, he examines his own philosophy of ministry and his understanding of the Christian life for the centrality of faith. Preaching for faith requires a foundation of faith in the preacher.

This same purpose is made clear as the writer of Hebrews describes the sweep of God's revelation, "In the past God spoke to our forefathers through the prophets at many times and in various ways, but in these last days he has spoken to us by his Son" (Heb. 1:1; 2, NIV). The writer later admonishes his readers not to fail in their proper response to the message as the Israelites did in the wilderness. "For we also have had the gospel preached to us, just as they did; but the message they heard was of no value to them, because those who heard did not combine it with faith" (4:2, NIV). The preaching goal was faith.

It seems reasonable to press for change in the hearer, whether that change is born of faith or not. But, as is often the case, what seems reasonable is not biblical. If the preacher hopes for obedience, he must preach for faith.

The concepts of faith and obedience are so inseparable in Scripture as to be two sides of one idea. There can be no authentic obedience without faith, just as there can be no authentic faith which does not result in obedience. To circumvent this biblical pattern and preach obedience without faith is to work against God's purposes.

True conversion comes only through faith. "Believe in the Lord Jesus, and you shall be saved, you and your household" (Acts 16:31). The only acceptable relationship with God is by trust in Him. "Without faith it is impossible to please Him, for he who comes to God must believe that He is, and that He is a rewarder of those who seek Him" (Heb 11:6). Faith is the basis for every aspect of the life of a believer. "The righteous will live by his faith" (Hab. 2:4, NIV).

The measure of a Christian is not the measure of his virtue, his ministry, his moral life, his stewardship, or any of the other criteria we usually cite. Though all these elements of character are important, the true measure of the Christian is his faith. Paul writes, "Do not think of yourself more highly than you ought, but rather think of yourself with sober judgment, in accordance with the measure of faith God has given you" (Rom. 12:3, NIV). Every other desirable quality or work must flow from faith.

How does one get such faith? It is a gift from God. And God's method of giving it is clear. "Faith comes from hearing, and hearing by the word of Christ" (10:17). This is because the message God has for man concerns Himself as He is revealed in Christ. That divine truth has an impact at the deepest level of man's spirit. "It is the power of God for salvation to everyone who believes" (Rom. 1:16, NIV).

As one is confronted with the revelation of God's truth, the Spirit ignites faith in his heart so that he can respond to that truth. The Spirit is saying, "What you are hearing is true. You can believe it. You can trust that God exists and that He rewards those who earnestly seek Him." As preachers, we are to work in harmony with that ministry of the Spirit as He confirms God's message to the hearer.

What a tremendous encouragement and relief this truth is to the preacher! I do not have to create changes and growth in the lives of my people. I am simply a messenger from God to present His truth to them—the truth about who He is and what He is doing in the world, the truth about His great love in Jesus Christ, the truth about a life of victory and grace. That is the truth which ignites faith, the truth which sets men free.

It is vital, therefore, that we look carefully at our preaching aims. Every desired result in the lives of people must spring from faith. Any other motivation—guilt, fear, pity, religious duty, dedication—is dead and carnal without faith. Paul even writes that "Whatever is not from faith is sin" (Rom. 14:23). Even though human motives are always mixed, our response to God must be based finally on our trust in Him as He makes Himself known in Christ.

Let me encourage you to look closely at every sermon you preach to see whether it is designed to evoke faith in the hearer. Look at your own intention in delivering the message for that same goal. I am confident that there is nothing God expects from His people that is not based on their faith in His adequacy. How do you preach for faith? A beginning point is calling attention to the One we trust.

Pleading the Credibility of God

"What percent of preaching do you think is 'dobetter' preaching and what proportion is 'trustGod' preaching?" I have repeatedly asked that question of preachers. By these terms I mean, of course, preaching which aims to get the congregation to "do better" in their moral behavior as opposed to preaching which aims to have the audience "trust God" more fully. Most preachers admit that 90 to 95 percent of preaching is aimed at getting the hearers to do better, while only 5 to 10 percent is aimed at enhancing their faith in God. This suggests that most preachers think the primary aim of preaching is moral reform.

It is my conviction that appealing to the people week after week to "do better" really accomplishes little. They are accustomed to hearing this kind of preaching. It is normally written off as the expected and not usually taken very seriously. We all know that we need to do better. And heaven knows we would like to do better. That is not the problem. The problem is how we are to do it.

This is where the challenge of preaching for faith has its great advantage. By preaching in the "trustGod" mode, the preacher will actually create an opportunity for the hearers to grow in their Christian lives. In fact, the only way they will really do better is to learn to trust God in the very specific areas of their own personal concerns. So every sermon should address real life concerns in terms of the adequacy of God for every need.

A young husband was about to purchase a medical insurance policy, but his wife said she did not feel right about it. She just did not trust the company. She insisted that he not buy that policy. How would you handle such a situation? On one hand the concerned husband could criticize her for her doubts. He could accuse her of being obstinate and urge her to be more trusting. He could tell her that she really should appreciate all the time he spent choosing this policy. This approach basically sees her opposition as an attitude problem.

On the other hand, he could address her doubts by focusing on the credibility of the insurance company. He could, for instance, tell her something about the character of the company and its founders. He could show her a financial statement and tell her how much money the company has in reserves. He could go over the policy with her and explain what the company has promised to do in case of a medical need in the family. He could call a friend who already has a policy with the company and let him tell how pleased he is with their service.

Which approach do you think is more likely to build confidence for the wife? That is easy enough to see. Turning his wife's attention away from her own uncertainty to the object of her faith, the young husband was able to solve the problem. If he had badgered her about her attitude and insisted she do better, he would only have succeeded in creating conflict while leaving the real issue unresolved.

It is the same with preaching. You will only build the faith that changes lives by pointing beyond the believer to the One to be believed. Faith is not created by calling for faith. It is not created by criticizing the faithless. It is not created by aiming for obedience. It is not created by aiming for guilt. It is only evoked by appealing to the credibility of the object of faith.

The object of faith is God Himself. He is the source of any and all resources for the living of the Christian life. "For this reason it is by faith, that it might be in accordance with grace" (Rom. 4:16). This principle prevails throughout the Bible. If anything is to be by grace, it must be by faith. If it is not by faith, it cannot be by grace. That leaves us with the clear choice of preaching for faith or pursuing a policy that actually leads our people out of the grace of God.

If preaching is to aim for "trustGod" rather than "dobetter" results, it must be planned for focusing attention on God and His credibility. This leads us to an examination of the credibility of God. We can plead His credibility in the same ways we cited in the insurance story.

Pleading the credibility of God means preaching on the character of God. This kind of preaching is in the indicative mood, emphasizing the reality that is. God is faithful. He is love. He is our Shepherd, our Rock and Fortress. God never changes. He is the loving Father, the Gardener, the King of heaven. All our faith is focused in who God is in His person. To preach the character of God is to plead His credibility.

Pleading the credibility of God also involves preaching about His capabilities. What is God able to do? If He cannot act in the lives of believers, our faith will be misplaced. If, however, He is able to do all that is needed, He is worthy of our trust. God is omnipotent, all powerful. He is omniscient, all knowing. He is omnibenevolent, all good and gracious toward man. He is able to hear us when we call, in any language. He is able to see us in any need. He is able to speak to us for any instruction. God is able.

Pleading the credibility of God calls for preaching about His intentions. Faith is awakened when we realize what God has promised us in Scripture. There are thousands of promises, for every need man can possibly experience. God intends us only good. Jeremiah wrote in 29:11, "'For I know the plans that I have for you,' declares the Lord, 'plans for welfare and not for calamity to give you a future and a hope.'" This timeless statement is the believer's assurance of God's intention, even for today.

Pleading the credibility of God involves preaching about His record. Any person worthy of trust establishes credibility with a positive track record. The Bible records the mighty deeds of God on behalf of His people. It was common in their sermons and psalms for the Hebrews to recount the wonderful works of God for Israel. They never tired of telling those stories over and over again. It was those very stories which gave Israel courage in the midst of her troubles. So it is with the preacher who would have his congregation grow in faith. He must preach God's record.

Let me urge you to commit yourself to trustGod preaching instead of dobetter preaching. To do this will require aiming for faith in every aspect of sermon design.

Sermon Design and Faith

"They seem to listen, but do they really hear?" That question, spoken or not, plagues the mind of the preacher. Since "faith comes from hearing, and hearing by the word of Christ" (Rom. 10:17), we preachers need to know how to "get a hearing." We need to know how to plan sermon design in keeping with our aim to preach for faith.

The word "hearing" does not mean a casual attention to what is said. The NIV translation for that verse is, "Consequently, faith comes from hearing the message, and the message is heard through the word of Christ." It means the receiving of the message rather than the sense of hearing. It is the "hearing of faith" mentioned in Galatians 3:2 and 5.

When you think of the barriers which must be crossed before a new idea is received, it is a wonder we ever get a hearing. "'My thoughts are not your thoughts, Neither are your ways My ways,' declares the Lord" (Isa. 55:8). People do not naturally think in God's ideas. But the preacher is aiming to have them accept those ideas after a half-hour presentation. He hopes for that hearing which receives the message, accepts it, assimilates it into present thinking and is moved to act on it.

At this point the dynamics of revelation mingle with the workings of human communication. The sermon is more than just a religious speech. It is a powerful means of igniting the faith which transforms. The preacher can keep this faith aim in mind from the beginning of his text interpretation. He can then plan the sermon idea and division statements for faith. Development, as well, can be planned for faith. Consider how the four functional elements work to remove barriers to faith.

Faith waits for new ideas to take root. To be really heard, a new idea first must be conceptualized. It must be presented clearly enough that it is generally understood. This is the role of explanation in sermon development. After stating a biblical principle as the division statement, we explain it so that the hearer could well respond, "I understand what you are talking about."

This does not mean that he accepts the idea yet. It merely means he basically understands it. And this is vitally needed in the revelation which results in faith. New knowledge is required, new insights and principles based on the reality of God and His purpose. This new knowledge must be stated and explained in terms the hearer understands.

The Work of Development			
Appeal	**Aim**	**Response**	**Faith**
Explanation intellect	clarity	understand	conceptulize
Illustration imagination	vividness	imagine	visualize
Argumentation reason	plausibility	accept	rationalize
Application volition	practicality	intend	actualize

This is the way revelation works. This is the way human nature works. This is the way faith is ignited. This is why our sermon concepts must be clearly and precisely worded. This is why our sermon development requires what we call explanation. In this element is carried the basic conceptualization which allows the message to be heard.

Faith waits to see the unseen. A person is likely to ignore any idea that does not make an impression on his imagination. This is a second barrier to effective communication and faith. Memory experts have proved that the best way to memorize is to visualize an idea. The things we soon forget were probably never "seen" in the imagination.

We are so accustomed to trusting our senses to tell us what is around us, we naturally feel that whatever we cannot see must not be real. Since the reality of the spiritual world is not accessible to the senses, our minds will accept its reality only if it can be imagined vividly enough. As the Bible writers have done, we must translate spiritual reality into earthly images which can be grasped by the mind of man. In a real sense, then, seeing is believing. Our faith calls for the truth to be visualized. So our preaching must not be abstract and general, but concrete and specific, with word pictures which the mind can "see."

Faith waits for rational validation. The mind of man is already made up. This is a third barrier to revelation and faith. He has accumulated, over a lifetime, a store of knowledge, ideas, opinions, and conclusions which he accepts as valid. If you come along with new information in your preaching, he will not readily accept it. It must be made to fit in with what he already "knows" is "true." Otherwise, it doesn't make sense to him.

The preacher does well, then, to know how his audience thinks. What are the generally accepted ideas? How do these ideas conflict with biblical truth? How can a case be made for the validity of the sermon truths in terms of the hearer's way of thinking? What points of common agreement can help bridge the gap?

Faith waits on this rationalizing process. Even though there may continue to be some loose ends, the mind must be able to make a rational case for any belief it accepts. In sermon development we call this argumentation. The path to spiritual transformation is the "renewing of your mind" (Rom. 12:2). Enough input, piece by piece, must be tied to what the hearer already accepts in order to create a new rationale for the biblical view.

Faith waits on specific directions. The mind of man does not welcome ideas that do not have practical meaning for his life. This erects yet another barrier to our preaching for faith. When faced with the irrelevancies of abstract religious ideas, he may ask, "But what does that have to do with me?" His own preoccupation with his personal concerns causes him to evaluate every new idea as to whether it can make a difference in his own life.

Biblical faith cannot be indifferent and philosophical. It is a matter of life and relationship. Bible truth is not to be debated and discussed for amusement and intellectual stimulation. It calls for response from the hearer, for him to actualize it in his own experience. This requires of sermons what we have called application.

James makes it emphatic. "Faith by itself, if it is not accompanied by action, is dead. . . . Show me your faith without deeds, and I will show you my faith by what I do" (Jas. 2:17–18, NIV). The Bible makes clear that belief and behavior must match. Faith which never acts is not biblical faith. This requires, of course, that preaching present clear and specific actions.

In summary, then, we can say that sermon development contributes toward building faith by helping to overcome the natural barriers to new thinking in the mind of man. If the truths of the Word of God are to have their powerful effect in a person's life, they must be conceptualized, visualized, rationalized, and actualized.

The Language of Faith

The language used by the preacher reveals his view of his audience and his expectations for them. Beyond that, his language reveals his own interpretations of the Christian life. Very often one sermon will tell more about the preacher's faith and attitude than he realizes. The basic perspective of language can be indicative, imperative, or subjunctive. You will recognize these three terms as designating grammatical mood.

Most preaching is in the imperative mood. It is essentially designed to tell the audience what to do, to give commands and instructions. This is what we have called dobetter preaching. This kind of preaching sees the congregation as falling short of the mark and the preacher's job as straightening them out. Common terms which mark imperative preaching are must, ought, and should.

The most common expression of all in this approach is "We need to. . . ." The constant use of this phrase indicates that the preacher is dissatisfied with the present performance of the congregation, including himself. The suggestion is, of course, that it is God who is really displeased. Week after week the people are barraged with "We need to . . ." statements, signaling the ongoing failure of the people to live up to expectations. Thus the Christian life is presented as a moral striving with no hope of meeting the standards.

Some preaching is also in the subjunctive mood. In grammar the subjunctive mood is used for statements which are "contrary to fact." This does not refer to lying, but rather to some condition which is not now a reality but is suggested or desired. Some examples: "If you and I would earnestly pray, we would see miracles." "If we were a more caring congregation, we would reach out to this neighborhood." "O, that the power of God might fall!"

Preaching in the subjunctive is focusing on what might be

rather than what is. The present realities of life are not addressed in practical terms, but are overlooked in favor of better conditions which may someday come. A prominent place is usually given to heaven. In one sense there is a skeptical idealism at work here which never quite accepts and comes to terms with the way things really are. A more thorough analysis of this kind of preaching is not possible in the space here. Suffice it to say it concentrates on what is not now a reality.

There is a place for imperative and subjunctive emphases in preaching. The commands and instructions throughout the Bible are to be obeyed. There is also hope for the time when God will set everything right according to His will. These perspectives should be taken seriously. But to interpret the Christian life only as commands or as deferred hopes is a failure to take the whole Bible into account.

The essential message of the Bible is that God is, that God can, that God will, and that God has already. These are indicative statements. You see in these statements of faith the four aspects of pleading the credibility of God: His character, His capabilities, His intentions, and His record. Any imperative or subjunctive emphasis must come in the context of a basically indicative approach to preaching. Everything is based on the credibility of God.

I am always a bit mystified that so much evangelical preaching is preoccupied with man. It seems to me that the Bible is about God. It is first theological, not anthropological. Rather than reflecting this emphasis on the nature of God, some preaching reflects a fascination with the sin of mankind. This may be coming from the discouragement of the preacher rather than the study of Scripture. He is not immune to the tendency to take out his frustrations on the people rather than ministering to them.

It is only in the context of the indicative that the needs of persons are really clear. God Himself must be the measure, particularly as seen in the person of Jesus Christ. Without indicative preaching about God, His character, capabilities, intentions, and record, there is no reference point for human attitudes and behavior. Neither is there any hope for improvement. The goal of the Christian is not moral rectitude. The goal is to glorify God! Anyone can try to be morally decent, but only a Christian can produce the fruit which glorifies the Father (John 15:8).

A Case for "Can"

If the essential message of Scripture is about God, the basic thrust of preaching should be indicative. In preaching the reality of the living God, we preach for faith. In pleading the credibility of God, we emphasize that He is, He can, He will, and He has already. These terms express the truth of His character, His capabilities, His intentions, and His record. In light of this, what then shall we say to our hearers? How can the preacher overcome the habit of constantly saying "We need to," "We ought," "We must," "We should"? The best term to use for maintaining the indicative perspective while challenging your audience is "can."

To say "You can" is to call for a faith response to the credibility of God. Because of all we have said about God, "You can." This does not diminish the truth that you are a new creature in Christ and that you will live eternally in Christ. But for right now, in the stress and struggle of life, the good news is "You can."

Instead of telling the people what they ought to do, we go beyond *ought* to *can*. Whereas *ought, must,* and *should* give obligation, can gives promise. "You ought to love your neighbor" becomes a new and exciting idea when it is "You can love your neighbor." This change of emphasis seems subtle, but it has an amazing effect. It places the emphasis on faith, believing you can do something because of what God will do. This is much more dynamic and exciting than hearing that you have an obligation you cannot fulfill.

Every *ought* in your sermon application can be translated into a *can*. As you do this, you will find yourself immediately pressed by the question, "How?" *Ought* doesn't seem to raise that question like *can* does. And in answer to that question, you will be forced to offer steps of faith which allow your hearer to tap into the resources of God for his obedience. "You can love your neighbor." "I can? Really? How can I do that? I mean, where do I start? Are there some secrets here I haven't seen? Why do you say with such confidence that I can do this?"

Even in addressing the issue of sin, we use the language of faith. "You need to deal with your pride" becomes "You can deal with your pride." This change in emphasis drives the preacher to prepare an answer to the "How?" he knows is coming. He will want to search the Scripture for answers to that question so he can tell his hearers how to overcome their pride.

To say "You need to" lays a burden on the hearer. He does not want to receive it. He already has enough to think about. He is already burdened enough with the responsibilities of life. He would really like to get some relief. He would like to cast some of these burdens on the Lord. To say "You can" creates an entirely different response. If you are addressing an issue he is concerned about as a Christian, he is suddenly alert to what you have to say next. Instead of a burden, you have given him a promise. Instead of an obligation, you have presented a possibility. This possibility awakens faith for the specific issue you are raising.

There are several different words for the idea of sin in the Bible. One means missing the mark. Another means breaking the law. Another means leaving the path. With the language of faith, we not only emphasize that our hearer can experience the forgiveness of God in Christ, we go further. We tell him he can hit the mark, keep the law, and walk the path in the grace of God.

Saying *can* instead of *need* to also gives a different interpretation of the person himself. Instead of an implied condemnation, you are offering a vote of confidence. "You need to" always suggests that you are not now doing what you should do. "You can" suggests that you are fully capable of doing what you really want to do. You are a new creation in Christ! You live by the grace of God! That timid and fearful Christian just may be willing to give it a try. As he takes some little steps of faith, he will find his trust growing. He will find his faith stronger for the next command which becomes a possibility.

Guidelines for the Exercise

The exercise, Preaching for Faith, is designed to strengthen your skill at planning every aspect of sermon design in harmony with the overall aim of a faith response. Here are some guidelines for the exercise and for preaching for faith.

Objectively examine your own philosophy of ministry for the faith element. This is too big a subject to deal with here at any length. Your philosophy of ministry includes your views of the church, the preacher's role, the nature of the Christian life, and other basic matters. Unless the underlying foundation of your operating assumptions is faith in the adequacy of God, your effort to preach for faith will be thwarted from the beginning.

Be alert to the faith element in your texts from the beginning of selection and study. Look for the content of the writer's faith as it is revealed in the text. Watch for indications of his faith assumptions which are only implied in the text. Trace admonitions and commands back to their foundation in the reality of God. Keep your faith aim in mind as you seek to name the textual idea.

Plan your sermon design with the aim of a faith response from your audience. We have already urged you to plan sermon design in light of three factors: the biblical text, the needs of the audience, and the nature of oral communication. Now add a fourth consideration, the overarching aim of a faith response in the hearer. This aim will affect sermon design in a number of ways, but particularly in the use of an indicative mood throughout.

Make a careful study of the faith implications of your particular sermon idea. Faith, as relationship with God, is not a general response. It is a particular response to a word from God in some specific area of personal concern. Your sermon will deal with a particular theological idea. Make sure that idea is clearly presented in terms of its underlying faith assumptions and the specific response that is appropriate.

Completing the Exercise

STEP 1: Identify in the text the ideas about God which would plead His credibility. These may be directly presented or only implied, but each should have some clear basis in the text.

STEP 2: Trace from instructions, arguments, applications, or figures in the text their foundation in the person of God. Always give the indicative basis for the imperative.

STEP 3: Test your sermon idea for its faith appeal. Is it in the indicative mood? Does it give assurance? Is it essentially theological?

STEP 4: Check each division statement for its faith appeal and reword as needed.

STEP 5: Examine development for balance in dealing with the barriers to faith in four areas: understanding, insight, reason, and intention.

STEP 6: Analyze the introductory and concluding segments for their faith appeal.

Summary

Preaching for faith means affirming and implementing the overarching aim of a faith response to your sermons. Whatever objectives a sermon may have, the foundational aim must be faith. Faith is the only appropriate response to God and His word. The Holy Spirit works to illumine the mind of the hearer to the truth of preaching claims and to awaken faith in response to them. The measure of a Christian is the measure of his faith.

Faith is enhanced by presenting the object of faith, God Himself. The preacher can plead the credibility of God by proclaiming His character, His capabilities, His intentions, and His record. This will require that the indicative serve as the foundation for the imperative, that who God is be the basis for what He requires of us. The language of faith will emphasize "can" to focus on the complete provision God makes for the believer in every aspect of the Christian life.

Study Questions

1. Why is faith the overarching aim of all preaching?
2. Why is "straightening them out" not a good aim for preaching?
3. Explain pleading the credibility of God.
4. What are the four areas emphasized in focusing on God as the object of faith?
5. Explain conceptualization, visualization, rationalization, and actualization.
6. Explain indicative, imperative, and subjunctive.
7. In what ways does "can" affect the hearer differently from "ought," "must," or "need to"?

1."A Lecture for Little-faith," in *Sermons of Rev. C. H. Spurgeon of London,* vol. 5 (London: Funk & Wagnalls, n. d.), 137–38.

Preaching for Faith

Text ___Psalm 1_____ Name ___W. McDill_____ Date_____

Preaching for Faith means planning every aspect of sermon design according to the overarching aim of a faith response in the hearer. This will require that the sermon focus on the person of God. Whatever the nature of the text material, the theological foundation of it is in God Himself. This exercise will help you plan for faith.

1. Identify in the text the ideas about God which would plead His credibility. These may be directly presented or only implied.

character _____judge, provider_____

capabilities _____knowledge of men's character and deeds, gives life and counsel_____

intentions _____to bless the godly, judge the wicked, produce fruit, separate_____

record _____

2. Trace from the text writer's material the theological assumptions behind his statements. Every instruction, interpretation, or application has its foundation in the person of God. The imperative is based on the indicative.

Because God is righteous, He judges men accordingly

The counsel of God through His Word makes worldly counsel foolish

God blesses and prospers those who live by His Word.

3. Write your sermon idea here as you have stated it. Test it for its faith appeal.
The life of the godly man is in sharp contrast with that of the wicked.

☑ Is it indicative in mood?   ☑ Does it give the hearer assurance?

☑ Does it present a faith principle?   ☑ Is it essentially theological?

☐ Does it use faith language?   ☑ Does it plead the credibility of God?

4. Check each division statement by the same tests. How does it measure up to the faith aim?

☑ Is it indicative in mood?   ☑ Does it give the hearer assurance?

☑ Does it present a faith principle?   ☑ Is it essentially theological?

☐ Does it use faith language?   ☐ Does it plead the credibility of God?

5. Examine development throughout and check it for balance in dealing with the barriers to faith.

☑ Conceptualization   ☑ Visualization

☑ Rationalization   ☑ Actualization

6. Analyze the introductory and concluding segments for their faith appeal according to the tests in item three above.

Preaching for Faith

Text   __Ephesians 1:3–6__   Name __W. McDill__   Date_____

Preaching for Faith means planning every aspect of sermon design according to the overarching aim of a faith response in the hearer. This will require that the sermon focus on the person of God. Whatever the nature of the text material, the theological foundation of it is in God Himself. This exercise will help you plan for faith.

1. Identify in the text the ideas about God which would plead His credibility. These may be directly presented or only implied.

character   __Father of Lord Jesus, goodness, grace, love, kindness__

capabilities __Power to provide everything, to make holy, fulfill His plans__

intentions   __holy and blameless, adopt, fulfill His will thru Jesus__

record   __predestined us, He chose us, blessed us__

2. Trace from the text writer's material the theological assumptions behind his statements. Every instruction, interpretation, or application has its foundation in the person of God. The imperative is based on the indicative.

__Assumes God is all good, all powerful, pouring out His grace__

__God can do all He plans; all through Jesus Christ__

3. Write your sermon idea here as you have stated it. Test it for its faith appeal.

__We are chosen by God's grace.__

☑ Is it indicative in mood?   ☑ Does it give the hearer assurance?

☑ Does it present a faith principle?   ☑ Is it essentially theological?

☑ Does it use faith language?   ☑ Does it plead the credibility of God?

4. Check each division statement by the same tests. How does it measure up to the faith aim?

☑ Is it indicative in mood?   ☑ Does it give the hearer assurance?

☑ Does it present a faith principle?   ☑ Is it essentially theological?

☐ Does it use faith language?   ☑ Does it plead the credibility of God?

5. Examine development throughout and check it for balance in dealing with the barriers to faith.

☑ Conceptualization   ☑ Visualization

☑ Rationalization   ☑ Actualization

6. Analyze the introductory and concluding segments for their faith appeal according to the tests in item three above.

Preaching for Faith

Text _____ Name _____ Date_____

Preaching for Faith means planning every aspect of sermon design according to the overarching aim of a faith response in the hearer. This will require that the sermon focus on the person of God. Whatever the nature of the text material, the theological foundation of it is in God Himself. This exercise will help you plan for faith.

1. Identify in the text the ideas about God which would plead His credibility. These may be directly presented or only implied.

character _____

capabilities _____

intentions _____

record _____

2. Trace from the text writer's material the theological assumptions behind his statements. Every instruction, interpretation, or application has its foundation in the person of God. The imperative is based on the indicative.

_____

_____

_____

3. Write your sermon idea here as you have stated it. Test it for its faith appeal.

_____

❑ Is it indicative in mood?　　　　❑ Does it give the hearer assurance?

❑ Does it present a faith principle?　　❑ Is it essentially theological?

❑ Does it use faith language?　　　❑ Does it plead the credibility of God?

4. Check each division statement by the same tests. How does it measure up to the faith aim?

❑ Is it indicative in mood?　　　　❑ Does it give the hearer assurance?

❑ Does it present a faith principle?　　❑ Is it essentially theological?

❑ Does it use faith language?　　　❑ Does it plead the credibility of God?

5. Examine development throughout and check it for balance in dealing with the barriers to faith.

❑ Conceptualization　　　　　　❑ Visualization

❑ Rationalization　　　　　　　❑ Actualization

6. Analyze the introductory and concluding segments for their faith appeal according to the tests in item three above.

Marshall thy notions into a handsome method. . . .
One will carry twice more weight packed up in
bundles, than when it lies flapping and hanging about
his shoulders.

Thomas Fuller, ca. 1650

CONCLUSION

PLANNING FOR BETTER PREACHING

The owner of a chain of restaurants was addressing us on human nature and better administrative methods. To illustrate his point, he told how it is necessary to place pictures of the menu dishes on the wall in the kitchens of his restaurants. Only then will the cook see constantly before him what he is to create.

He went on to say, however, that there was an assistant manager who was to go back and point to the pictures to remind the cook to look at them. Beyond that, he said, he had a manager in each restaurant who was assigned to send the assistant manager back to the kitchen to remind the cook to look at the pictures.

The point of that vivid and humorous story was simple. Our human nature tends to go astray. He quoted that Old Testament verse about our being like sheep which go astray, turning every one to his own way. There is a "drift factor" in our nature which does not take us to excellence. We always drift away from our best ideas and intentions.

As we deal with the task of sermon preparation, we must confront the same tendency to drift. No matter how much we may have learned about effective sermon preparation, we drift away from those ideas. We forget. We fall into habits which we do not even stop to examine. We get into a rut which does not utilize our best knowledge.

To overcome this tendency to drift away from our best work, you will have to plan your preaching program. This planning includes not only sermon preparation methods, but also study habits, ongoing improvement, time management, and other related areas. Before we consider the planning needed in those areas, let's consider why planning is necessary.

The Importance of Planning

Little of any value comes to pass without someone planning it. I like the saying we use in discussing sermon purpose, "Aim at nothing and you're sure to hit it." We can use that same idea for planning: "Plan for nothing and you're sure to accomplish it." Planning is an essential part of the way life works in this world. God created the universe in such a way that planning fits. This includes, of course, planning for your preaching in every aspect of it. Here are some reasons for the importance of planning in your preaching program.

The lordship of Christ calls for the discipline of planning. Being under the rule of our Lord calls for continual choices on our part. At every point we want to seek His will. Even so, you and I have great freedom under the lordship of Christ. We are the ones making the choices. His reign will be a reality in our experience to the extent we choose it. This truth applies to our preaching ministry as well. If we are to honor Christ in preaching, we will have to take an intentional approach to it. We never stumble or drift into the will of God. We move into it intentionally because we plan to do so.

The priority of the preaching task calls for planning. Of all the work to be done in ministry, preaching is surely one of the most important. There is no other aspect of the pastoral work which has as much potential for good as preaching. What else does the pastor do in any other half-hour which can affect as many people in a positive way? The Blizzard study found that pastors listed preaching as their most important task.[1] But they also indicated that they did not give it the first priority in their use of time. That discrepancy can only be corrected by careful planning.

Planning is vital to the well-being of the preacher. A positive and enthusiastic attitude toward your ministry can be spoiled quickly by another poor sermon. This discouragement and guilt then affect the preacher's attitude about the whole of his ministry. Preaching is too close to the heart of the preacher's calling and commitments to be done poorly without serious regrets. Planning carefully will change those regrets into rejoicing.

The needs of the preacher's family call for careful planning in his preaching ministry. By this I do not mean they need to hear good preaching from father and husband. I rather mean they deserve his undivided attention at those hours when "family time" is the agenda. When the family is home in the evening, the preacher should not have to think about his sermon. Because he has planned his study and preparation so well, he is free to give them his full attention.

The needs of the congregation call for careful planning. The pastor is not preacher only. He is also counselor, chaplain, friend, referee, administrator, teacher, and other varied roles. Whatever he does, however, his preaching and teaching will provide the overall conceptual framework for his ministry. It is there he interprets the Christian life and the mission of the church. It is there he addresses the people at the point of their personal needs. Without careful planning this preaching ministry will not touch these needs.

The time pressures of the pastorate require the pastor to plan his preaching carefully. There is always more to do than can be done in any pastoral role. These secondary tasks will dominate the time needed for sermon preparation. The pastor can give adequate time to sermon preparation only if he plans on it. In fact, he must plan for more than he can get by with because of the interruptions and emergencies which will inevitably come. Without careful planning he will all too often find himself with the "Saturday night panics."

The call for excellence in ministry requires careful planning. No one answers God's call to ministry with the intention of doing a poor job. This is the most important work in the world. Lives hang in the balance. A great price has been paid to make the ministry of Christ a reality. We must give it our best. But to do so will call for planning. Again, we never drift into excellence. Let's consider now some of the areas in which planning is needed.

Planning for Ongoing Training

This book is designed as a tool for ongoing training. It assumes we never finally arrive at excellence in our preaching. We are to be growing and continuing to sharpen our skills as long as we continue to preach. No matter which end of your calling you are on, you can still learn, still do a better job of proclaiming the Word of God.

The first barrier to overcome is the assumption that you are already really good at what you do. Most preachers I meet think they are pretty good preachers. Some of them think they are very good. And some are. I have never met one, however, who had arrived. There is always room for improvement. Preaching is a very complex subject. It involves hermeneutics (Bible interpretation), homiletics (sermon planning), and speech communication. The basic principles in these three disciplines offer much territory for growth for any preacher.

In spite of the many opportunities for skills development, most preachers are reluctant to involve themselves with anything that suggests their preaching is not up to par. As we have noted, preaching is as close to the heart of our calling and commitments as possible. It is a divine/human endeavor. Our sermons come from God Himself. We pray over them. We are inspired with a subject and its treatment. Surely this is from God. How could anyone think to tinker with that, and presume to improve upon it?

Besides this sense of God's involvement in our preaching, our own ego is on the line. Are we effective students? Can we communicate effectively? Do we have anything worthwhile to say? Too much emotional and spiritual energy goes into your preaching for you to be nonchalant about it. It is your life and your calling. To fail at preaching is to fail, period. To be told you should work to improve your preaching is tantamount to being told to find another profession.

An important decision for ongoing training is to commit yourself to a growing competency in expository preaching. This suggestion obviously reflects my own bias about text-based preaching. The riches of the Bible are fresh and exciting material to believers today, many of whom have not been exposed to expository preaching. In a sense you will be on the cutting edge of something "new." This is why many of the nationally known preachers of the day are careful expositors of Scripture.

One of the most helpful things you can do is to plan systems for feedback and critique for your preaching. There are many ways this can be done, and it is best to have several avenues for feedback. As simple a matter as listening to tapes of your sermons can help. Video is even better. Enlisting a group of church members to meet with you about your preaching can provide feedback. Pastors can also meet together regularly to share ideas and offer suggestions for improvement.

Growth in preaching skills is a lifelong pursuit. Some of the most effective steps you can take are on your own. One of these is the ongoing development of a preparation system which works for you.

A Preparation System

Good sermon preparation is hard work. There are no shortcuts, no gimmicks which will eliminate that work. It is, however, possible to develop systems of preparation which will make most effective use of your time. Necessary to everything we are describing here will be a serious commitment to put in the effort for good preaching.

What is needed is a system for preparing sermons which remains constant as a reference point and guide. Whether you think of yourself as an organized person or not, you will find such a system directing and enhancing your work. You will use your time more effectively. You will have much better content in your preaching.

Some preachers are lazy, while others do not know what to do.

Some rationalize their poor preparation with pious talk about "inspiration" and "just letting the Spirit speak." The biblical fact is that God has decided to use preachers. Our laziness does not help the Holy Spirit; it hinders Him. There is nothing particularly spiritual about poor sermon preparation.

I challenge you to work at your sermon preparation in direct proportion to your estimate of the value of preaching. Determine to strengthen the skills you need most. You will find yourself much more inspired as you see progress, and as your hearers see it. Here are some suggestions.

Commit yourself to the thorough spade work necessary to good preparation. If you think preaching is not important, then I can understand why you don't want to give it much effort. If, however, you think God has decided to do vital work through the preaching of His Word, then give it the time and sweat that priority deserves. This hard work will include a continual effort to strengthen the necessary skills. Skills development calls for practice, but it must be the practice of good methods.

The chapters in this study are all linked together as one overlaps another. That is the way preaching skills are. For the sake of discussion, however, we have identified twelve skills. You can focus on any group of these skills or on any one. Read over the material again. Make notes. Mark the pages. Study the exercise sheet. Then work at it. Use text after text to practice the particular skill.

Develop systematic procedures which employ your most effective methods.

Over the course of time you have noticed that certain things you do in sermon preparation work pretty well. Other approaches are not so effective. If we were to sit down and talk about it, you would be able to describe a plan for preparing sermons which includes your best methods. Chances are, however, that you do not follow that plan yourself.

Most of us know a good deal more about effective preparation than we actually practice. If asked to explain to a young preacher how to prepare a sermon, you would doubtless be able to do so.

But do you practice your own best plan? Or do you "wing it" week after week, relying on the habits you have fallen into over the years?

What I am suggesting is this: write up a set of instructions for yourself. Put the best you know about sermon preparation into a plan to follow every week. Instead of assuming that what you are doing is all you know, jot down suggestions for yourself that you will review every week for more effective work. Prepare planning tools, lists, and other helps which will systemize your preparation approach.

Prepare worksheets which provide step-by-step guidance. One of the most useful planning tools you can prepare is a worksheet for any phase of your preparation. Like the exercise sheets in this study, this is simply a form to fill out as you do your preparation work. You can use worksheets for your Bible study, your outlining, your sermon development. They will force your work into productive channels of activity. They will get you started and keep you going when you bog down.

Let's face it. Sermon preparation is hard work. As we have heard so often, "Creative genius is 10 percent inspiration and 90 percent perspiration." There are times when you aren't caught up in a vision of great truths from God. But you are slogging along so you will have something to preach Sunday. This is when worksheets will keep you on the track with productive effort.

Even at times when you are inspired and can hardly wait to preach the ideas you have, the worksheets will keep you on track. They will fence you in to solid study. They will direct you to careful exegesis. They will guide you to an outline and development which comes from the teaching of the text instead of some peripheral idea. They will keep you from forgetting those study methods most effective for you.

Take every phase of sermon preparation into account. Though you should start with the phase of your preparation you most need to systemize, ultimately aim to include every phase of the work in your system. This means you will want to develop a plan for preparing a preaching calendar. If you have a step-by-step procedure planned out, you will find calendar planning a manageable task.

Another key phase is the study of the text. Instead of a haphazard rummaging through your text, plan a step-by-step procedure which will produce the most effective exegesis and exposition. As you know, I personally prefer an inductive approach to Bible study which allows you to discover the truths of the text for yourself.

After you have carefully studied the text, you need a system for moving from the teachings of the text to the sermon outline. This phase is critical if you want your sermon to communicate the same truths that are in the text. Next you need a plan for preparing your outline for clear and timeless truths. After that you will work on sermon development, and you need a system for assuring balanced and effective development.

Continually revise your preparation system to serve you better. Your preparation system is your plan. You are developing it to serve you. I have found that my system is never finally set, as I continually learn new ways to do a better job in my sermon preparation. Some parts of my system prove to be too cumbersome, so I discard them. Other parts need to be fine-tuned for sharper focus. The key is to use what works best for you.

I have found two errors to be common as I urge preachers to develop a preparation system. One error is the idea that you cannot improve on what you are doing. This response usually indicates to me that the person is arrogant and unteachable. The second error is to let the system use you. This is the "tail wagging the dog." You must stay in charge and use your system as a set of tools, not as a tyrant to obey.

Be on the lookout for new ideas. Read books on preaching which will lead you into new insights. Keep revising your system of preparation for better results and more effective use of your time. Exchange ideas with friends. Share your approach with other preachers eager to get a handle on good preparation habits. And don't get into a rut.

Develop a study routine which insures adequate preparation. When your preparation system begins to take fuller shape, you will find that you are more eager to get at the work of weekly sermon preparation. Having a plan gives security and a sense of progress. It allows you to get right to work so that you make better use of your time. Even though the system may seem mechanical at times, you know that it provides you the structure you need to do your best work.

Setting aside regular study time is a must. Just as you would not flippantly break an important appointment, so must you guard your study time. You will find the constant temptation to "bump" your scheduled study time in favor of something you know is not as important. Your own human nature will often look for interruptions because the hard work of sermon preparation requires buckling down and applying yourself.

Some of us take more naturally to study than others. Temperament and inherited personality traits may have a lot to do with this. But whatever the reason for neglecting and postponing the needed study, it is vital to counter with a plan for devoting the time and effort you know is necessary. So a part of your preparation system must be a weekly study schedule.

Design checklists to monitor the quality of your preparation. My final suggestion for your system is that you summarize the various aspects of your methods into checklists. Like a pilot preparing for a takeoff, you need to have a checklist to see that you are ready to preach. A pilot does not trust his memory or assume that all the plane's necessary systems are working properly. He methodically goes over a flight checklist item by item. He knows his life is at stake.

Many a weakness in your sermon outline can be detected if you write out the standard you want to set for yourself. You may detect imbalanced sermon development if you go over your checklist for development. You may find wording which can be sharpened. You may note weakness in your introduction or that your conclusion is not as strong as you would like. You may find that you have not used faith language.

These checklists will give you the assurance that you have done what you intended. You will go to the pulpit with the confidence that your preparation is good. You are free to present the sermon without the struggling and stumbling of poor preparation.

You may have never heard of a sermon preparation system. Maybe you are saying that you already have your own system, it's just not written down. Let me urge you to write it down. If necessary, tack it to the wall like the menu picture in the restaurant kitchen and look at it every week. Your preaching will be better for it.

Preparing a Year's Preaching Calendar

The Saturday night panics is a disease peculiar to preachers. The symptoms include a knot in your stomach, a backache from bending over the desk, a tendency toward fervent prayer and muttering to yourself about how you will never again wait this late to prepare your Sunday morning sermon.

I hope you have never suffered from this distressing ailment, but chances are you have. You are busy with so many people to see. You have so many details to cover in administrative duties. Though sermon preparation is of great importance, it doesn't seem to be urgent until Saturday. One wise man has called this "the tyranny of the urgent," concentrating on the urgent matters instead of the important ones.

The initial phase of any good sermon preparation system will be calendar planning. By this I mean you plan your preaching program for a year at a time, or at least a quarter. In putting the broad strokes of your year's preaching together, you avoid the discomfort your weekly struggle causes.

With a long-term preaching plan you choose your texts ahead so there is no frantic search for a text to go with your Saturday night sermon idea. You avoid preaching half-baked sermons because you are always thinking ahead. You avoid sporadic planning, and you avoid being surprised by events like Mother's Day.

Here is a suggested plan for preparing a preaching calendar. Perhaps some of these steps will work well for you.[2]

Take an extended period of hours to plan a yearly or a quarterly calendar. One hour in this kind of planning will save you multiple hours later on. Once you get into it, the long-term planning will begin to come together. Seeing the long look stimulates ideas for many of your sermons at once. That will result in less preparation time later on and less stress, because your text and subject are already chosen.

Using one calendar sheet for each month, make date, events, and services columns for each week. This form is quite easy to prepare. Using a standard-sized sheet of paper, draw lines for a column down the left side of the sheet. Follow this with four more columns. The left column will be for the date, the second for calendar events, the third for the morning service, the fourth for the evening service, and the fifth for a midweek Bible study. Now draw lines for five spaces down the page, one for each Sunday of the month. You will mark twelve of the forms we have just designed with the months of the coming year. Now in the left column place the Sunday dates on each month's sheet.

From the calendar for the coming year, indicate all holidays and emphases. In the second column write in the holidays of that week, such as New Year's Day, Valentine's Day, Easter, Mother's Day, Independence Day, Labor Day, etc. Write them all down, even though some may not affect your preaching at all.

From the denominational calendar, indicate special emphasis by Sundays. In that same events column write in all the special Sundays and other emphases, even those only remotely related to your preaching. These might include missions offerings, Youth Week, Sunday School Preparation Week, Sanctity of Human Life Sunday, Witness Commitment Sunday, etc.

From your own church calendar, indicate planned church activities. Some church emphases will be the same as on the denominational calendar. Now add those specific events you know are coming up for your church. Here you will include revival dates, the Lord's Supper, high attendance days, the church picnic, a film series, guest speakers scheduled, music programs, etc.

Identify the differences in style, audience, and purpose of services. Morning and evening worship services usually appeal to different audiences. They may have a different style and feel about them. If the morning is when most of the unchurched are present, plan accordingly. If the evening is the time for going deeper with the inner circle of members, give it the emphasis needed. You may be planning for a midweek service as well.

Plan a book series for one service. Preaching through a book of the Bible is a good way to plan long-term. If you plan to do this, read over the entire book several times. Then choose an overall theme. Use paragraphs as sermon text units. Prepare a page for preliminary notes on each text. Write the text and topic for each sermon, even if you know you may revise it later. Then as you near the preaching date, complete the preparation.

Plan a theme series for one service. You may choose a theme for a topical series to use in the other service. Or you may choose a section to preach through, like the Ten Commandments or the Beatitudes. Contemporary themes often create interest: Seven Keys to Success, Learning to Love, Attitudes that Change Your World, The Secrets of Answered Prayer. Keep each series short enough to maintain interest and long enough to deal adequately with the subject. Choose all texts and write them into your calendar.

Consider using outside plans for a preaching calendar. A few preachers have set out to preach through the whole Bible. Some use a preaching annual with texts and sermon ideas already selected. I found it challenging to follow the texts of the Sunday School Bible Book curriculum for several years in morning services. For special occasions I would go to a more appropriate text if needed.

Go over your plan with your music director for worship planning. Without long-range planning it is seldom possible to coordinate the music with the theme of the sermon. But if you plan long-term, the music director will be able to choose special music and plan the worship to follow the text and theme of the day. Scripture readings, hymns, testimonies, and other features can all be planned in harmony.

Be ready to suspend your plan when necessary rather than serving it. Your preaching plan is to serve you. It should be suspended any time special events require a change of emphasis. When that is necessary, just pick up with the plan the following week.

Continue to look ahead and anticipate upcoming subjects each week. As you follow through with your plan, you will be looking over upcoming texts and themes each week. You may do a little spade work on several texts in a series. Early in the week you will want to go over plans for the coming Sunday so that you can "walk around" on the subjects during the week. Spending some time on this each day will make final preparations easy toward the end of the week.

Much more can be said about how to plan a year's pulpit work. The book by Pierce cited above will be most helpful for the details of calendar planning.

Planning for Personal Growth

"Preaching is the communication of truth by man to men. It has in it two essential elements, truth and personality."[3] That classic definition of preaching by Phillips Brooks focuses our attention on the person of the preacher himself as a major factor in preaching. Planning for better preaching must include personal growth. Christianity is such that the integrity of the preacher is necessary to effective preaching. What the preacher says must be what he lives.

Does "truth and personality" mean that the person of the preacher is half the preaching mix? It is an unsettling realization for the preacher that who he is personally may well be as important as what he says in a sermon. It is not that most preachers fear being found out to be rascals. The challenge lies in the difficulty of becoming all we ought to be. My own weaknesses are often blind spots to me. I am so used to being who I am, warts and all, that I am not at all sure how to be a better person.

Character is the issue. Preaching is not merely a performance. I cannot just play the part of the preacher in sermon delivery. I have to live the role of a godly person. Image is not the issue so much as integrity. Character and integrity are huge subjects. Character means essential quality, nature, or kind. It means an individual's pattern of behavior or personality, his moral constitution. Integrity means the quality of sound moral principle like uprightness, honesty, and sincerity.

Growth in character must be a specific matter, a concrete and particular quality being cultivated. It cannot be a general, abstract growth without intention. Nineteenth-century preacher G. D. Boardman put it in these familiar words, "Sow an act, and you reap a habit; sow a habit and you reap a character; sow a character and you reap a destiny." One key to character is *intentionality*, or "sowing." It is making choices, hard choices, right choices. A second key is *action*. It is intentional action which develops positive character. A third key is *habit*. When chosen patterns of right behavior become habitual, character has been established.

It is easy to give so much attention to management activities in the pastorate that you neglect the disciplines of Christian character. There are devotional disciplines necessary for maintaining intimacy with Christ. There are moral disciplines necessary for godliness. There are relational disciplines for living out the servant love of our Lord. There are intellectual disciplines for growth in knowledge. There are vocational disciplines for the various duties of the pastorate. There are physical disciplines for health and stamina. Every one of these areas affects the preaching ministry.

In his book, *The Seven Habits of Highly Effective People*, Stephen R. Covey says that a habit arises at the intersection of knowledge, skill, and desire.[4] Knowledge provides the what and why of a course of action. Skill gives the how to. Desire contributes the want to. As one has the knowledge, the skill, and the desire to pursue a behavior, he can see it become habitual, a matter of character.

These three factors which converge to establish new habits are very much like the three areas of learning we cited in the Introduction to this study: *knowledge, values,* and *skills.* It is my hope that this brief study has contributed somewhat to your knowledge of the principles for text-based preaching. I also hope that these chapters have stimulated your desire to be a wordcrafter and to do the necessary hard work for effective preaching. As we indicated in the beginning, this study focuses on skills development. Based on sound knowledge and sincere desire, skills in the tasks discussed here can lead you to better preaching.

Growth in Christian character or in preaching skills comes one action at a time until habits are developed which become normal to us. As you plan for better preaching, you will never arrive. With the goal ever before you, you find that the dynamic is in the journey. There is always some way to do a better job of communicating the matchless truth of the gospel of Christ. May He walk with you step for step in that journey!

---

1. Cited by H. C. Brown, Jr., Gordon Clinard, and Jesse J. Northcutt, *Steps to the Sermon* (Nashville: Broadman, 1963), 10–11.

2. These steps and the diagram are adapted from ideas in J. Winston Pierce, *Planning Your Preaching* (Nashville: Broadman, 1967). Also see Andrew Blackwood, *Planning A Year's Pulpit Work* (New York: Abingdon-Cokesbury, 1942).

3. Phillips Brooks, *Lectures on Preaching* (New York: E. P. Dutton, 1891), 5.

4. Stephen R. Covey, *The Seven Habits of Highly Effective People* (New York: Simon & Schuster, 1989), 47.

Preaching Calandar for_____

Date	Calendar events	Sunday A.M.	Sunday P.M.	Midweek

OTHER ABLE ASSISTANTS FOR YOUR MINISTRY...

This bonus section offers you help from several specially chosen assistants in the Broadman & Holman group of professional books. The excerpts that follow have been chosen from our other Professional Development Books to give you helpful insights on additional subjects of particular interest to ministers.

THE ANTIOCH EFFECT:

8 Characteristics of Highly Effective Churches
by Ken Hemphill

The "Antioch effect" is what made the church in Acts grow—nurturing the spiritual character of the church. This book helps you focus on developing that character in your church as the foundation for growth, rather than on implementing techniques to make church growth happen.

The Antioch Effect

"Church growth" has become a field of study, a topic of considerable interest and debate, and big business. Growth conferences are sponsored by virtually all evangelical denominations, and at levels from the local church to the national convention. Centers for church growth abound, and seminaries and colleges are getting on the bandwagon. Books, tapes, marketing studies, and models abound. More people are attending more conferences and buying more materials than at any time in the history of the church, and yet little visible results can be detected. Certainly some churches are growing. The mega-church has become the cinderella story of this decade. New churches are being added to a growing list daily. But is the church growing? Are people being added to the kingdom of God through all this activity? That is another question and one which must be honestly addressed.

In truth, we cannot show substantial church growth. The brutal truth is that church growth is not keeping pace with population increase. Total members in U.S. evangelical churches increased by 28 percent from 1960 to 1990, while population increased by 39 percent. If membership had kept pace with population, we would have 12 million more church members today in the United States.

Our growth in number of churches has not kept pace with the population increase either. The number of churches in the U.S. increased by 7 percent from 1960 to 1990. If the number of churches had grown at the same percentage as population, we would have today an additional 96,000 churches.

Other church growth authors and statisticians have ma•de the same observation. Ken Sidey, in an article in *Christianity Today* acknowledged that our church growth principles don't seem to be working. Statisticians such as Gallup and Barna have consistently and faithfully documented the woeful results of the evangelical community to reach America. Such results have caused some to conclude that the church growth movement is simply not working. While there may be some validity to that accusation, we must ask what would have been the state of the church if there had been no conferences or books to give encouragement and new ideas?

With our focus on methods, models, and marketing strategies, we're only treating the symptoms of the illness that is robbing the church of its vitality. We're not looking at the true source of the illness. As long as we continue to talk about symptoms, we will persist in thinking that we can heal the sickness with another prescription in the form of a new program, method, or model. These too, whether they be traditional or non-traditional, will only provide a surface cure to a problem that is bone deep. If we want to cure the problem that is keeping church growth from taking place, we must go much deeper. It is not so much that our programs, methods, and marketing strategies are out of date. Our primary problem is a spiritual one, not a methodological one.

Church growth is not produced by a program, plan, or marketing strategy. The greatest need of your church is not a clearer understanding of its demographics. The greatest need is a clearer understanding of its God. Church growth is not something we do or produce in the church. Church growth is not the result of any program or plan. Church growth is the by-product of a right relationship with the Lord of the Church. Church growth is by definition a supernatural activity and thus is accomplished through the church by the Lord Himself. When Jesus founded the church He promised that He Himself would build the church (Matt. 16:18). Paul, in recounting his ministry in Corinth, declared that

He planted, Apollos water, but that God gave the increase (1 Cor. 3:7).

The solution then will not be found in methods, models, or marketing strategies. These are not unimportant issues; they simply are not the primary issue. The church growth movement may have inadvertently produced a subtle sense of carnality in the church. It may have caused some to think that a method or program could produce church growth. Such thinking is both wrong and carnal. "It," whatever cherished program, model, method, or marketing strategy "It" may be, cannot cause your church to grow. Scripture is clear and insistent that God alone can grow His church. The attempt to produce church growth results through a certain method is an attempt to do supernatural work in natural power. This has led to great confusion in many congregations where model after model and method after method have been espoused as the solution to the stagnancy of the church. It has in many cases heaped failure upon failure. So much so that many churches recoil at the very mention of the term "church growth."

Lest you overreact, or think that I am overreacting, I am not arguing against methods, models, marketing strategies, or programs. God is not a God of confusion. He works through human beings and uses strategy and organization. The Scripture is full of illustrations of God working supernaturally through persons with clear strategies. I am simply suggesting that the program is not the first or most crucial issue in relationship to church growth. The vast variety of methods and programs being employed successfully across our nation will bear powerful testimony to this truth. The critical issue is the supernatural empowering of the church which occurs when the church dwells in right relationship with its Head, Christ.

Thus this book is a foundational book to other books on church growth methodology. It focuses on the character of the church. It addresses the primary question, "What is the character of the church that God has chosen to work through?" We have long recognized and taught that it is the character of an individual that ultimately determines the actions and fruitfulness of that person. I think it is equally true that the character of a church will ultimately determine the ability of that church to grow.

POWER HOUSE:

A Step-by-Step Guide to Building a Church that Prays
by Glen Martin & Dian Ginter

In *Power House,* you'll learn how to unleash the power of prayer—the single most effective force for energizing a church. You'll discover how to assess your congregation's prayer skills and develop a step-by-step strategy for renewal and outreach based on prayer. *Power House* also includes inspiring examples of churches transformed by prayer.

Power House

A well-oiled machine is a joy to behold—intricate parts of all sizes and shapes, close together and yet working smoothly as one. However, the very parts that were designed to work together in perfect, close harmony will tear each other up without proper lubrication. So it is in the church.

Prayer—God's Oil for Relationships

God has provided the wonderful "oil" of prayer, which if properly applied, can help all members work together in spite of the differences. Prayer provides the lubrication so that as a church, made up of different parts, all members can fit together perfectly, working together without friction to perform a job which they could never accomplish on their own.

The same principle is true of the component parts of the church. When heavy duty prayer is applied, the various leadership elements—deacons, trustees, councils, laity, mission groups, etc.—can work in harmony. This means prayer that is enough to saturate the decision-making process, not just a "drop" of prayer at the beginning of a meeting, not just token praying for relationships that do not reach the need, but in-depth praying that not only reaches the needs, but also applies God's oil to the problems, to the points of friction that would otherwise damage or destroy things of value. This really means the whole machine needs oil on an ongoing basis.

Looking further at this illustration, in the world of machinery different kinds of oils—various grades and different weights—are used for a specific need. To apply too light an oil when a heavy duty one is needed can lead to trouble. Too heavy an oil where a light one is called for may gum up the works or be overkill.

The same concept applies to prayer. There are different kinds of prayer for different kinds of situations. God has shown us how to pray for certain results, confess when appropriate, intercede for others, and do spiritual warfare in specific situations. Each fills a need and, when used appropriately, can be the very oil to make our lives and our churches run their best.

A powerful house of prayer is a church that knows the value of the oil of prayer. It is using prayer to maximize all of its ministries and to maintain a smooth running operation. Prayer is acting as a shield against any of the enemy's attacks on all ministries and relationships.

Prayer Ministry vs. House of Prayer

At this point a distinction should be drawn between having a prayer ministry and desiring to be a house of prayer. A prayer ministry involves a portion of the congregation in ministry, as with a youth ministry. A limited number will be involved—usually, those with a greater burden for prayer. Such a ministry may take the form of missionary prayer circles; times of prayer open to the whole church such as a Wednesday night prayer meeting; or men's/women's/youth's prayer meeting; a prayer room; an intercessory team; prayer ministry before/during/after the church service; or a prayer chain. In such cases, prayer will be seen as something done by some but not all of the membership. It will be just another, although important, ministry, as is evangelism or choir.

Some churches have tried to solve this problem by creating a prayer room in their facility, thinking this is the equivalent of becoming a house of prayer. The prayer room can be a very helpful component of the prayer life of a church but should not be the main focus. It is only a part of the overall prayer picture.

All prayer ministries are important for they lay the foundation for becoming a house of prayer since there is already an acknowledgment of the strategic importance of prayer in the church. God will help you build on your current ministry and help you go to the next level of prayer, until you truly become a powerful house of prayer.

THE ISSACHAR FACTOR:

Understanding Trends that Confront Your Church
and Designing a Strategy for Success
by Glen Martin & Gary McIntosh

Martin and McIntosh help you learn how to meet the
needs of a modern congregation in a biblical way by
transforming troubling trends into ministry opportunities. The title is taken from 1 Chronicles: "The sons of
Issachar . . . understood the times and knew what
Israel should do."

The Issachar Factor

During the last half century, we have lived in a virtual
explosion of information. More information has been produced
in the last thirty years than in the previous five thousand.
Today, information doubles every five years. By the year 2000 it
will be doubling every four years! For example, note the following signs of the information explosion experienced since the
1940s.

• Computers: Between 1946 and 1960 the number of computers grew from one to ten thousand, and from 1960 to 1980 to ten
million. By the year 2000 there will be over eighty million
computers in the United States alone. The number of components that can be programmed into a computer chip is doubling
every eighteen months.

• Publications: Approximately ninety-six hundred different
periodicals are published in the United States each year, and
about one thousand books are published internationally every
day. Printed information doubles every eight years. A weekday
edition of the *New York Times* contains more information than
the average person was likely to come across in a lifetime in
seventeenth-century England.

• Libraries: The world's great libraries are doubling in size
every fourteen years. In the early 1300s, the Sorbonne Library
in Paris contained only 1,338 books and yet was thought to be the
largest library in Europe. Today several libraries in the world

---

have an inventory of well over eight million books each.

• Periodicals: The Magazine Publishers Association notes that 265 more magazines were published in 1988 than in 1989, which works out to about one a day if magazine creators take weekends off. Newsstands offer a choice of twenty-five hundred different magazines.

• Reference works: The Pacific Bell Yellow Pages are used about 3.5 million times a day. There are thirty-three million copies of 108 different directories with forty-one billion pages of information. The new second edition of the Random House Dictionary of the English Language contains more than 315,000 words, has twenty-five hundred pages, weighs 13.5 pounds, and has fifty thousand new entries.

All of this information is good. Right? Wrong! Today we must deal with new challenges like overload amnesia, which occurs when an individual's brain shuts down to protect itself. Did you ever forget simple information like a friend's name when trying to introduce them to another person? That's overload amnesia. Or have you ever crammed for an exam only to forget what it was about less than one hour later? That's "Chinese-dinner memory dysfunction"—an undue emphasis on short-term memory. Or have you ever read about an upcoming event in a church program only to forget about it later? That's a result of "informational cacophony"—too much exposure to information so that you end up reading or hearing something but not remembering it. Finally, consider VCRitis—buying a high-technology product, getting it home, and then not being able to program it.

Exposure to this proliferation of information has created a generation of people with different needs, needs which require new models of ministry. The problem is that many churches continue to use models of ministry which do not address the different needs people have today. Examine the following effects of the informa-tion age. Ministry must change to meet people's needs today.

• People have less free time, and are more difficult to recruit.

• People oppose change, resist making friends, and are lonely.

• People are bombarded by so much information that they find it difficult to listen to more information.

• People cannot see the big picture, tie the ends together, or see how the pieces relate.

• People hear more than they understand, forget what they

already know, and resist learning more.

• People don't know how to use what they learn, make mistakes when they try, and fell guilty about it.

• People know information is out there, have difficulty getting it, and make mistakes without it.

Changing Models

Even though we minister in the information age, churches continue to reflect their agricultural and industrial age roots. This leads to stress as programs that worked in the past are not as effective today. Consider these two examples.

Worship services at 11:00 A.M. are a throwback to the agricultural age when churches had to give farmers time to complete the morning chores, hitch the horse to the wagon, and drive into town. The time most farmers completed this routine, 11:00 A.M., was the logical choice for morning church services to begin. Today, however, many churches find earlier hours for worship services often attract more people.

The evening service is a throwback to the industrial age when electric lights were first developed. Initially not every home or business establishment was able to have lights installed. Some enterprising church leaders found that by installing electric lights they could attract crowds to evening evangelistic church services. Today many churches find that smaller groups meeting in homes attract more people than evening services.

Let's face it: Most church models of ministry were developed in an entirely different age. The models of ministry developed in the agricultural and industrial ages are colliding head-on with the information age. That's what this book is all about. Our nation has changed; people have changed; and we must develop new models of ministry relevant for today's society if we are to fulfill Christ's commission to "make disciples."

While it is not possible to cover every aspect of ministry, throughout this book you'll find not only insight as to what changes have taken place, but also practical ideas you can use immediately to be more effective in your own ministry .

To get the best value from this book first overview the entire contents. You will find that each chapter focuses on areas of ministry commonly found in churches. If you are involved in a ministry specifically addressed by one chapter, read that chapter first and begin to use some of the practical suggestions immediately. Then go back through the other chapters, carefully noting insights and ideas applicable to other ministries in your church.

People of Issachar

In the Old Testament there's an interesting story in 1 Chronicles 12. David had been running from Saul, and while he was hiding, God sent some men to him who are described as mighty men of valor. The first group of men were skilled with the bow, with the arrow, and with the sling. These men would stand behind the lines and shoot arrows and fling stones over the front lines to inflict wounds on the enemy. Other men were skilled in the use of the shield and the sword, moved swiftly, and had a tenacious spirit. They would fight one on one with the enemy at the front lines. A third category of men understood the times and knew what Israel should do. They were the strategists who developed the master plan for the battle. We today need to be like men of Issachar. We need to be people who understand our times, know what we should do, and have the courage to do it.

We trust that *The Issachar Factor* will help you understand the times in which you are called to minister and know what to do to increase your church's effectiveness.

EATING THE ELEPHANT:
Bite-sized Steps
to Achieve Long-term Growth in Your Church
by Thom S. Rainer

Eating the Elephant shows why, in many cases, "contemporary" church growth plans can do more harm than good. It also explains how the long road to lasting growth is best traveled in tiny steps—through creating sensitive change at a comfortable pace.

Eating the Elephant

Most pastors realize that some type of change must take place in their churches in order to reach effectively a growing unchurched population. Many pastors face two major obstacles: lack of know-how and the inability to apply known principles of change.

Generally, innovations can be implemented with relative ease in three cases: (1) a newly-planted church; (2) a church that has experienced rapid growth due to relocation; or (3) a church that still has its founding pastor. Churches in these three categories account for less than 10 percent of all Christian churches in America. What do the remaining 90-percent-plus churches do? Can they be effective? Can they make a difference in their communities? Can they reached the unchurched? Can they implement change without destroying their fellowship?

Such is the tension that exists in many of the so-called traditional churches. How can the church be relevant to both the growing unchurched population and to the members for whom church relevance is grounded in old hymns and long-standing methodologies? The good news is that the traditional church can grow. Through my contact with hundreds of such churches in America, I have discovered that many pastors are leading traditional churches to growth. I will share with you their principles and struggles. And I will share with you my own successes and failures of leading traditional churches to growth.

Eating the Elephant

Many of my church members know that I love a good, clean joke. One of them shared with me a series of elephant jokes. One of the jokes asked the question: "How do you eat an elephant?" The answer: "One bite at a time." Later I would realize that the joke describes well the task before any leader in a traditional church. The process of leading a traditional church to growth is analogous to "eating an elephant." It is a long-term deliberate process that must be implemented "one bite at a time."

If the task before us is eating an elephant, then we must avoid two extremes. The first extreme is to ignore the task at hand. I remember when my son Sam had a monumental science project to complete. He was overwhelmed by the enormity of the task. Working together, we established a list of items to be completed and the date by which each item had to be finished. Instead of being a burden, the project became a joy because he could see his daily progress. Much to his amazement and delight, Sam finished the assignment several days before the deadline.

If we acknowledge that our churches are far from effective, the challenge to change may seem overwhelming. You are in the same situation as most pastors in America. But with God's anointing, you can lead toward change and growth one step at a time.

On the other hand, we must avoid the other extreme of eating the elephant in just a few bites. Massive and sudden change (I realize "massive" is a relative term but, for many church members, their "massive" is the pastor's "slight") can divide and demoralize a traditional church. Remember, church members who hold tenaciously to the old paradigms are not "wrong" while you are "right." They are children of God loved no less by the Father than those who prefer a different style.